NEURODEVELOPMENTAL DISEASES - LABORATORY AND CLINICAL RESEARCH

AUTISM SPECTRUM DISORDERS

GUIDANCE, RESEARCH AND FEDERAL ACTIVITY

NEURODEVELOPMENTAL DISEASES - LABORATORY AND CLINICAL RESEARCH

Additional books in this series can be found on Nova's website under the Series tab.

Additional E-books in this series can be found on Nova's website under the E-book tab.

NEURODEVELOPMENTAL DISEASES - LABORATORY AND CLINICAL RESEARCH

AUTISM SPECTRUM DISORDERS

GUIDANCE, RESEARCH AND FEDERAL ACTIVITY

GREGORY L. CAMPBELL
AND
ANTHONY O. PHILLIPS
EDITORS

NOVA BIOMEDICAL

Nova Science Publishers, Inc.
New York

Library of Congress Cataloging-in-Publication Data

Library of Congress Control Number: 2012939743

ISBN: 978-1-62257-076-8

Published by Nova Science Publishers, Inc. †New York

CONTENTS

PREFACE

Autism spectrum disorders (ASDs) are a group of developmental disabilities characterized by impairments in social interaction and communication and by restricted, repetitive, and stereotyped patterns of behavior. Symptoms typically are apparent before age 3 years. The complex nature of these disorders, coupled with a lack of biologic markers for diagnosis and changes in clinical definitions over time, creates challenges in monitoring the prevalence of ASDs. Accurate reporting of data is essential to understand the prevalence of ASDs in the population and can help direct research. This book provides a parent's guide to autism spectrum disorder with a focus on prevalence; suggested environmental factors; and federal financing research.

Chapter 1 - Autism is a group of developmental brain disorders, collectively called autism spectrum disorder (ASD). The term “spectrum” refers to the wide range of symptoms, skills, and levels of impairment, or disability, that children with ASD can have. Some children are mildly impaired by their symptoms, but others are severely disabled.

ASD is diagnosed according to guidelines listed in the *Diagnostic and Statistical Manual of Mental Disorders, Fourth Edition - Text Revision* (DSM-IV-TR).[1] The manual currently defines five disorders, sometimes called pervasive developmental disorders (PDDs), as ASD:

- Autistic disorder (classic autism)
- Asperger’s disorder (Asperger syndrome)
- Pervasive developmental disorder not otherwise specified (PDD-NOS)
- Rett’s disorder (Rett syndrome)
- Childhood disintegrative disorder (CDD).

This information packet will focus on autism, Asperger syndrome, and PDD-NOS, with brief descriptions of Rett syndrome and CDD in the section, “Related disorders.” Information can also be found on the *Eunice Kennedy Shriver* National Institute of Child Health and Human Development website a t http://www.nichd.nih.gov and the Centers for Disease Control and Prevention website at http://www.cdc.gov/ncbddd/autism/index.html.

Chapter 2 - Autism is a group of developmental brain disorders, collectively called autism spectrum disorder (ASD). The term “spectrum” refers to the wide range of symptoms, skills, and levels of impairment, or disability, that children with ASD can have. Some children are mildly impaired by their symptoms, but others are severely disabled.

ASD is diagnosed according to guidelines listed in the *Diagnostic and Statistical Manual of Mental Disorders, Fourth Edition - Text Revision* (DSM-IV-TR).[1] The manual currently defines five disorders, sometimes called pervasive developmental disorders (PDDs), as ASD:

- Autistic disorder (classic autism)
- Asperger's disorder (Asperger syndrome)
- Pervasive developmental disorder not otherwise specified (PDD-NOS)
- Rett's disorder (Rett syndrome)
- Childhood disintegrative disorder (CDD).

This information packet will focus on autism, Asperger syndrome, and PDD-NOS, with brief descriptions of Rett syndrome and CDD in the section, "Related disorders." Information can also be found on the *Eunice Kennedy Shriver* National Institute of Child Health and Human Development website a t http://www.nichd.nih.gov and the Centers for Disease Control and Prevention website at http://www.cdc.gov/ncbddd/autism/index.html.

Chapter 3 - *Problem/Condition:* Autism spectrum disorders (ASDs) are a group of developmental disabilities characterized by impairments in social interaction and communication and by restricted, repetitive, and stereotyped patterns of behavior. Symptoms typically are apparent before age 3 years. The complex nature of these disorders, coupled with a lack of biologic markers for diagnosis and changes in clinical definitions over time, creates challenges in monitoring the prevalence of ASDs. Accurate reporting of data is essential to understand the prevalence of ASDs in the population and can help direct research.

Period Covered: 2008.

Description of System: The Autism and Developmental Disabilities Monitoring (ADDM) Network is an active surveillance system that estimates the prevalence of ASDs and describes other characteristics among children aged 8 years whose parents or guardians reside within 14 ADDM sites in the United States. ADDM does not rely on professional or family reporting of an existing ASD diagnosis or classification to ascertain case status. Instead, information is obtained from children's evaluation records to determine the presence of ASD symptoms at any time from birth through the end of the year when the child reaches age 8 years. ADDM focuses on children aged 8 years because a baseline study conducted by CDC demonstrated that this is the age of identified peak prevalence. A child is included as meeting the surveillance case definition for an ASD if he or she displays behaviors (as described on a comprehensive evaluation completed by a qualified professional) consistent with the American Psychiatric Association's Diagnostic and Statistical Manual-IV, Text Revision (DSM-IV-TR) diagnostic criteria for any of the following conditions: Autistic Disorder; Pervasive Developmental Disorder–Not Otherwise Specified (PDD-NOS, including Atypical Autism); or Asperger Disorder. The first phase of the ADDM methodology involves screening and abstraction of comprehensive evaluations completed by professional providers at multiple data sources in the community. Multiple data sources are included, ranging from general pediatric health clinics to specialized programs for children with developmental disabilities. In addition, many ADDM sites also review and abstract records of children receiving special education services in public schools. In the second phase of the study, all abstracted evaluations are reviewed by trained clinicians to determine ASD case status. Because the case definition and surveillance methods have remained consistent across all ADDM surveillance years to date, comparisons to results for earlier surveillance years can be made. This report provides updated ASD prevalence estimates from the 2008 surveillance year, representing 14 ADDM areas in the United States. In addition to prevalence estimates, characteristics of the population of children with ASDs are described, as well as detailed comparisons of the 2008 surveillance year findings with those for the 2002 and 2006 surveillance years.

Results: For 2008, the overall estimated prevalence of ASDs among the 14 ADDM sites was 11.3 per 1,000 (one in 88) children aged 8 years who were living in these communities during 2008. Overall ASD prevalence estimates varied widely across all sites (range: 4.8–21.2 per 1,000 children aged 8 years). ASD prevalence estimates also varied widely by sex and by racial/ethnic group. Approximately one in 54 boys and one in 252 girls living in the ADDM Network communities were identified as having ASDs. Comparison of 2008 findings with those for earlier surveillance years indicated an increase in estimated ASD prevalence of 23% when the 2008 data were compared with the data for 2006 (from 9.0 per 1,000 children aged 8 years in 2006 to 11.0 in 2008 for the 11 sites that provided data for both surveillance years) and an estimated increase of 78% when the 2008 data were compared with the data for 2002 (from 6.4 per 1,000 children aged 8 years in 2002 to 11.4 in 2008 for the 13 sites that provided data for both surveillance years). Because the ADDM Network sites do not make up a nationally representative sample, these combined prevalence estimates should not be generalized to the United States as a whole.

Interpretation: These data confirm that the estimated prevalence of ASDs identified in the ADDM network surveillance populations continues to increase. The extent to which these increases reflect better case ascertainment as a result of increases in awareness and access to services or true increases in prevalence of ASD symptoms is not known. ASDs continue to be an important public health concern in the United States, underscoring the need for continued resources to identify potential risk factors and to provide essential supports for persons with ASDs and their families.

Public Health Action: Given substantial increases in ASD prevalence estimates over a relatively short period, overall and within various subgroups of the population, continued monitoring is needed to quantify and understand these patterns. With 5 biennial surveillance years completed in the past decade, the ADDM Network continues to monitor prevalence and characteristics of ASDs and other developmental disabilities for the 2010 surveillance year. Further work is needed to evaluate multiple factors contributing to increases in estimated ASD prevalence over time. ADDM Network investigators continue to explore these factors, with a focus on understanding disparities in the identification of ASDs among certain subgroups and on how these disparities have contributed to changes in the estimated prevalence of ASDs. CDC is partnering with other federal and private partners in a coordinated response to identify risk factors for ASDs and to meet the needs of persons with ASDs and their families.

Chapter 4 - [Last week] the CDC reported a 78 percent increase in autism prevalence since 2002. This week's autism news is about genetics—*three papers in Nature* describe new genes associated with autism. For many people, these two stories seem contradictory or, at best, unrelated. Increasing prevalence suggests environmental factors like chemicals and microbes changing over the past decade, whereas genes change over generations. Why is anyone looking for genetic causes when there is such a rapid increase in prevalence? Shouldn't every research dollar be invested in finding the environmental culprit rather than searching for rare gene variants?

The simple answer is that *some* autism is genetic. Autism, like *schizophrenia* and *mood disorders*, includes many syndromes. Indeed, we should probably speak of the "autisms." Some of these autisms are single gene disorders, such as *Fragile X*, *tuberous sclerosis*, and

Rett *syndrome*. While these rare genetic disorders account for less than 5 percent of children within the autism spectrum, children with any of these disorders are at high risk for autism, roughly a 30-fold higher risk than the general population and higher than any of the other known risk factors. Recent genomics research has discovered that many children diagnosed within the autism spectrum have other genetic mutations that have not yet been designated as named syndromes. Each of these mutations is rare, but in aggregate they may account for 10 - 20 percent or more of what we have been calling the autisms.

Chapter 5 - Two decades ago, autism was a little-known, uncommon disorder. Today, autism is more common in the United States than childhood cancer, juvenile diabetes, and pediatric AIDS combined, and the increasing numbers of children being diagnosed with autism has created a national health emergency. In a speech at the National Institutes of Health on September 30, 2009, President Obama specifically cited autism, along with cancer and heart disease, as one of three health conditions targeted for major scientific research investment through the American Recovery and Reinvestment Act. The President expressed his hope that research into genetic and environmental factors would result in strides in early intervention, treatments, and therapies to help people affected by autism achieve their fullest potential.

Chapter 6 - Autism spectrum disorder (ASD) and autism are general terms for a group of developmental disabilities that cause impairments in social skills and communication, and are often characterized by certain atypical behaviors. The federal government has a role in the financing (through Medicaid and State Children's Health Insurance Programs) and delivery (through funding of developmental disabilities programming in schools, Title V Maternal and Child Health funding, and other sources) of treatment for ASD. The number of autism cases and their appropriate diagnosis and treatment affect federal and state expenditures. As such, Congress has shown interest in financing research on ASD prevalence, causes, and optimal treatment for individuals with ASD.

On September 26, 2011, the 112th Congress passed the Combating Autism Reauthorization Act (CARA, P.L. 112-32), which reauthorized funding for autism research authorized under the Combating Autism Act of 2006 (CAA, P.L. 109-416). The CAA was enacted to address public and congressional concern with growing rates of autism; to increase existing autism research funding authorizations; and to stimulate state-level coordination of health, education, and disability programs. The CAA authorizes funding for ASD surveillance, research, and education at the Department of Health and Human Services (HHS), at the Centers for Disease Control and Prevention (CDC), the Health Resources and Services Administration (HRSA), and the National Institutes of Health (NIH).

The CAA authorizes funding for the CDC to administer a grant program for states and other entities to conduct surveillance on ASD and developmental disabilities, and to establish regional centers of excellence in ASD epidemiology. These funds have been used to develop a multi-state network for the collection, analysis, and reporting multiple years of state and local data on ASD prevalence to the CDC.

The CAA authorizes funding for the HRSA to support autism education, intervention, and early detection. These activities are designed to increase ASD awareness, to reduce barriers to screening and diagnosis, and to promote evidence-based interventions.

NIH is authorized under the CAA to conduct and fund basic scientific research on autism and other developmental disabilities. In addition, NIH is tasked with the coordination of all research, screening, intervention, and education efforts through the Interagency Autism Coordinating Committee.

The Combating Autism Act authorized appropriations for these activities from FY2007 through FY2011. The Combating Autism Reauthorization Act of 2011 extends authorizations of appropriations at FY2011 levels for FY2012 through FY2014. This report presents an overview of the CAA and CARA, HHS funding and activities under the CAA and CARA for FY2007 through FY2012 and the FY2013 President's budget request, other federal activities related to autism, and selected issues for Congress.

In: Autism Spectrum Disorders ISBN 978-1-62257-076-8
Editors: Gregory L. Campbell and Anthony O. Phillips

Chapter 1

A PARENT'S GUIDE TO AUTISM SPECTRUM DISORDER*

U.S. Department of Health and Human Services

WHAT IS AUTISM SPECTRUM DISORDER (ASD)?

Autism is a group of developmental brain disorders, collectively called autism spectrum disorder (ASD). The term "spectrum" refers to the wide range of symptoms, skills, and levels of impairment, or disability, that children with ASD can have. Some children are mildly impaired by their symptoms, but others are severely disabled.

ASD is diagnosed according to guidelines listed in the *Diagnostic and Statistical Manual of Mental Disorders, Fourth Edition - Text Revision* (DSM-IV-TR).[1] The manual currently defines five disorders, sometimes called pervasive developmental disorders (PDDs), as ASD:

- Autistic disorder (classic autism)
- Asperger's disorder (Asperger syndrome)
- Pervasive developmental disorder not otherwise specified (PDD-NOS)
- Rett's disorder (Rett syndrome)
- Childhood disintegrative disorder (CDD).

This information packet will focus on autism, Asperger syndrome, and PDD-NOS, with brief descriptions of Rett syndrome and CDD in the section, "Related disorders." Information can also be found on the *Eunice Kennedy Shriver* National Institute of Child Health and Human Development website a t http://www.nichd.nih.gov and the Centers for Disease Control and Prevention website at http://www.cdc.gov/ncbddd/autism/index.html.

* This is an edited, reformatted and augmented version of the U.S. Department of Health & Human Services, National Institutes of Health. NIH Publication No. 11-5511, dated 2011.

WHAT ARE THE SYMPTOMS OF ASD?

Symptoms of autism spectrum disorder (ASD) vary from one child to the next, but in general, they fall into three areas:

- Social impairment
- Communication difficulties
- Repetitive and stereotyped behaviors.

Children with ASD do not follow typical patterns when developing social and communication skills. Parents are usually the first to notice unusual behaviors in their child. Often, certain behaviors become more noticeable when comparing children of the same age.

In some cases, babies with ASD may seem different very early in their development. Even before their first birthday, some babies become overly focused on certain objects, rarely make eye contact, and fail to engage in typical back-and-forth play and babbling with their parents. Other children may develop normally until the second or even third year of life, but then start to lose interest in others and become silent, withdrawn, or indifferent to social signals. Loss or reversal of normal development is called regression and occurs in some children with ASD.[2]

Social Impairment

Most children with ASD have trouble engaging in everyday social interactions. According to the *Diagnostic and Statistical Manual of Mental Disorders, Fourth Edition - Text Revision*, some children with ASD may:

- Make little eye contact
- Tend to look and listen less to people in their environment or fail to respond to other people
- Do not readily seek to share their enjoyment of toys or activities by pointing or showing things to others
- Respond unusually when others show anger, distress, or affection.

Recent research suggests that children with ASD do not respond to emotional cues in human social interactions because they may not pay attention to the social cues that others typically notice. For example, one study found that children with ASD focus on the mouth of the person speaking to them instead of on the eyes (article at http://www.nimh.nih.gov/science-news/2008/lack-of-eye-contactmay-predict-level-of-social-disability-in-two-year-olds-with-autism.shtml), which is where children with typical development tend to focus.[3] A related study showed that children with ASD appear to be drawn to repetitive movements linked to a sound, such as hand-clapping during a game of pat-a-cake (article at http://www.nimh.nih.gov/science-news/2009/autism-skews-developing-brain-withsynchronous-motion-and-sound.shtml).[4] More research is needed to confirm these findings, but such studies suggest that children with ASD may misread or not notice subtle social cues—a smile, a wink, or a grimace—that could help them understand social relationships and interactions. For these children, a question such as, "Can you wait a minute?" always means the same thing, whether the speaker is joking, asking a real question, or issuing a firm request. Without the ability to interpret another person's tone of voice as well as gestures, facial expressions, and other nonverbal communications, children with ASD may not properly respond.

Likewise, it can be hard for others to understand the body language of children with ASD. Their facial expressions, movements, and gestures are often vague or do not match what they are saying. Their tone of voice may not reflect their actual feelings either. Many older children with ASD speak with an unusual tone of voice and may sound sing-song or flat and robotlike.[1]

Children with ASD also may have trouble understanding another person's point of view. For example, by school age, most children understand that other people have different information, feelings, and goals than they have. Children with ASD may lack this understanding, leaving them unable to predict or understand other people's actions.

Communication Issues

According to the American Academy of Pediatrics' developmental milestones, by the first birthday, typical toddlers can say one or two words, turn when they hear their name, and point when they want a toy. When offered something they do not want, toddlers make it clear with words, gestures, or facial expressions that the answer is "no."

For children with ASD, reaching such milestones may not be so straightforward. For example, some children with autism may:

- Fail or be slow to respond to their name or other verbal attempts to gain their attention
- Fail or be slow to develop gestures, such as pointing and showing things to others
- Coo and babble in the first year of life, but then stop doing so
- Develop language at a delayed pace
- Learn to communicate using pictures or their own sign language
- Speak only in single words or repeat certain phrases over and over, seeming unable to combine words into meaningful sentences
- Repeat words or phrases that they hear, a condition called echolalia
- Use words that seem odd, out of place, or have a special meaning known only to those familiar with the child's way of communicating.

Even children with ASD who have relatively good language skills often have difficulties with the back and forth of conversations. For example, because they find it difficult to understand and react to social cues, children with Asperger syndrome often talk at length about a favorite subject, but they won't allow anyone else a chance to respond or notice when others react indifferently.[1]

Children with ASD who have not yet developed meaningful gestures or language may simply scream or grab or otherwise act out until they are taught better ways to express their needs. As these children grow up, they can become aware of their difficulty in understanding others and in being understood. This awareness may cause them to become anxious or depressed. For more information on mental health issues in children with ASD, see the section: What are some other conditions that children with ASD may have?

Repetitive and Stereotyped Behaviors

Children with ASD often have repetitive motions or unusual behaviors. These behaviors may be extreme and very noticeable, or they can be mild and discreet. For example, some children may repeatedly flap their arms or walk in specific patterns, while others may subtly move their fingers by their eyes in what looks to be a gesture. These repetitive actions are sometimes called "stereotypy" or "stereotyped behaviors."

Children with ASD also tend to have overly focused interests. Children with ASD may become fascinated with moving objects or parts of objects, like the wheels on a moving car. They might spend a long time lining up toys in a certain way, rather than playing with them. They may also become very upset if someone accidentally moves one of the toys. Repetitive behavior can also take the form of a persistent, intense preoccupation.[1] For example, they might be obsessed with learning all about vacuum cleaners, train schedules, or lighthouses. Children with ASD often have great interest in numbers, symbols, or science topics.

While children with ASD often do best with routine in their daily activities and surroundings, inflexibility may often be extreme and cause serious difficulties. They may insist on eating the same exact meals every day or taking the same exact route to school. A slight change in a specific routine can be extremely upsetting.[1] Some children may even have emotional outbursts, especially when feeling angry or frustrated or when placed in a new or stimulating environment.

No two children express exactly the same types and severity of symptoms. In fact, many typically developing children occasionally display some of the behaviors common to children with ASD. However, if you notice your child has several ASD-related symptoms, have your child screened and evaluated by a health professional experienced with ASD.

Related Disorders

Rett syndrome and childhood disintegrative disorder (CDD) are two very rare forms of ASD that include a regression in development. Only 1 of every 10,000 to 22,000 girls has Rett syndrome.[5, 6] Even rarer, only 1 or 2 out of 100,000 children with ASD have CDD.[7]

Unlike other forms of ASD, Rett syndrome mostly affects girls. In general, children with Rett syndrome develop normally for 6–18 months before regression and autism-like symptoms begin to appear. Children with Rett syndrome may also have difficulties with coordination, movement, and speech. Physical, occupational, and speech therapy can help, but no specific treatment for Rett syndrome is available yet.

With funding from the *Eunice Kennedy Shriver* National Institute of Child Health and Human Development, scientists have discovered that a mutation in the sequence of a single gene is linked to most cases of Rett syndrome.[8] This discovery may help scientists find ways to slow or stop the progress of the disorder. It may also improve doctors' ability to diagnose and treat children with Rett syndrome earlier, improving their overall quality of life.

CDD affects very few children, which makes it hard for researchers to learn about the disease. Symptoms of CDD may appear by age 2, but the average age of onset is between age 3 and 4. Until this time, children with CDD usually have age-appropriate communication and social skills. The long period of normal development before regression helps to set CDD apart from Rett syndrome. CDD may affect boys more often than girls.[9]

Children with CDD experience severe, wide-ranging and obvious loss of previously-obtained motor, language, and social skills.[10] The loss of such skills as vocabulary is more dramatic in CDD than in classic autism.[11] Other symptoms of CDD include loss of bowel and bladder control.[1]

How Is ASD Diagnosed?

ASD diagnosis is often a two-stage process. The first stage involves general developmental screening during well-child checkups with a pediatrician or an early childhood health care provider. Children who show some developmental problems are referred for additional evaluation. The second stage involves a thorough evaluation by a team of doctors and other health professionals with a wide range of specialities.[12] At this stage, a child may be diagnosed as having autism or another developmental disorder.

Children with autism spectrum disorder (ASD) can usually be reliably diagnosed by age 2, though research suggests that some screening tests can be helpful at 18 months or even younger.[12,13]

Many people—including pediatricians, family doctors, teachers, and parents—may minimize signs of ASD at first, believing that children will "catch up" with their peers. While you may be concerned about labeling your young child with ASD, the earlier the disorder is diagnosed, the sooner specific interventions may begin. Early intervention can reduce or prevent the more severe disabilities associated with ASD. Early intervention may also improve your child's IQ, language, and everyday functional skills, also called adaptive behavior.[14]

Screening

A well-child checkup should include a developmental screening test, with specific ASD screening at 18 and 24 months as recommended by the American Academy of Pediatrics.[14] Screening for ASD is not the same as diagnosing ASD. Screening instruments are used as a first step to tell the doctor whether a child needs more testing. If your child's pediatrician does not routinely screen your child for ASD, ask that it be done.

Types of ASD Screening Instruments

Sometimes the doctor will ask parents questions about the child's symptoms to screen for ASD. Other screening instruments combine information from parents with the doctor's own observations of the child. Examples of screening instruments for toddlers and preschoolers include:

- Checklist of Autism in Toddlers (CHAT)
- Modified Checklist for Autism in Toddlers (M-CHAT)
- Screening Tool for Autism in Two-Year-Olds (STAT)
- Social Communication Questionnaire (SCQ)
- Communication and Symbolic Behavior Scales (CSBS).

To screen for mild ASD or Asperger syndrome in older children, the doctor may rely on different screening instruments, such as:

- Autism Spectrum Screening Questionnaire (ASSQ)
- Australian Scale for Asperger's Syndrome (ASAS)
- Childhood Asperger Syndrome Test (CAST).

Some helpful resources on ASD screening include the Center for Disease Control and Prevention's General Developmental Screening tools and ASD Specific Screening tools on their website at http://cdc.gov/ ncbddd/autism/screening.html.

For parents, your own experiences and concerns about your child's development will be very important in the screening process. Keep your own notes about your child's development and look through family videos, photos, and baby albums to help you remember when you first noticed each behavior and when your child reached certain developmental milestones.

Comprehensive Diagnostic Evaluation

The second stage of diagnosis must be thorough in order to find whether other conditions may be causing your child's symptoms. For more information, see the section: What are some other conditions that children with ASD may have?

A team that includes a psychologist, a neurologist, a psychiatrist, a speech therapist, or other professionals experienced in diagnosing ASD may do this evaluation. The evaluation may assess the child's cognitive level (thinking skills), language level, and adaptive behavior (age-appropriate skills needed to complete daily activities independently, for example eating, dressing, and toileting).

Because ASD is a complex disorder that sometimes occurs along with other illnesses or learning disorders, the comprehensive evaluation may include brain imaging and gene tests, along with in-depth memory, problem-solving, and language testing.[12] Children with any delayed development should also get a hearing test and be screened for lead poisoning as part of the comprehensive evaluation.

Although children can lose their hearing along with developing ASD, common ASD symptoms (such as not turning to face a person calling their name) can also make it seem that children cannot hear when in fact they can. If a child is not responding to speech, especially to his or her name, it's important for the doctor to test whether a child has hearing loss.

The evaluation process is a good time for parents and caregivers to ask questions and get advice from the whole evaluation team. The outcome of the evaluation will help plan for treatment and interventions to help your child. Be sure to ask who you can contact with follow-up questions.

WHAT ARE SOME OTHER CONDITIONS THAT CHILDREN WITH ASD MAY HAVE?

Sensory Problems

Many children with autism spectrum disorder (ASD) either overreact or underreact to certain sights, sounds, smells, textures, and tastes. For example, some may:

- Dislike or show discomfort from a light touch or the feel of clothes on their skin
- Experience pain from certain sounds, like a vacuum cleaner, a ringing telephone, or a sudden storm; sometimes they will cover their ears and scream
- Have no reaction to intense cold or pain.

Researchers are trying to determine if these unusual reactions are related to differences in integrating multiple types of information from the senses.

Sleep Problems

Children with ASD tend to have problems falling asleep or staying asleep, or have other sleep problems.[15] These problems make it harder for them to pay attention, reduce their ability to function, and lead to poor behavior. In addition, parents of children with ASD and sleep problems tend to report greater family stress and poorer overall health among themselves.

Fortunately, sleep problems can often be treated with changes in behavior, such as following a sleep schedule or creating a bedtime routine. Some children may sleep better using medications such as melatonin, which is a hormone that helps regulate the body's sleep-wake cycle. Like any medication, melatonin can have unwanted side effects. Talk to your child's doctor about possible risks and benefits before giving your child melatonin. Treating sleep problems in children with ASD may improve the child's overall behavior and functioning, as well as relieve family stress.[16]

Intellectual Disability

Many children with ASD have some degree of intellectual disability. When tested, some areas of ability may be normal, while others—especially cognitive (thinking) and language abilities—may be relatively weak. For example, a child with ASD may do well on tasks related to sight (such as putting a puzzle together) but may not do as well on language-based problem-solving tasks. Children with a form of ASD like Asperger syndrome often have average or above-average language skills and do not show delays in cognitive ability or speech.

Seizures

One in four children with ASD has seizures, often starting either in early childhood or during the teen years.[17] Seizures, caused by abnormal electrical activity in the brain, can result in

- A short-term loss of consciousness, or a blackout
- Convulsions, which are uncontrollable shaking of the whole body, or unusual movements
- Staring spells.

Sometimes lack of sleep or a high fever can trigger a seizure. An electroencephalogram (EEG), a nonsurgical test that records electrical activity in the brain, can help confirm whether a child is having seizures. However, some children with ASD have abnormal EEGs even if they are not having seizures.

Seizures can be treated with medicines called anticonvulsants. Some seizure medicines affect behavior; changes in behavior should be closely watched in children with ASD. In most cases, a doctor will use the lowest dose of medicine that works for the child. Anticonvulsants usually reduce the number of seizures but may not prevent all of them.

For more information about medications, see the NIMH online booklet, "Medications" at http://www.nimh.nih.gov/health/publications/mental-health-medications/index. shtml. None of these medications have been approved by the FDA to specifically treat symptoms of ASD.

Fragile X Syndrome

Fragile X syndrome is a genetic disorder and is the most common form of inherited intellectual disability,[18] causing symptoms similar to ASD. The name refers to one part of the X chromosome that has a defective piece that appears pinched and fragile when viewed with a microscope. Fragile X syndrome results from a change, called a mutation, on a single gene. This mutation, in effect, turns off the gene. Some people may have only a small mutation and not show any symptoms, while others have a larger mutation and more severe symptoms.[19]

Around 1 in 3 children who have Fragile X syndrome also meet the diagnostic criteria for ASD, and about 1 in 25 children diagnosed with ASD have the mutation that causes Fragile X syndrome.[19]

Because this disorder is inherited, children with ASD should be checked for Fragile X, especially if the parents want to have more children. Other family members who are planning to have children may also want to be checked for Fragile X syndrome. For more information on Fragile X, see the *Eunice Kennedy Shriver* National Institute of Child Health and Human Development website at http://www.nichd.nih.gov/health/topics/fragile_x_ syndrome.cfm.

Tuberous Sclerosis

Tuberous sclerosis is a rare genetic disorder that causes noncancerous tumors to grow in the brain and other vital organs. Tuberous sclerosis occurs in 1 to 4 percent of people with ASD.[18, 20] A genetic mutation causes the disorder, which has also been linked to mental retardation, epilepsy, and many other physical and mental health problems. There is no cure for tuberous sclerosis, but many symptoms can be treated.

Gastrointestinal Problems

Some parents of children with ASD report that their child has frequent gastrointestinal (GI) or digestion problems, including stomach pain, diarrhea, constipation, acid reflux, vomiting, or bloating. Food allergies may also cause problems for children with ASD.[21] It's unclear whether children with ASD are more likely to have GI problems than typically developing children.[22, 23] If your child has GI problems, a doctor who specializes in GI problems, called a gastroenterologist, can help find the cause and suggest appropriate treatment.

Some studies have reported that children with ASD seem to have more GI symptoms, but these findings may not apply to all children with ASD. For example, a recent study found that children with ASD in Minnesota were more likely to have physical and behavioral difficulties related to diet (for example, lactose intolerance or insisting on certain foods), as well as constipation, than children without ASD.[23] The researchers suggested that children with ASD may not have underlying GI problems, but that their behavior may create GI symptoms—for example, a child who insists on eating only certain foods may not get enough fiber or fluids in his or her diet, which leads to constipation.

Some parents may try to put their child on a special diet to control ASD or GI symptoms. While some children may benefit from limiting certain foods, there is no strong evidence that these special diets reduce ASD symptoms.[24] If you want to try a special diet, first talk with a doctor or a nutrition expert to make sure your child's nutritional needs are being met.

Co-occurring Mental Disorders

Children with ASD can also develop mental disorders such as anxiety disorders, attention deficit hyperactivity disorder (ADHD), or depression. Research shows that people with ASD are at higher risk for some mental disorders than people without ASD.[25] Managing these co-occurring conditions with medications or behavioral therapy, which teaches children how to control their behavior, can reduce symptoms that appear to worsen a child's ASD symptoms. Controlling these conditions will allow children with ASD to focus more on managing the ASD.[26]

HOW IS ASD TREATED?

While there's no proven cure yet for autism spectrum disorder (ASD), treating ASD early, using school-based programs, and getting proper medical care can greatly reduce ASD symptoms and increase your child's ability to grow and learn new skills.

Early Intervention

Research has shown that intensive behavioral therapy during the toddler or preschool years can significantly improve cognitive and language skills in young children with ASD.[27,28] There is no single best treatment for all children with ASD, but the American Academy of Pediatrics recently noted common features of effective early intervention programs.[29] These include:

- Starting as soon as a child has been diagnosed with ASD
- Providing focused and challenging learning activities at the proper developmental level for the child for at least 25 hours per week and 12 months per year
- Having small classes to allow each child to have one-on-one time with the therapist or teacher and small group learning activities
- Having special training for parents and family
- Encouraging activities that include typically developing children, as long as such activities help meet a specific learning goal
- Measuring and recording each child's progress and adjusting the intervention program as needed
- Providing a high degree of structure, routine, and visual cues, such as posted activity schedules and clearly defined boundaries, to reduce distractions
- Guiding the child in adapting learned skills to new situations and settings and maintaining learned skills
- Using a curriculum that focuses on
    - Language and communication
    - Social skills, such as joint attention (looking at other people to draw attention to something interesting and share in experiencing it)
    - Self-help and daily living skills, such as dressing and grooming
    - Research-based methods to reduce challenging behaviors, such as aggression and tantrums
    - Cognitive skills, such as pretend play or seeing someone else's point of view
    - Typical school-readiness skills, such as letter recognition and counting.

One type of a widely accepted treatment is applied behavior analysis (ABA). The goals of ABA are to shape and reinforce new behaviors, such as learning to speak and play, and reduce undesirable ones. ABA, which can involve intensive, one-on-one child-teacher interaction for up to 40 hours a week, has inspired the development of other, similar interventions that aim to help those with ASD reach their full potential.[30, 31] ABA-based interventions include:

- **Verbal Behavior**—focuses on teaching language using a sequenced curriculum that guides children from simple verbal behaviors (echoing) to more functional communication skills through techniques such as errorless teaching and prompting[32]
- **Pivotal Response Training**—aims at identifying pivotal skills, such as initiation and self-management, that affect a broad range of behavioral responses. This intervention incorporates parent and family education aimed at providing skills that enable the child to function in inclusive settings.[33, 34]

Other types of early interventions include:

- **Developmental, Individual Difference, Relationship-based(DIR)/ Floortime Model**—aims to build healthy and meaningful relationships and abilities by following the natural emotions and interests of the child.[35] One particular example is the Early Start Denver Model, which fosters improvements in communication, thinking, language, and other social skills and seeks to reduce atypical behaviors. Using developmental and relationship-based approaches, this therapy can be delivered in natural settings such as the home or pre-school.[33, 34]
- **TEACCH (Treatment and Education of Autistic and related Communication handicapped Children)**—emphasizes adapting the child's physical environment and using visual cues (for example, having classroom materials clearly marked and located so that students can access them independently). Using individualized plans for each student, TEACCH builds on the child's strengths and emerging skills.[34, 36]
- **Interpersonal Synchrony**—targets social development and imitation skills, and focuses on teaching children how to establish and maintain engagement with others.

For children younger than age 3, these interventions usually take place at home or in a child care center. Because parents are a child's earliest teachers, more programs are beginning to train parents to continue the therapy at home.

Students with ASD may benefit from some type of social skills training program.[37] While these programs need more research, they generally seek to increase and improve skills necessary for creating positive social interactions and avoiding negative responses. For example, Children's Friendship Training focuses on improving children's conversation and interaction skills and teaches them how to make friends, be a good sport, and respond appropriately to teasing.[38]

Working with Your Child's School

Start by speaking with your child's teacher, school counselor, or the school's student support team to begin an evaluation. Each state has a Parent Training and Information Center and a Protection and Advocacy Agency that can help you get an evaluation. A team of professionals conducts the evaluation using a variety of tools and measures. The evaluation will look at all areas related to your child's abilities and needs.

Once your child has been evaluated, he or she has several options, depending on the specific needs. If your child needs special education services and is eligible under the Individuals with Disabilities Education Act (IDEA), the school district (or the government agency administering the program) must develop an individualized education plan, or IEP specifically for your child within 30 days.

IDEA provides free screenings and early intervention services to children from birth to age 3. IDEA also provides special education and related services from ages 3 to 21. Information is available from the U.S. Department of Education at http://idea.ed.gov.

If your child is not eligible for special education services—not all children with ASD are eligible—he or she can still get free public education suited to his or her needs, which is available to all public-school children with disabilities under Section 504 of the Rehabilitation Act of 1973, regardless of the type or severity of the disability.

The U.S. Department of Education's Office for Civil Rights enforces Section 504 in programs and activities that receive Federal education funds. For more information on Section 504, please see http://www.ed.gov/about/ offices/list/ocr/504faq.html.

More information about U.S. Department of Education programs for children with disabilities is available at http://www.ed.gov/parents/needs/ speced/edpicks.jhtml?src=ln.

During middle and high school years, your child's teachers will begin to discuss practical issues such as work, living away from a parent or caregiver's home, and hobbies. These lessons should include gaining work experience, using public transportation, and learning skills that will be important in community living.[29]

Medications

Some medications can help reduce symptoms that cause problems for your child in school or at home. Many other medications may be prescribed off-label, meaning they have not been approved by the U.S. Food and Drug Administration (FDA) for a certain use or for certain people. Doctors may prescribe medications off-label if they have been approved to treat other disorders that have similar symptoms to ASD, or if they have been effective in treating adults or older children with ASD. Doctors prescribe medications off-label to try to help the youngest patients, but more research is needed to be sure that these medicines are safe and effective for children and teens with ASD.

At this time, the only medications approved by the FDA to treat aspects of ASD are the antipsychotics risperidone (Risperdal) and aripripazole (Abilify). These medications can help reduce irritability—meaning aggression, self-harming acts, or temper tantrums—in children ages 5 to 16 who have ASD.

Some medications that may be prescribed off-label for children with ASD include the following:

- **Antipsychotic medications** are more commonly used to treat serious mental illnesses such as schizophrenia. These medicines may help reduce aggression and other serious behavioral problems in children, including children with ASD. They may also help reduce repetitive behaviors, hyper-activity, and attention problems.[29]

- **Antidepressant medications**, such as fluoxetine (Prozac) or sertraline (Zoloft), are usually prescribed to treat depression and anxiety but are sometimes prescribed to reduce repetitive behaviors. Some antidepressants may also help control aggression and anxiety in children with ASD.[29] However, researchers still are not sure if these medications are useful; a recent study suggested that the antidepressant citalopram (Celexa) was no more effective than a placebo (sugar pill) at reducing repetitive behaviors in children with ASD (see article at http://www. nimh.nih.gov/science-news/2009/ citalopram-no-better-than-placebo-treatment-for-children-with-autism -spectrum-disorders.shtml).[39] http://www. nimh. nih.gov/ science-news/2009/ citalopram-no-better-than-placebo-treatment-for-children-with-autism-spectrum-disorders.shtml
- **Stimulant medications**, such as methylphenidate (Ritalin), are safe and effective in treating people with attention deficit hyperactivity disorder (ADHD). ethylphenidate has been shown to effectively treat hyperactivity in children with ASD as well. But not as many children with ASD respond to treatment, and those who do have shown more side effects than children with ADHD and not ASD.[40]

All medications carry a risk of side effects. For details on the side effects of common psychiatric medications, see the NIMH website on "Medications" at http://www.nimh.nih. gov/health/publications/mental-health-medications/ index. shtml.

FDA Warning about Antidepressants

Antidepressants are safe and popular, but some studies have suggested that they may have unintended effects on some people, especially in teens and young adults. The FDA warning says that patients of all ages taking antidepressants should be watched closely, especially during the first few weeks of treatment. Possible side effects to look for are depression that gets worse, suicidal thinking or behavior, or any unusual changes in behavior such as trouble sleeping, agitation, or withdrawal from normal social situations. Families and caregivers should report any changes to the doctor. The latest information from the FDA can be found at http://www.fda.gov.

A child with ASD may not respond in the same way to medications as typically developing children. You should work with a doctor who has experience treating children with ASD. The doctor will usually start your child on the lowest dose that helps control problem symptoms. Ask the doctor about any side effects of the medication and keep a record of how your child reacts to the medication. The doctor should regularly check your child's response to the treatment.

You have many options for treating your child's ASD. However, not all of them have been proven to work through scientific studies. Read the patient information that comes with your child's medication. Some people keep these patient inserts along with their other notes for easy reference. This is most useful when dealing with several different prescription medications. You should get all the facts about possible risks and benefits and talk to more than one expert when possible before trying a new treatment on your child.

How Common Is ASD?

Studies measuring autism spectrum disorder (ASD) prevalence—the number of children affected by ASD over a given time period—have reported varying results, depending on when and where the studies were conducted and how the studies defined ASD.

In a 2009 government survey on ASD prevalence, the Centers for Disease Control and Prevention (CDC) found that the rate of ASD was higher than in past U.S. studies. Based on health and school records of 8-year-olds in 14 communities throughout the country, the CDC survey found that around 1 in 110 children has ASD.[41] Boys face about four to five times higher risk than girls.

Experts disagree about whether this shows a true increase in ASD prevalence. Since the earlier studies were completed, guidelines for diagnosis have changed. Also, many more parents and doctors now know about ASD, so parents are more likely to take their children to be diagnosed, and more doctors are able to properly diagnose ASD. These and other changes may help explain some differences in prevalence numbers. Even so, the CDC report confirms other recent studies showing that more children are being diagnosed with ASD than ever before. For more information, please visit the autism section of the CDC website at http://www.cdc.gov/ncbddd/autism.

What Causes ASD?

Scientists don't know the exact causes of autism spectrum disorder (ASD), but research suggests that both genes and environment play important roles.

Genetic Factors

In identical twins who share the exact same genetic code, if one has ASD, the other twin also has ASD in nearly 9 out of 10 cases. If one sibling has ASD, the other siblings have 35 times the normal risk of also developing the disorder. Researchers are starting to identify particular genes that may increase the risk for ASD.[42,43]

Still, scientists have only had some success in finding exactly which genes are involved. For more information about such cases, see the section, "What are some other conditions that children with ASD may also have?" which describes Fragile X syndrome and tuberous sclerosis.

Most people who develop ASD have no reported family history of autism, suggesting that random, rare, and possibly many gene mutations are likely to affect a person's risk.[44,45] Any change to normal genetic information is called a mutation. Mutations can be inherited, but some arise for no reason. Mutations can be helpful, harmful, or have no effect.

Having increased genetic risk does not mean a child will definitely develop ASD. Many researchers are focusing on how various genes interact with each other and environmental factors to better understand how they increase the risk of this disorder.

Environmental Factors

In medicine, "environment" refers to anything outside of the body that can affect health. This includes the air we breathe, the water we drink and bathe in, he food we eat, the medicines we take, and many other things that our bodies may come in contact with. Environment also includes our surroundings in the womb, when our mother's health directly affects our growth and earliest development.

Researchers are studying many environmental factors such as family medical conditions, parental age and other demographic factors, exposure to toxins, and complications during birth or pregnancy.[29, 46-48]

As with genes, it's likely that more than one environmental factor is involved in increasing risk for ASD. And, like genes, any one of these risk factors raises the risk by only a small amount. Most people who have been exposed to environmental risk factors do not develop ASD. The National Institute of Environmental Health Sciences is also conducting research in this area. More information is available at http://www.niehs.nih.gov/health/topics/conditions/autism/index.cfm.

Scientists are studying how certain environmental factors may affect certain genes—turning them on or off, or increasing or decreasing their normal activity. This process is called epigenetics and is providing researchers with many new ways to study how disorders like ASD develop and possibly change over time.

ASD and Vaccines

Health experts recommend that children receive a number of vaccines early in life to protect against dangerous, infectious diseases, such as measles. Since pediatricians in the United States started giving these vaccines during regular checkups, the number of children getting sick, becoming disabled, or dying from these diseases has dropped to almost zero.

Children in the United States receive several vaccines during their first 2 years of life, around the same age that ASD symptoms often appear or become noticeable. A minority of parents suspect that vaccines are somehow related to their child's disorder. Some may be concerned about these vaccines due to the unproven theory that ASD may be caused by thimerosal. Thimerosal is a mercury-based chemical once added to some, but not all, vaccines to help extend their shelf life. However, except for some flu vaccines, no vaccine routinely given to preschool aged children in the United States has contained thimerosal since 2001. Despite this change, the rate of children diagnosed with ASD has continued to rise.

Other parents believe their child's illness might be linked to vaccines designed to protect against more than one disease, such as the measles-mumps-rubella (MMR) vaccine, which never contained thimerosal.

Many studies have been conducted to try to determine if vaccines are a possible cause of autism. As of 2010, none of the studies has linked autism and vaccines.[49,50]

Following extensive hearings, a special court of Federal judges ruled against several test cases that tried to prove that vaccines containing thimerosal, either by themselves or combined with the MMR vaccine, caused autism. More information about these hearings is available on the U.S. Court of Federal Claims' website at http://www.uscfc.uscourts.gov/ omnibus-autism-proceeding.

The latest information about research on autism and vaccines is available from the Centers for Disease Control and Prevention at http://cdc.gov/ncbddd/ autism/topics.html. This website provides information from the Federal Government and independent organizations.

WHAT EFFORTS ARE UNDER WAY TO IMPROVE THE DETECTION AND TREATMENT OF ASD?

Many recent research studies have focused on finding the earliest signs of autism spectrum disorder (ASD). These studies aim to help doctors diagnose children at a younger age so they can get needed interventions as quickly as possible.

For example, one early sign of ASD may be increased head size or rapid head growth. Brain imaging studies have shown that abnormal brain development beginning in an infant's first months may have a role in ASD. This theory suggests that genetic defects in growth factors, which direct proper brain development, cause the brain abnormalities seen in autism. It's possible that an infant's sudden, rapid head growth may be an early warning signal, which could help in early diagnosis and treatment or possible prevention of ASD.[51]

Current studies on ASD treatment are exploring many approaches, such as:

- A computer-based training program designed to teach children with ASD how to create and respond to facial expressions appropriately[52]
- A medication that may help improve functioning in children with Fragile X syndrome[53]
- New social interventions that can be used in the classroom or other "everyday" settings
- An intervention parents can follow to reduce and pre-vent ASD-related disability in children at high risk for the disorder.[54]

For more information about clinical trials on ASD funded by the National Institute of Mental Health, go to http://www.nimh.nih.gov/health/trials/ autism-spectrum-disorders-pervasive-developmental-disorders.shtml.

You can read about future research plans on the Interagency Autism Coordinating Committee's (IACC's) website at http://iacc.hhs.gov. The IACC is made up of representatives of Federal agencies and members of the public and coordinates efforts within the U.S. Department of Health and Human Services concerning ASD.

HOW CAN I HELP A CHILD WHO HAS ASD?

After your child is diagnosed with autism spectrum disorder (ASD), you may feel unprepared or unable to provide your child with the necessary care and education. Know that there are many treatment options, social services and programs, and other resources that can help.

Some tips that can help you and your child are:

- Keep a record of conversations, meetings with health care providers and teachers, and other sources of information. This will help you remember the different treatment options and decide which would help your child most.
- Keep a record of the doctors' reports and your child's evaluation. This information may help your child qualify for special programs.
- Contact your local health department or autism advocacy groups to learn about the special programs available in your state and local community.
- Talk with your child's pediatrician, school system, or an autism support group to find an autism expert in your area who can help you develop an intervention plan and find other local resources.

Understanding Teens with ASD

The teen years can be a time of stress and confusion for any growing child, including teenagers with autism spectrum disorder (ASD).

During the teenage years, adolescents become more aware of other people and their relationships with them. While most teenagers are concerned with acne, popularity, grades, and dates, teens with ASD may become painfully aware that they are different from their peers. For some, this awareness may encourage them to learn new behaviors and try to improve their social skills. For others, hurt feelings and problems connecting with others may lead to depression, anxiety, or other mental disorders. One way that some teens with ASD may express the tension and confusion that can occur during adolescence is through increased autistic or aggressive behavior. Teens with ASD will also need support to help them understand the physical changes and sexual maturation they experience during adolescence.

If your teen seems to have trouble coping, talk with his or her doctor about possible co-occurring mental disorders and what you can do. Behavioral therapies and medications often help.

Preparing for Your Child's Transition to Adulthood

The public schools' responsibility for providing services ends when a child with ASD reaches the age of 22. At that time, some families may struggle to find jobs to match their adult child's needs. If your family cannot continue caring for an adult child at home, you may need to look for other living arrangements. For more information, see the section, "Living arrangements for adults with ASD."

Long before your child finishes school, you should search for the best programs and facilities for young adults with ASD. If you know other parents of adults with ASD, ask them about the services available in your community. Local support and advocacy groups may be able to help you find programs and services that your child is eligible to receive as an adult.

Another important part of this transition is teaching youth with ASD to self-advocate. This means that they start to take on more responsibility for their education, employment, health care, and living arrangements. Adults with ASD or other disabilities must self-advocate for their rights under the Americans with Disabilities Act at work, in higher education, in the community, and elsewhere.

Living Arrangements for Adults with ASD

There are many options for adults living with ASD. Helping your adult child choose the right one will largely depend on what is available in your state and local community, as well as your child's skills and symptoms. Below are some examples of living arrangements you may want to consider:

- **Independent living.** Some adults with ASD are able to live on their own. Others can live in their own home or apartment if they get help dealing with major issues, such as managing personal finances, obtaining necessary health care, and interacting with government or social service agencies. Family members, professional agencies, or other types of providers can offer this assistance.
- **Living at home.** Government funds are available for families who choose to have their adult child with ASD live at home. These programs include Supplemental Security Income, Social Security Disability Insurance, and Medicaid waivers. Information about these programs and others is available from the Social Security Administration (SSA). Make an appointment with your local SSA office to find out which programs would be right for your adult child.
- **Other home alternatives.** Some families open their homes to provide long-term care to adults with disabilities who are not related to them. If the home teaches self-care and housekeeping skills and arranges leisure activities, it is called a "skill-development" home.
- **Supervised group living.** People with disabilities often live in group homes or apartments staffed by professionals who help with basic needs. These needs often include meal preparation, housekeeping, and personal care. People who are more independent may be able to live in a home or apartment where staff only visit a few times a week. Such residents generally prepare their own meals, go to work, and conduct other daily activities on their own.
- **Long-term care facilities.** This alternative is available for those with ASD who need intensive, constant supervision.

CITATIONS

[1] *American Psychiatric Association. Diagnostic and Statistical Manual of Mental Disorders, Fourth Edition – Text Revision* (DSM-IV-TR) (2000). Washington, DC: American Psychiatric Publishing, Inc.

[2] Wiggins, L. D., Rice, C. E. & Baio, J. (2009). Developmental regression in children with an autism spectrum disorder identified by a population-based surveillance system. *Autism*, Jul; *13*(4), 357–74.

[3] Jones, W., Carr, K. & Klin, A. (2008). Absence of preferential looking to the eyes of approaching adults predicts level of social disability in 2-year-old toddlers with autism spectrum disorder. *Archives of General Psychiatry*, Aug; *65*(8), 946–54.

[4] Klin, A., Lin, D. J., Gorrindo, P., Ramsay, G. & Jones, W. (2009). Two-year-olds with autism orient to non-social contingencies rather than biological motion. *Nature*, May 14; *459*(7244), 257–61.

[5] Ben Zeev Ghidoni B. Rett syndrome (2007). *Child and Adolescent Psychiatric Clinics of North America*, Jul; *16*(3),723–43.

[6] Percy A. K. Rett syndrome (2002). Current status and new vistas. *Neurologic Clinics*, Nov; *20*(4), 1125–41.

[7] Fombonne, E. (2002). Prevalence of childhood disintegrative disorder. *Autism*, Jun; *6*(2),149–57.

[8] *Eunice Kennedy Shriver* National Institute of Child Health and Human Development, NIH, DHHS (2006). *Rett Syndrome*. Washington, DC: U.S. Government Printing Office, NIH-065590.

[9] Fombonne, E. (2005). Epidemiologyof autistic disorder and other pervasive developmental disorders. *Journal of Clinical Psychiatry*, *66* (Suppl 10), 3–8.

[10] Volkmar, F. R. & Rutter, M. (1995). Childhood disintegrative disorder: results of the DSM-IV autism field trial. Journal of the *American Academy of Child and Adolescent Psychiatry*, Aug; *34*(8), 1092–5.

[11] Volkmar, FR. (1994). "*Childhood Disintegrative Disorder-Case Report*." In Spitzer RL. (ed) *DSM-IV Casebook*. Washington, DC: American Psychiatric Press.

[12] Filipek, P. A., Accardo, P. J., Ashwal, S., Baranek, G. T., Cook, E. H., Jr., Dawson, G., Gordon, B., Gravel, J. S., Johnson, C. P., Kallen, R. J., Levy, S. E., Minshew, N. J., Ozonoff, S., Prizant, B. M., Rapin, I., Rogers, S. J., Stone, W. L., Teplin, S. W., Tuchman, R. F. & Volkmar, F. R. (2000). Practice parameter: screening and diagnosis of autism: report of the Quality Standards Subcommittee of the American Academy of Neurology and the Child Neurology Society. *Neurology*, Aug 22; *55*(4), 468–79.

[13] Landa, R. J., Holman, K. C. & Garrett-Mayer, E. (2007). Social and communication development in toddlers with early and later diagnosis of autism spectrum disorders. *Archives of General Psychiatry*, Jul; *64*(7), 853–64.

[14] Johnson, C. P. & Myers, S. M. (). Identification and evaluation of children with autism spectrum disorders. *Pediatrics*, 2007 Nov; *120*(5), 1183–215.

[15] Krakowiak, P., Goodlin-Jones, B., Hertz-Picciotto, I., Croen, L. A. & Hansen, R. L. (2008). Sleep problems in children with autism spectrum disorders, developmental delays, and typical development: a population-based study. *Journal of Sleep Research*, Jun; *17*(2),197–206.

[16] Johnson, K. P., Giannotti, F. & Cortesi, F. (2009). Sleep patterns in autism spectrum disorders. *Child and Adolescent Psychiatric Clinics of North America*, Oct; *18*(4), 917–28.

[17] Volkmar, F. R. (2000). "Medical Problems, Treatments and Professionals." in Powers MD. (ed) *Children with Autism: A Parent's Guide, Second Edition*. Bethesda: Woodbine House.

[18] Zafeiriou, D. I., Ververi, A. & Vargiami, E. (2007). Childhood autism and associated comorbidities. *Brain and Development*, Jun; *29*(5), 257–72.

[19] *Eunice Kennedy Shriver* National Institute of Child Health and Human Development, NIH, PHS, DHHS *Families and Fragile X Syndrome* (2003). Washington, DC: U.S. Government Printing Office, NIH-96-3402.

[20] Smalley, S. L. (1998). Autism and tuberous sclerosis. *Journal of Autism and Developmental Disorders*, Oct; *28*(5), 407–14.

[21] Xue, M., Brimacombe, M., Chaaban, J., Zimmerman-Bier, B. & Wagner, G. C. (2008). Autism spectrum disorders: concurrent clinical disorders. *Journal of Child Neurology*, Jan; *23*(1), 6–13.

[22] Kuddo, T. & Nelson, K. B. (2003). How common are gastrointestinal disorders in children with autism? *Current Opinion in Pediatrics*, Jun; *15*(3), 339–43.

[23] Nikolov, R. N., Bearss, K. E., Lettinga, J., Erickson, C., Rodowski, M., Aman, M. G., McCracken, J. T., McDougle, C. J., Tierney, E., Vitiello, B., Arnold, L. E., Shah, B., Posey, D. J., Ritz, L. & Scahill L. (2009). Gastrointestinal symptoms in a sample of children with pervasive developmental disorders. *Journal of Autism and Developmental Disorders*, Mar; *39*(3), 405–13.

[24] Buie, T., Campbell, D. B., Fuchs, G. J., 3rd, Furuta, G. T., Levy, J, Vandewater, J, Whitaker, A. H., Atkins, D., Bauman, M. L., Beaudet A. L., Carr, E. G., Gershon, M. D., Hyman, S. L., Jirapinyo, P., Jyonouchi, H., Kooros, K., Kushak, R., Levitt, P., Levy, S. E., Lewis, J. D., Murray K. F., Natowicz, M. R., Sabra, A., Wershil, B. K., Weston, S. C., Zeltzer, L. & Winter, H. (2010). Evaluation, diagnosis, and treatment of gastrointestinal disorders in individuals with ASDs: a consensus report. *Pediatrics*, Jan; *125*Suppl 1, S1–18.

[25] Leyfer, O. T., Folstein, S. E., Bacalman, S., Davis, N. O., Dinh, E., Morgan, J., Tager-Flusberg, H. & Lainhart, J. E. (2006). Comorbid psychiatric disorders in children with autism: interview development and rates of disorders. *Journal of Autism and Developmental Disorders*, Oct; *36*(7), 849–61.

[26] Simonoff, E., Pickles, A., Charman, T., Chandler, S., Loucas, T. & Baird, G. (2008). Psychiatric disorders in children with autism spectrum disorders: prevalence, comorbidity, and associated factors in a population-derived sample. *Journal of the American Academy of Child and Adolescent Psychiatry*, Aug; *47*(8), 921–9.

[27] Reichow, B. & Wolery, M. (2009). Comprehensive synthesis of early intensive behavioral interventions for young children with autism based on the UCLA young autism project model. *Journal of Autism and Developmental Disorders*, Jan; *39*(1), 23–41.

[28] Rogers, S. J. & Vismara, L.A. (2008). Evidence-based comprehensive treatments for early autism. *Journal of Clinical Child and Adolescent Psychology*, Jan; *37*(1), 8–38.

[29] Myers, S. M. & Johnson, C. P. (2007). Management of children with autism spectrum disorders. *Pediatrics*, Nov; *120*(5),1162–82.

[30] McEachin, J. J., Smith, T. & Lovaas, O. I. (1993). Long-term outcome for children with autism who received early intensive behavioral treatment. *American Journal of Mental Retardation*, Jan; *97*(4), 359-72; discussion 73–91.

[31] Couper, J. J. & Sampson, A. J. (2003). Children with autism deserve evidence-based intervention. *Medical Journal of Australia*, May 5; *178*(9), 424–5.

[32] Levy, S. E., Mandell, D. S. & Schultz RT. Autism. *Lancet*, 2009 Nov 7; 374(9701), 1627–38.

[33] Paul R. (2008). Interventions to improve communication in autism. *Child and Adolescent Psychiatric Clinics of North America*, Oct; *17*(4), 835-56, ix–x.

[34] Autism Speaks (2010). How Is Autism Treated? http://www.autism speaks.org/docs/ family_services_docs/100day2/Treatment_Version_2_0.pdf. Accessed on October 22.

[35] The Interdisciplinary Council on Developmental and Learning Disorders (2009). *Floortime overview*. http://www.icdl.com/dirFloortime/overview/index.shtml. Accessed on Jun 17.

[36] TEACCH – UNC School of Medicine. What is TEACCH? http://teacch.com/about-us-1 /what-is-teacch. Accessed on Jun 17, 2009.

[37] Bellini, S. & Peters, J. K. (2008). Social skills training for youth with autism spectrum disorders. *Child and Adolescent Psychiatric Clinics of North America*, Oct; *17*(4), 857–73.

[38] Frankel, F., Myatt, R., Sugar, C., Whitham, C., Gorospe, C. M. & Laugeson, E. (2010). A Randomized Controlled Study of Parentassisted Children's Friendship Training with Children having Autism Spectrum Disorders. *Journal of Autism and Developmental Disorders*, Jul; *40*(7), 827–42.

[39] King, B. H., Hollander, E., Sikich, L., McCracken, J. T., Scahill, L., Bregman, J. D., Donnelly, C. L., Anagnostou, E., Dukes, K., Sullivan, L., Hirtz, D., Wagner, A. & Ritz, L. (2009). Lack of efficacy of citalopram in children with autism spectrum disorders and high levels of repetitive behavior: citalopram ineffective in children with autism. *Archives of General Psychiatry*, Jun; *66*(6), 583–90.

[40] Research Units on Pediatric Psychopharmacology Autism Network. (2005). Randomized, controlled, crossover trial of methylphenidate in pervasive developmental disorders with hyperactivity. *Archives of General Psychiatry*, Nov; *62*(11), 1266–74.

[41] Prevalenceof autism spectrum disorders- Autism and Developmental Disabilities Monitoring Network, United States, (2006). *MMWR Surveillance Summaries*, 2009 Dec 18; *58*(10), 1–20.

[42] Campbell, D. B., Sutcliffe, J. S., Ebert, P. J., Militerni, R., Bravaccio, C., Trillo, S., Elia, M., Schneider, C., Melmed, R., Sacco, R., Persico, A. M. & Levitt, P. (2006). A genetic variant that disrupts MET transcription is associated with autism. *Proceedings of the National Academy of Sciences of the United States of America*, Nov 7; *103*(45), 16834–9.

[43] Arking, D. E., Cutler, D. J., Brune, C. W., Teslovich, T. M., West, K., Ikeda, M., Rea, A., Guy, M., Lin, S., Cook, E. H. & Chakravarti, A. (2008). A common genetic variant in the neurexin superfamily member CNTNAP2 increases familial risk of autism. *American Journal of Human Genetics*, Jan; *82*(1), 160–4.

[44] Sebat, J., Lakshmi, B., Malhotra, D., Troge, J., Lese-Martin, C., Walsh, T., Yamrom, B., Yoon, S., Krasnitz, A., Kendall, J., Leotta, A., Pai, D., Zhang, R., Lee, Y. H., Hicks, J., Spence, S. J., Lee, A. T., Puura, K., Lehtimaki, T., Ledbetter, D., Gregersen, P. K., Bregman, J., Sutcliffe, J. S., Jobanputra, V., Chung, W., Warburton, D., King, M. C., Skuse, D., Geschwind, D. H., Gilliam, T. C., Ye, K. & Wigler, M. (2007). Strong association of de novo copy number mutations with autism. *Science*, Apr 20; *316*(5823), 445–9.

[45] Morrow, E. M., Yoo, S. Y., Flavell, S. W., Kim, T. K., Lin, Y., Hill, R. S., Mukaddes, N. M., Balkhy, S., Gascon, G., Hashmi, A., Al-Saad, S., Ware, J., Joseph, R. M., Greenblatt, R., Gleason, D., Ertelt, J. A., Apse, K. A., Bodell, A., Partlow, J. N., Barry,

B., Yao, H., Markianos, K., Ferland, R. J., Greenberg, M. E. & Walsh, C. A. (2008). Identifying autism loci and genes by tracing recent shared ancestry. *Science*, Jul 11; *321*(5886), 218–23.

[46] Kolevzon, A., Gross, R. & Reichenberg, A. (2007). Prenatal and perinatal risk factors for autism: a review and integration of findings. *Archives of Pediatric and Adolescent Medicine*, Apr; *161*(4), 326–33.

[47] Lawler, C. P., Croen, L. A., Grether, J. K. & Van de Water, J. (2004). Identifying environmental contributions to autism: provocative clues and false leads. *Mental Retardation and Developmental Disabilities Research Reviews*, *10*(4), 292–302.

[48] Daniels, J. L., Forssen, U., Hultman, C. M., Cnattingius, S., Savitz, D. A., Feychting, M. & Sparen, P. (2008). Parental psychiatric disorders associated with autism spectrum disorders in the offspring. *Pediatrics*, May; *121*(5), e1357–62.

[49] Immunization Safety Review Committee (2004). Immunization Safety Review: Vaccines and Autism. Washington, DC: The National Academies Press.

[50] Interagency Autism Coordinating Committee (2010). Question 3: what caused this to happen and can this be prevented? *The 2010 Interagency Autism Coordinating Committee Strategic Plan for Autism Spectrum Disorders Research – January, 19, 2010*. Washington, DC: Interagency Autism Coordinating Committee, U.S. Department of Health and Human Services.

[51] Courchesne, E., Carper, R. & Akshoomoff, N. (2003). Evidence of brain overgrowth in the first year of life in autism. *JAMA*. Jul 16; *290*(3), 337–44.

[52] National Institute of Mental Health (2010). Recovery act grant aims to teach kids with autism how to better express themselves. http://www. nimh.nih.gov/sciencenews/2009/ recovery-actgrant-aims-to-teach-kids-with-autism-how-to-better-expressthemselves. shtml. Accessed on March 23.

[53] National Institute of Mental Health. Clinical tests begin on medication to correct Fragile X defect (2010). http://www.nimh.nih.gov/science-news/ 2009/clinical-tests-begin-on-medication-tocorrect-fragile-x-defect.shtml. Accessed on March 23.

[54] National Institute of Mental Health (2010). NIH awards more than 50 grants to boost search for causes, improve treatments for autism. http://www.nimh.nih.gov/science-news/2009/nih-awards-more-than-50-grants-to-boost-search-for-causesimprove-treatments-for-autism.shtml. Accessed on March 23.

In: Autism Spectrum Disorders ISBN 978-1-62257-076-8
Editors: Gregory L. Campbell and Anthony O. Phillips

Chapter 2

AUTISM PREVALENCE: MORE AFFECTED OR MORE DETECTED?*

U. S. Department of Health and Human Services

Autism is always surprising. Earlier today, the CDC released new numbers from their ongoing surveillance of autism prevalence, the *Autism and Developmental Disability Monitoring (ADDM) Network*. What was once considered a rare disorder is now reported as affecting 1 in 88 children, 1 in 54 boys. These new numbers, up 78 percent from 2002 and 23 percent from 2006, raise immediate questions. Are more children affected or more detected? Does the increase reflect a growing problem, or do these new numbers reflect an improvement in our ability to diagnose and serve those affected?

These new data do not answer these questions. The CDC surveillance project focuses on 8-year-olds identified in 2008; that is, children who were born in 2000. By definition, autism begins before age 3, so a focus on 8-year-olds should capture anyone who was identified and still has a diagnosis. The prevalence numbers are based on a standardized assessment of descriptions of behaviors culled from administrative or health records from select communities, not on standardized diagnostic interviews in the general population. The strength of this approach is its wide reach, allowing a comparison across 14 states. The CDC reports a four-fold variation across sites. These new results, as with those from other records-based surveillance systems, do not answer questions related to why the identified prevalence of autism has changed over time.

Other research suggests a complicated picture. A total population study of all 7–12-year-olds in a town in South Korea (more than 55,000 children) used standardized diagnostic instruments for children who screened positive and reported a prevalence of 2.64 percent.[1] That is 1 in 38 children! There is no reason to expect that this prevalence is unique to this community. To be sure, two-thirds of these children had never received a diagnosis of autism spectrum disorder (ASD), meaning that the identified prevalence was closer to 1 percent or one in 100, roughly the same prevalence reported in the United States. From this perspective, the increase reported by the CDC might mean we are better at detecting children who meet

* This is an edited, reformatted and augmented version of the National Institute of Mental Health, dated March 29, 2012.

criteria for ASD, but potentially we still are only halfway to the actual prevalence in the general population. Indeed, the biggest increase in the CDC surveillance report was in Hispanic and African American children, groups which previously had low rates of detection.

But can we be certain that more children are not affected? Data from the Developmental Disability Services registry in California demonstrates a 12-fold increase in the number of children receiving services for autism over the past 20 years, with a continuing rise recently. But these data, while dramatic, cannot rule out increased use of the diagnosis. *Bearman and colleagues* who have studied the California trends suggest that only about 26 percent of this increase can be explained by diagnostic substitution, especially for the most severe cases — children with intellectual deficits — which may not have been identified as autism in an earlier era. Another fraction can be attributed to better ascertainment or detection especially for children at the less severe end of the spectrum. Together these factors explain only a part of the linear increase observed in the California registry. In the absence of other explanations they and others suggest that a real increase is quite likely.[2, 3, 4]

Which makes a recent report from England especially surprising. In a careful epidemiological study based on a national sample (n = 7,461 adults) from 2007, Brugha and colleagues did careful diagnostic assessments based on standardized interviews. They found that familiar rate of about 1 percent in adults across the entire age range without a significant reduction in the older part of the sample as one would expect if the prevalence had increased in recent years.[5]

This takes us back to the central question: has the number of children with ASD increased or not? Total population epidemiological studies suggest much or all of the increase is due to better and wider detection. Studies of administrative and services data suggest that better detection cannot fully explain the profound and continuing increase. Are we seeing more affected or more detected? The question is vitally important, but there is not one, simple answer just as autism is not a single, simple disorder.

If there is an increase in the number affected, then we need to find the causal factors to bend the curve. Analogous increases in food allergies, asthma, and Type 1 diabetes have provoked an aggressive search for environmental causes. If the number of children with ASD has not changed, but we are diagnosing and serving 12-fold more of them over the past two decades, then we need to focus on better diagnosis and treatments rather than looking for new environmental factors driving the precipitous increase.

Science can resolve this dilemma, but the methods to examine this question as well as the answers will be complex. While it is never possible to go back in time, longitudinal population based studies and even careful retrospective studies can determine if more children are affected and if the nature of the disorder is changing over time. The changes in prevalence of other developmental disorders, measured with biomarkers (Type 1 diabetes) or emergency room visits (food allergies), appear to be true increases in the number of children affected. As diagnostic changes and ascertainment fail to explain the majority of the increase in autism prevalence, it seems prudent to assume that there are indeed more children affected and continue an aggressive search for causes while striving to improve detection, treatments, and services. Our working assumption is that there are both more children affected and more detected.

REFERENCES

[1] Kim, YS; Leventhal, BL; Koh, YJ; Fombonne, E; Laska, E; Lim, EC; Cheon, KA; Kim, SJ; Kim, YK; Lee, H; Song, DH; Grinker, RR. Prevalence of autism spectrum disorders in a total population sample. Am J Psychiatry. 2011 Sep; 168(9), 904-12. Epub 2011 May 9. PubMed PMID: 21558103.

[2] King, M; Bearman, P. Diagnostic change and the increased prevalence of autism. *Int J Epidemiol.* 2009 Oct; 38(5), 1224-34. Epub 2009 Sep 7. PubMed PMID: 19737791; PubMed Central PMCID: PMC2800781.

[3] Keyes, KM; Susser, E; Cheslack-Postava, K; Fountain, C; Liu, K; Bearman, PS. Cohort effects explain the increase in autism diagnosis among children born from 1992 to 2003 in California. *Int J Epidemiol.* 2011 Dec 7. [Epub ahead of print] PubMed PMID: 22253308.

[4] Bresnahan, M; Li, G; Susser, E. Hidden in plain sight. *Int J Epidemiol.* 2009 Oct; 38(5), 1172-4. PubMed PMID: 19797336.

[5] Brugha, TS; McManus, S; Bankart, J; Scott, F; Purdon, S; Smith, J; Bebbington, P; Jenkins, R; Meltzer, H. Epidemiology of autism spectrum disorders in adults in the community in England. *Arch Gen Psychiatry.* 2011 May; 68(5),459-65. PubMed PMID: 21536975.

In: Autism Spectrum Disorders ISBN 978-1-62257-076-8
Editors: Gregory L. Campbell and Anthony O. Phillips

Chapter 3

PREVALENCE OF AUTISM SPECTRUM DISORDERS: AUTISM AND DEVELOPMENTAL DISABILITIES MONITORING NETWORK, 14 SITES, UNITED STATES, 2008*

Centers for Disease Control and Prevention

ABSTRACT

Problem/Condition: Autism spectrum disorders (ASDs) are a group of developmental disabilities characterized by impairments in social interaction and communication and by restricted, repetitive, and stereotyped patterns of behavior. Symptoms typically are apparent before age 3 years. The complex nature of these disorders, coupled with a lack of biologic markers for diagnosis and changes in clinical definitions over time, creates challenges in monitoring the prevalence of ASDs. Accurate reporting of data is essential to understand the prevalence of ASDs in the population and can help direct research.

Period Covered: 2008.

Description of System: The Autism and Developmental Disabilities Monitoring (ADDM) Network is an active surveillance system that estimates the prevalence of ASDs and describes other characteristics among children aged 8 years whose parents or guardians reside within 14 ADDM sites in the United States. ADDM does not rely on professional or family reporting of an existing ASD diagnosis or classification to ascertain case status. Instead, information is obtained from children's evaluation records to determine the presence of ASD symptoms at any time from birth through the end of the year when the child reaches age 8 years. ADDM focuses on children aged 8 years because a baseline study conducted by CDC demonstrated that this is the age of identified peak prevalence. A child is included as meeting the surveillance case definition for an ASD if he or she displays behaviors (as described on a comprehensive evaluation completed by a qualified professional) consistent with the American Psychiatric

* This is an edited, reformatted and augmented version of the 14 Sites, United States, 2008. MMWR, SS Vol. 61 (No. 3), dated March 30, 2012.

Association's Diagnostic and Statistical Manual-IV, Text Revision (DSM-IV-TR) diagnostic criteria for any of the following conditions: Autistic Disorder; Pervasive Developmental Disorder–Not Otherwise Specified (PDD-NOS, including Atypical Autism); or Asperger Disorder. The first phase of the ADDM methodology involves screening and abstraction of comprehensive evaluations completed by professional providers at multiple data sources in the community. Multiple data sources are included, ranging from general pediatric health clinics to specialized programs for children with developmental disabilities. In addition, many ADDM sites also review and abstract records of children receiving special education services in public schools. In the second phase of the study, all abstracted evaluations are reviewed by trained clinicians to determine ASD case status. Because the case definition and surveillance methods have remained consistent across all ADDM surveillance years to date, comparisons to results for earlier surveillance years can be made. This report provides updated ASD prevalence estimates from the 2008 surveillance year, representing 14 ADDM areas in the United States. In addition to prevalence estimates, characteristics of the population of children with ASDs are described, as well as detailed comparisons of the 2008 surveillance year findings with those for the 2002 and 2006 surveillance years.

Results: For 2008, the overall estimated prevalence of ASDs among the 14 ADDM sites was 11.3 per 1,000 (one in 88) children aged 8 years who were living in these communities during 2008. Overall ASD prevalence estimates varied widely across all sites (range: 4.8–21.2 per 1,000 children aged 8 years). ASD prevalence estimates also varied widely by sex and by racial/ethnic group. Approximately one in 54 boys and one in 252 girls living in the ADDM Network communities were identified as having ASDs. Comparison of 2008 findings with those for earlier surveillance years indicated an increase in estimated ASD prevalence of 23% when the 2008 data were compared with the data for 2006 (from 9.0 per 1,000 children aged 8 years in 2006 to 11.0 in 2008 for the 11 sites that provided data for both surveillance years) and an estimated increase of 78% when the 2008 data were compared with the data for 2002 (from 6.4 per 1,000 children aged 8 years in 2002 to 11.4 in 2008 for the 13 sites that provided data for both surveillance years). Because the ADDM Network sites do not make up a nationally representative sample, these combined prevalence estimates should not be generalized to the United States as a whole.

Interpretation: These data confirm that the estimated prevalence of ASDs identified in the ADDM network surveillance populations continues to increase. The extent to which these increases reflect better case ascertainment as a result of increases in awareness and access to services or true increases in prevalence of ASD symptoms is not known. ASDs continue to be an important public health concern in the United States, underscoring the need for continued resources to identify potential risk factors and to provide essential supports for persons with ASDs and their families.

Public Health Action: Given substantial increases in ASD prevalence estimates over a relatively short period, overall and within various subgroups of the population, continued monitoring is needed to quantify and understand these patterns. With 5 biennial surveillance years completed in the past decade, the ADDM Network continues to monitor prevalence and characteristics of ASDs and other developmental disabilities for the 2010 surveillance year. Further work is needed to evaluate multiple factors contributing to increases in estimated ASD prevalence over time. ADDM Network investigators continue to explore these factors, with a focus on understanding disparities in the identification of ASDs among certain subgroups and on how these disparities have contributed to changes in the estimated prevalence of ASDs. CDC is partnering with other federal and private partners in a coordinated response to identify risk factors for ASDs and to meet the needs of persons with ASDs and their families.

Corresponding author: Jon Baio, EdS, National Center on Birth Defects and Developmental Disabilities, CDC, 1600 Clifton Road, MS E-86, Atlanta, GA 30333. Telephone: 404-498-3873; Fax: 404-498-3550; E-mail: jbaio@cdc.gov.

INTRODUCTION

Autism spectrum disorders (ASDs) are a group of developmental disabilities characterized by impairments in social interaction and communication and by restricted, repetitive, and stereotyped patterns of behavior [1]. Symptoms typically are apparent before age 3 years. Since the early 1990s, elevated public concern about continued reported increases in the number of children receiving services for ASDs and reports of higher-than-expected ASD prevalence estimates have underscored the need for systematic public health monitoring of ASDs [2]. Tracking the prevalence of ASDs over time poses unique challenges because of the complex nature of these disorders, a lack of biologic markers for diagnosis, and changes in clinical definitions over time.

In 2000, CDC established the Autism and Developmental Disabilities Monitoring (ADDM) Network to collect data that would provide estimates of the prevalence of ASDs and other developmental disabilities in the United States [2]. Initial reports from the ADDM Network provided ASD prevalence estimates from six sites for the 2000 surveillance year [3] and from 14 sites for the 2002 surveillance year [4]. Estimates of ASD prevalence among children aged 8 years were similar for both surveillance years. Data combined from all sites in each respective surveillance year yielded overall ASD prevalence estimates of 6.7 per 1,000 children aged 8 years in 2000 (range: 4.5–9.9) and 6.6 per 1,000 in 2002 (range: 3.3–10.6), or one in every 150 children aged 8 years.

The subsequent ADDM Network report provided data on estimated ASD prevalence among children aged 8 years for 2004 (eight sites) and 2006 (11 sites) [5]. When data from all sites were combined, overall estimated ASD prevalence was 8.0 per 1,000 children aged 8 years in 2004 (range: 4.6–9.8), or one in every 125 children, and 9.0 per 1,000 in 2006 (range: 4.2–12.1), or one in every 110 children aged 8 years. ASD prevalence estimates for the 2002 and 2006 surveillance years were compared [5]. All 10 ADDM sites that provided data for both surveillance years reported an increase in estimated ASD prevalence (range: 27%–95%). By 2006, the combined estimated prevalence of ASDs in ADDM Network sites approached 1% of children aged 8 years, a 4-year increase of 57% among sites that provided data for both the 2002 and 2006 surveillance years [5]. Some of the increase in estimated ASD prevalence might be attributed to improved identification, particularly among certain subgroups (e.g., children without intellectual disability and Hispanic children). These data indicated the importance of continuing to monitor trends in ASD prevalence and of accelerating the pace of research into risk factors and effective interventions.

Certain studies from the United States, Europe, and Asia have reported ASD prevalence estimates based on national survey data, statewide administrative data, or community screening approaches [6-10]. Results from these studies are generally consistent with those reported by the ADDM Network, although some international prevalence estimates are higher. In the United States, parent-reported data from the 2007 National Survey of Children's Health indicated an overall estimated prevalence of 11.0 per 1,000 children aged 3–17 years [6], and data from the National Health Interview Survey demonstrated a nearly fourfold increase in estimated ASD prevalence between the 1997–1999 and the 2006–2008 surveillance periods [7]. A British study that employed both a questionnaire and direct screening methods estimated an ASD prevalence of close to 1% of children aged 5–9 years during the 2003 and 2004 school years [8,9]. A recent study based on population screening and direct assessment in South Korea estimated overall ASD prevalence of 26.4 per 1,000 children aged 7–12 years in 2006 [10].

This report provides updated ASD prevalence estimates from the ADDM Network for the 2008 surveillance year, representing 14 sites in the United States. In addition to prevalence estimates, characteristics of the population of children with ASDs are described. This report is intended to communicate the latest available ASD prevalence estimates from the ADDM Network and to provide basic comparisons with estimates for earlier ADDM surveillance years. More focused efforts are underway to analyze available data on multiple factors influencing the identification of children with ASDs and potential changes in risk factors over time.

METHODS

Study Sites

The Children's Health Act of 2000 [11] authorized CDC to create the ADDM Network, the only collaborative network to estimate the prevalence of ASDs in the United States. ADDM has multiple goals: 1) to obtain as complete a count as possible of the number of children with ASDs in each project area, 2) to report comparable population-based ASD prevalence estimates from different sites and determine if these rates are changing over time, 3) to study whether autism is more common among some groups of children than among others, and 4) to provide descriptive data on the population of children with ASDs. Since the ADDM Network's inception in 2000, CDC has funded grantees in 14 states (Alabama, Arizona, Arkansas, Colorado, Florida, Maryland, Missouri, New Jersey, North Carolina, Pennsylvania, South Carolina, Utah, West Virginia, and Wisconsin). The ADDM Network implements a multisite, multiple-source, records-based surveillance methodology based on a model originally implemented by CDC's Metropolitan Atlanta Developmental Disabilities Surveillance Program (MADDSP) [12]. The case definition and surveillance methods, which have been described in detail previously [2-5,12,13], have remained consistent over time, enabling comparisons across multiple surveillance years. ADDM focuses on children aged 8 years because a baseline ASD prevalence study conducted by MADDSP demonstrated that this is the age of identified peak prevalence[12]. MADDSP represents one ADDM site in Georgia, and the remaining ADDM projects are administered through state health departments or through universities working on behalf of their state health departments to collect or receive information used for protecting public health. Sites were selected through a competitive objective review process on the basis of their ability to conduct active, records-based surveillance of ASDs; they were not selected to be a nationally representative sample. Each ADDM site participating in the 2008 surveillance year functioned as a public health authority under the HIPAA Privacy Rule and met applicable local Institutional Review Board and privacy/confidentiality requirements under 45 CFR 46 [14].

Case Ascertainment

ADDM is an active surveillance system that does not rely on professional or family reporting of an existing diagnosis or classification to ascertain ASD case status. Case determination is completed in two phases. The first phase involves screening and abstraction of records at multiple data sources in the community. All abstracted evaluations then are compiled and reviewed by trained clinicians to determine ASD case status in the second phase of the study. In the first phase, a broad net is cast to screen thousands of records and identify a subset of children with general symptoms of ASDs, whereas a much more strict case definition is applied during the second phase of the study. Because children's records are screened at multiple data sources, developmental assessments completed by a wide range of health and education providers are included. Data sources are categorized as either 1) education source type, including evaluations to determine eligibility for special education services or 2) health source type, including diagnostic and developmental assessments from psychologists, neurologists, developmental pediatricians, physical therapists, occupational therapists, speech/language pathologists, and other providers. Agreements to access records are made at the institutional level in the form of contracts, memoranda, or other formal agreements. All ADDM Network sites have agreements in place to access records at health sources; however, four ADDM sites (Alabama, Florida, Missouri, and Wisconsin) have not been granted access to records at education sources, and in one site (Colorado), parents are notified directly about the study and may request that their children's education records be excluded.

In the first phase of the study, ADDM Network sites identify source records to review based on a child's year of birth and either 1) eligibility classifications in special education or 2) International Classification of Diseases, Ninth Revision (ICD-9) billing codes (Box) for select childhood disabilities or psychological conditions. Children's records are screened to confirm year of birth and residency in the surveillance area at some time during the surveillance year. For children meeting age and residency requirements, the source files are screened for certain behavioral or diagnostic descriptions defined by ADDM as "triggers" for abstraction (e.g., child does not initiate interactions with others, prefers to play alone or engage in solitary activities, or has received a documented ASD diagnosis). If abstraction "triggers" are found, evaluation information from birth through the current surveillance year is abstracted into a single composite record for each child.

In the second phase of the ADDM methodology, the abstracted composite evaluation files are de-identified and reviewed systematically by trained clinicians to determine ASD case status using a coding scheme based on the American Psychiatric Association's Diagnostic and Statistical Manual-IV, Text Revision (DSM-IV-TR) [1] criteria for ASDs. A child is included as meeting the surveillance case definition for ASD if he or she displays behaviors at any time from birth through the end of the year when the child reaches age 8 years, as described on a comprehensive evaluation by a qualified professional, that are consistent with the DSM-IV-TR diagnostic criteria for any of the following conditions: Autistic Disorder; Pervasive Developmental Disorder–Not Otherwise Specified (PDD-NOS, including Atypical Autism); or Asperger Disorder.

Box. Core list of International Classification of Diseases, Ninth Revision billing codes used by all Autism and Developmental Disabilities Monitoring Network sites to identify records for review at health sources

299.0	Autistic disorder
299.1	Childhood disintegrative disorder
299.8	Other specified pervasive developmental disorders
299.9	Unspecified pervasive developmental disorder
315.30	Developmental speech or language disorder
315.31	Expressive language disorder
315.32	Mixed receptive-expressive language disorder
315.4	Developmental coordination disorder
315.5	Mixed development disorder
315.8	Other specified delays in development
315.9	Unspecified delay in development
317.0	Mild mental retardation
318.0	Moderate mental retardation
318.1	Severe mental retardation
318.2	Profound mental retardation
319.0	Unspecified mental retardation
330.8	Other specified cerebral degenerations in childhood
348.3	Encephalopathy, not elsewhere classified
348.8	Other conditions of brain
348.9	Unspecified condition of brain
759.5	Tuberous sclerosis
759.83	Fragile X syndrome
771.0	Congenital rubella
783.42	Delayed milestones
V79.2	Screening, mental retardation
V79.3	Screening, developmental handicaps in early childhood
V79.8	Screening, other specified mental disorders and developmental handicaps
V79.9	Screening, unspecified mental disorder and developmental handicap

Descriptive Characteristics

In addition to coding DSM-IV-TR diagnostic criteria for determining ASD case status, clinician reviewers systematically record additional findings from each abstracted evaluation. For example, reviewers note any concerns regarding the child's development by age 3 years, with specific focus on the development of social, language, and imaginative play skills as well as any mention of regression or plateau in skill development. The diagnostic conclusions from each evaluation record also are summarized for each child, including notation of any

ASD diagnosis by subtype, when available. Children are considered to have a previously documented ASD classification if they received a diagnosis of Autistic Disorder, PDD-NOS, Asperger Disorder, or ASD that was documented in an abstracted evaluation or by an ICD-9 billing code at any time from birth through the end of the year when they reached age 8 years, or if they received special education services under an autism eligibility during the surveillance year.

Information on children's functional skills also is abstracted from source records, when available, including scores on tests of intellectual ability. Children are classified as having intellectual disability if they had an intelligence quotient (IQ) score of ≤70 on their most recent test available in the record. Borderline intellectual ability is defined as having an IQ score of 71–85, and average or above-average intellectual ability is defined as having an IQ score of >85. In the absence of a specific IQ score, an examiner's statement about the child's intellectual ability, if available, is used to classify the child in one of these three levels.

Quality Assurance

All sites follow the same quality assurance standards established by the ADDM Network. For Phase 1, screening and abstraction of source records are monitored for accuracy on a periodic basis. In Phase 2, ongoing inter-rater reliability checks are conducted on a blinded, random sample of ≥10% of records undergoing clinician review. For the 2008 surveillance year, when comparison samples from all sites are combined, inter-rater agreement on case status (confirmed ASD versus not ASD) was 90.2% (k = 0.8); this exceeds the minimal quality assurance standards established by the ADDM Network for all surveillance years.

Analytic Methods

Population denominators for calculating ASD prevalence estimates were obtained from CDC's National Center for Health Statistics (NCHS) vintage 2009 bridged-race postcensal population estimates for calculating vital rates [15]. NCHS provides estimated population counts by state, county, single year of age, race, ethnic origin, and sex. Population denominators for the 2008 surveillance year were compiled from the postcensal estimates of children aged 8 years living in the counties under surveillance by each ADDM site (Table 1).

For two sites (Arizona and Utah), partial counties were included in the 2008 surveillance area, so geographic boundaries were defined by the school district(s) included in the surveillance area. Counts of children residing in outlying school districts were subtracted from the county-level postcensal denominators using school enrollment data from the U.S. Department of Education's National Center for Education Statistics [16]. Enrollment counts of students in third grade during the 2008–09 school year were noted to differ from NCHS postcensal population estimates; this difference was attributable primarily to children being enrolled out of the customary grade for their age, in private schools, or home-schooled. Because these differences varied by race and sex within the applicable counties, a race-and sex-specific adjustment factor based on enrollment data was applied to the NCHS data to derive school district–specific denominators for these two states.

For comparison of prevalence estimates across multiple time points, population estimates also were obtained from the NCHS vintage 2009 bridged-race postcensal population estimates [15] using the number of children aged 8 years living in the surveillance counties during 2002, 2006, and 2008. These population estimates differ slightly from those used in previous ADDM reports but represent the most recent available data [17] for evaluating changes in the prevalence of ASDs across multiple time points.

The race/ethnicity of each child whose records were abstracted was determined from information contained in source records or, if not found in the source file, from birth certificates (when available). Race- or ethnicity-specific prevalence estimates were calculated for five populations: non-Hispanic white, non-Hispanic black, Hispanic, Asian/Pacific Islander, and American Indian/Alaska Native. Prevalence results are reported as the total number of children meeting the ASD case definition per 1,000 children aged 8 years in the population in each race/ethnicity group. ASD prevalence also was calculated separately for males and females, as well as within each level of intellectual ability. Overall prevalence estimates include all children identified with ASDs regardless of sex, race/ethnicity, or level of intellectual ability and thus are not affected by the availability of data on these characteristics.

Confidence intervals (CIs) for prevalence estimates were derived under the assumption that the observed counts of children identified with ASDs are random variables drawn from an underlying Poisson distribution. For the current report, chi-square tests, rate ratios (RRs), and percentage differences were calculated to compare prevalence estimates within and across sites and between surveillance years. A maximum value of $p<0.05$ was used for all tests of statistical significance. Results for all sites combined were based on pooled numerator and denominator data from all sites, in total and stratified by race/ethnicity, sex, and level of intellectual ability.

Evaluation Methods

Certain education and health records could not be located for review. An analysis of the effect of these missing records on case ascertainment was conducted. This also included records affected by the passive consent process unique to the Colorado site. All children initially identified for screening were first stratified by two factors highly associated with final case status: information source (education type source only, health type source only, or both types of sources) and the presence or absence of either an ICD-9 code for ASD or autism special education eligibility. The potential number of cases missed because of missing records was estimated under the assumption that within each of these six strata, the proportion of children with missing records who ultimately would be confirmed as having ASDs would have been similar to that of children for whom no records were missing. Within each stratum, the proportion of children with no missing records who were confirmed as having ASDs was applied to the number of children with missing records to estimate the number of missed cases, and the estimates from all six strata were summed to calculate the total for each site.

Table 1. Number[*] and percentage of children aged 8 years, by race/ethnicity and site — Autism and Developmental Disabilities Monitoring Network, 14 sites, United States, 2008

Site	Site/ Institution	Surveillance area	Total	White, non-Hispanic		Black, non-Hispanic		Hispanic		API		AI/AN	
			No.	No.	(%)	No.	(%)	No.	(%)	No.	(%)	No.	(%)
Alabama	Univ of Alabama at Birmingham	32 counties in north and central Alabama	36,566	24,516	(67.0)	9,295	(25.4)	2,112	(5.8)	489	(1.3)	154	(0.4)
Arizona[†]	Univ of Arizona	Part of 1 county in metropolitan Phoenix	32,601	15,022	(46.1)	1,804	(5.5)	14,227	(43.6)	893	(2.7)	655	(2.0)
Arkansas	Univ of Arkansas for Medical Sciences	1 county (Pulaski) in metropolitan Little Rock	4,940	2,371	(48.0)	2,112	(42.8)	296	(6.0)	123	(2.5)	38	(0.8)
Colorado[§]	Colorado Dept of Public Health and Environment	1 county (Arapahoe) in metropolitan Denver	7,725	3,990	(51.7)	1,051	(13.6)	2,233	(28.9)	387	(5.0)	64	(0.8)
Colorado[¶]	Colorado Dept of Public Health and Environment	6 counties in metropolitan Denver (excludes Arapahoe)	29,336	16,923	(57.7)	1,390	(4.7)	9,660	(32.9)	1,179	(4.0)	184	(0.6)
Florida	Univ of Miami	1 county (Miami–Dade) in south Florida	29,366	7,013	(23.9)	6,328	(21.5)	15,540	(52.9)	445	(1.5)	40	(0.1)
Georgia	CDC	5 counties including metropolitan Atlanta	50,427	18,725	(37.1)	20,690	(41.0)	7,875	(15.6)	2,958	(5.9)	179	(0.4)
Maryland	Johns Hopkins Univ	6 counties in suburban Baltimore	27,022	18,337	(67.9)	5,796	(21.4)	1,347	(5.0)	1,467	(5.4)	75	(0.3)

Table 1. (Continued)

Site	Site/ Institution	Surveillance area	Total	White, non-Hispanic		Black, non-Hispanic		Hispanic		API		AI/AN	
			No.	No.	(%)	No.	(%)	No.	(%)	No.	(%)	No.	(%)
Missouri	Washington Univ–St. Louis	5 counties including metropolitan St. Louis	25,668	17,718	(69.0)	6,153	(24.0)	891	(3.5)	816	(3.2)	90	(0.4)
New Jersey	Univ of Medicine and Dentistry of New Jersey	1 county (Union) in metropolitan Newark	7,082	3,096	(43.7)	1,601	(22.6)	2,050	(28.9)	322	(4.5)	13	(0.2)
North Carolina	Univ of North Carolina–Chapel Hill	11 counties in central North Carolina	36,913	21,038	(57.0)	9,414	(25.5)	4,977	(13.5)	1,353	(3.7)	131	(0.4)
Pennsyl-vania	Univ of Pennsylvania	1 metropolitan county (Philadelphia)	18,440	5,180	(28.1)	9,060	(49.1)	3,067	(16.6)	1,067	(5.8)	66	(0.4)
South Carolina	Medical Univ of South Carolina	23 counties in Coastal and Pee Dee regions	23,769	12,506	(52.6)	9,566	(40.2)	1,285	(5.4)	295	(1.2)	117	(0.5)
Utah[†]	Univ of Utah	Part of 1 county in northern Utah	2,123	899	(42.3)	116	(5.5)	902	(42.5)	171	(8.1)	35	(1.6)
Wisconsin	Univ of Wisconsin–Madison	10 counties in south eastern Wisconsin	34,451	22,479	(65.2)	5,818	(16.9)	4,720	(13.7)	1,264	(3.7)	170	(0.5)

Abbreviations: API = Asian/Pacific Islander; AI/AN = American Indian/ Alaska Native.

* Total numbers of children aged 8 years in each surveillance area were obtained from CDC's National Center for Health Statistics vintage 2009 postcensal population estimates.

† Denominator excludes school districts that were not included in the surveillance area, calculated from National Center on Education Statistics enrollment counts of third graders during the 2008–2009 school year.

§ Colorado health and education source type surveillance area.

¶ Expanded Colorado health source type only surveillance area.

All 2008 ADDM sites identified records to review at most health sources by searching based on a common list of ICD-9 billing codes. However, several sites reviewed records based on an expanded list of ICD-9 codes because they were conducting surveillance for other developmental disabilities in addition to ASDs (i.e., one or more of the following: cerebral palsy, intellectual disability, hearing loss, and vision impairment) or, in the case of Colorado, because they identified an additional billing code (781.3, lack of coordination) that is commonly used for children with ASDs in that community. To evaluate the potential impact on ASD prevalence, analysts calculated the proportion of children meeting the ASD surveillance case definition whose records were obtained solely on the basis of those additional codes.

Funding for most ADDM Network sites participating in the 2008 surveillance year was awarded for a 4-year cycle during 2006–2010, during which time data were collected for the 2006 and 2008 surveillance years. However, three additional sites (Arkansas, New Jersey, and Utah) were funded during 2009–2010 to collect data for the 2008 surveillance year only. These three sites also had participated in the ADDM 2002 surveillance year and were able to compare their 2008 prevalence results to those from 2002. However, because only 1 year of funding was available to complete the study, these three sites covered smaller surveillance areas in 2008 compared with other sites and with the earlier surveillance year(s) in which these three returning sites participated. This enabled the three sites to complete surveillance year 2008 on the same timeline as other ADDM Network sites. However, this abbreviated timeline required that population denominators for each of the three returning sites be fewer than 10,000 children, potentially yielding less representative prevalence estimates for Arkansas, New Jersey, and Utah. Results from the ADDM 2004 surveillance year were not compared with 2008 results because only eight of the 14 sites completed both studies, and the 2004 surveillance year represented a smaller scale, optional effort based on available resources.

Seven of the 14 sites participating in the 2008 surveillance year included a different mix of counties or school districts in 2008 compared with 1 or more previous surveillance years. For these sites, numerators and denominators for between-year comparisons were restricted systematically to residents of the core surveillance area that were common across all surveillance years in a given analysis (i.e., 2008-to-2002 ratios, 2008-to-2006 ratios, and statistics that include all 3 surveillance years). Numerators for these comparisons were selected based on the child's county of residency or, for sites with surveillance areas defined by school districts, based on the child's census block group of residency within school district boundaries. Denominators for between-year comparisons were based on county-level NCHS postcensal estimates for the core surveillance area that was included during both surveillance years in a given comparison. For sites with surveillance areas defined by school districts, only those school districts included in both surveillance years were included when denominators for between-year comparisons were calculated. For these sites, county-level population estimates were adjusted according to school enrollment data in the same manner as denominators for the 2008 surveillance year were computed but further restricted to the school districts included in both surveillance years in a given comparison. Sites adjusting their denominators in this manner included Arizona for both the 2008-to-2006 and the 2008-to-2002 comparisons, as well as New Jersey and Utah for the 2008-to-2002 comparisons (school districts were used in defining surveillance areas for New Jersey in 2002 and Utah in 2008). Comparisons between surveillance years were not affected by any changes in sites' agreements to access education records because no sites had access to education sources for one surveillance year but not for the other.

RESULTS

The 14 ADDM sites that provided data for the 2008 surveillance year covered a total population of 337,093 children aged 8 years, which represented 8.4% of the U.S. population of children that age in 2008 [13]. A total of 48,247 source records for 38,253 children were reviewed at education and health sources. Of these, the source records of 6,739 children met the criteria for abstraction, which was 17.5% of the total number of children whose source records were reviewed and 2% of the total population under surveillance (range: 1.0% [Alabama]–6.3% [Utah]). During clinician review, 3,820 children (57%) were confirmed as meeting the ASD surveillance case definition (range: 30% [Arkansas]–74% [North Carolina]). The number of evaluations abstracted for each child ultimately identified as having an ASD varied (median: 5; range: 3 [Florida and North Carolina]–10 [Utah].

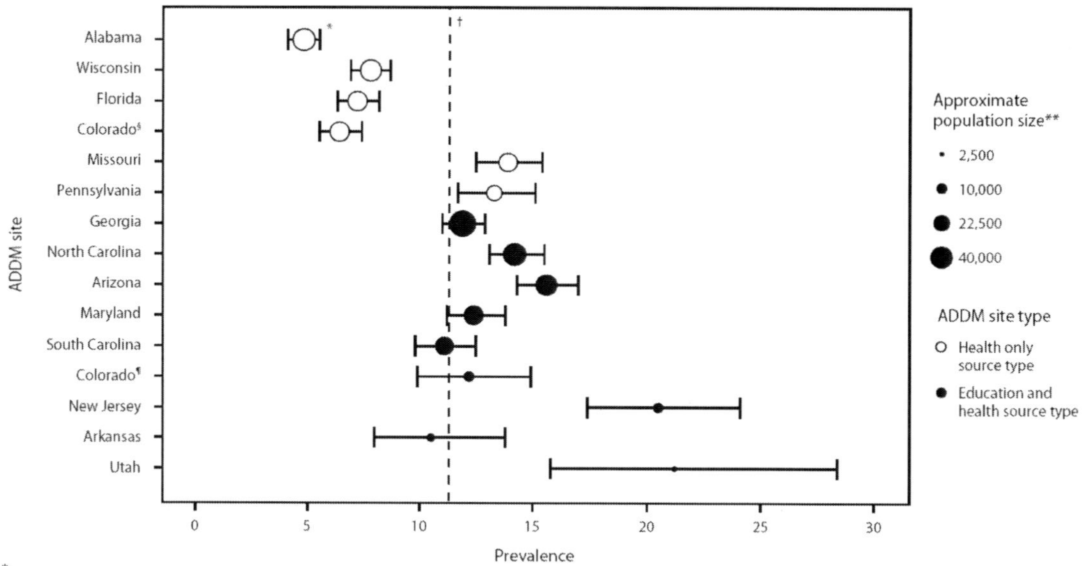

* 95% confidence intervals.

† Overall weighted ASD prevalence.

§ Expanded Colorado health source type only surveillance area.

¶ Colorado health and education source type surveillance area.

** Size of dot represents total population of children aged 8 years residing in the surveillance area.

Figure 1. Estimated prevalence (per 1,000 population) of autism spectrum disorders (ASDs) among children aged 8 years, by access to education records and population size covered — Autism and Developmental Disabilities Monitoring Network (ADDM), 14 sites, United States, 2008.

Overall ASD Prevalence Estimates

When data from all 14 ADDM sites in the 2008 surveillance year were combined, overall estimated ASD prevalence was 11.3 per 1,000 (one in 88) children aged 8 years (range: 4.8 [Alabama]–21.2 [Utah]) (Table 2). Overall estimated prevalence of ASDs was significantly lower in Alabama (4.8 per 1,000) than in any other site. Utah had the highest estimated ASD prevalence (21.2 per 1,000), which was significantly higher than all other sites except Arizona and New Jersey. The overall estimated ASD prevalence in New Jersey (20.5 per 1,000) was significantly higher than in any other site except Utah.

On average, estimated ASD prevalence was significantly higher in ADDM sites that had access to education sources compared with sites that relied solely on health sources to identify cases (RR: 1.5; 95% CI = 1.4–1.7; $p<0.01$). Relative differences among sites in prevalence estimates and 95% CIs are compared by access to education records and population size covered (Figure 1). In sites with access to both health and education sources, the proportion of ASD cases identified exclusively from education sources ranged from 10% in Arkansas to 72% in Arizona. One site (Colorado) was able to access education records in only one county but completed the study in six additional counties based on health records alone. In the one Colorado county with access to both education and health records, estimated ASD prevalence was almost twice as high (11.8 per 1,000) as in the six Colorado counties with access to health sources only (6.4 per 1,000). For this reason, Colorado results from the one county with access to both education and health records are considered to represent all children with ASDs more completely than results from the remaining six counties.

Prevalence by Sex and Race/Ethnicity

Combining data from all 14 ADDM sites, estimated ASD prevalence was 18.4 per 1,000 (one in 54) males and 4.0 per 1,000 (one in 252) females (RR: 4.6 for all sites combined). ASD prevalence estimates were significantly ($p<0.01$) higher among boys than among girls in all 14 ADDM sites, with male-to-female prevalence ratios ranging from 2.7 in Utah to 7.2 in Alabama.

Estimated ASD prevalence also varied by race and ethnicity (Table 2). When data from all sites were combined, the estimated prevalence among non-Hispanic white children (12.0 per 1,000) was significantly greater than that among non-Hispanic black children (10.2 per 1,000) and Hispanic children (7.9 per 1,000). Estimated ASD prevalence was significantly lower among Hispanic children than among non-Hispanic white children in nine sites and significantly lower than among non-Hispanic black children in five sites. Only one site (Florida) identified a significantly higher ASD prevalence among Hispanic children compared with either non-Hispanic white or non-Hispanic black children. New Jersey was the only site that identified approximately the same estimated ASD prevalence among non-Hispanic white children, non-Hispanic black children, and Hispanic children. Estimates for Asian/Pacific Islander children ranged from 2.2 to 19.0 per 1,000 although wide confidence intervals suggest that these findings should be interpreted with caution.

Table 2. Estimated prevalence[*] of autism spectrum disorders (ASDs) per 1,000 children aged 8 years, by sex and race/ethnicity — Autism and Developmental Disabilities Monitoring Network, 14 sites, United States, 2008

Site	Total no.	Total no. with ASDs	Sex						Male-to-female prev ratio[§]
			Total[†]		Male		Female		
			Prev	95% CI	Prev	95% CI	Prev	95% CI	
Alabama	**36,566**	**174**	**4.8**	**(4.1–5.5)**	8.1	(7.0–9.5)	1.1	(0.7–1.8)	7.2
Arizona	**32,601**	**507**	**15.6**	**(14.3–17.0)**	25.1	(22.8–27.6)	5.4	(4.4–6.7)	4.6
Arkansas	**4,940**	**52**	**10.5**	**(8.0–13.8)**	17.5	(13.0–23.6)	3.6	(1.9–7)	4.8
Colorado[¶]	**7,725**	**91**	**11.8**	**(9.6–14.5)**	20.1	(16.1–25.0)	2.9	(1.6–5.3)	6.8
Colorado[**]	**29,336**	**188**	**6.4**	**(5.6–7.4)**	10.4	(8.9–12.2)	2.2	(1.6–3.1)	4.7
Florida	**29,366**	**211**	**7.2**	**(6.3–8.2)**	11.3	(9.7–13.1)	2.9	(2.1–3.9)	3.9
Georgia	**50,427**	**601**	**11.9**	**(11.0–12.9)**	19.6	(18.0–21.4)	3.8	(3.1–4.6)	5.2
Maryland	**27,022**	**336**	**12.4**	**(11.2–13.8)**	20.5	(18.3–23.1)	3.9	(2.9–5.1)	5.3
Missouri	**25,668**	**357**	**13.9**	**(12.5–15.4)**	21.6	(19.2–24.3)	5.9	(4.7–7.4)	3.7
New Jersey	**7,082**	**145**	**20.5**	**(17.4–24.1)**	34.2	(28.7–40.7)	5.8	(3.8–9.1)	5.8
North Carolina	**36,913**	**525**	**14.2**	**(13.1–15.5)**	23.1	(21.0–25.3)	5.1	(4.1–6.2)	4.5
Pennsylvania	**18,440**	**245**	**13.3**	**(11.7–15.1)**	22.2	(19.4–25.4)	4.3	(3.1–5.8)	5.2
South Carolina	**23,769**	**264**	**11.1**	**(9.8–12.5)**	18.3	(16.1–20.9)	3.5	(2.6–4.8)	5.2
Utah	**2,123**	**45**	**21.2**	**(15.8–28.4)**	31.7	(22.4–44.8)	11.7	(6.8–20.1)	2.7
Wisconsin	**34,451**	**267**	**7.8**	**(6.9–8.7)**	11.7	(10.2–13.4)	3.7	(2.9–4.7)	3.2
Total	**337,093**	**3,820**	**11.3**	**(11.0–11.7)**	**18.4**	**(17.7–19.0)**	**4.0**	**(3.7–4.3)**	**4.6**

Site	Race/Ethnicity								Prev ratio		
	White, non-Hispanic		Black, non-Hispanic		Hispanic		API		White-to-black	White-to-Hispanic	Black-to-Hispanic
	Prev	95% CI	Prev	95% CI	Prev	95% CI	Prev	95% CI			
Alabama	5.0	(4.2–6.0)	4.0	(2.9–5.5)	1.4	(0.5–4.4)	4.1	(1.0–16.4)	1.3	3.5[††]	2.8
Arizona	20.7	(18.5–23.1)	16.1	(11.2–23.1)	8.9	(7.5–10.6)	19.0	(11.8–30.6)	1.3	2.3[§§]	1.8[§§]
Arkansas	13.5	(9.5–19.1)	7.1	(4.3–11.8)	10.1	(3.3–31.4)	—[¶¶]	—	1.9[††]	1.3	0.7

Site	Race/Ethnicity								Prev ratio		
	White, non-Hispanic		Black, non-Hispanic		Hispanic		API		White-to-black	White-to-Hispanic	Black-to-Hispanic
	Prev	95% CI	Prev	95% CI	Prev	95% CI	Prev	95% CI			
Colorado[¶]	14.8	(11.5–19.1)	10.5	(5.8–18.9)	6.7	(4.1–11.1)	2.6	(0.4–18.3)	1.4	2.2[§§]	1.6[§§]
Colorado[**]	7.3	(6.1–8.7)	6.5	(3.4–12.4)	3.5	(2.5–4.9)	0.9	(0.1–6.0)	1.1	2.1[§§]	1.8
Florida	4.6	(3.2–6.5)	3.0	(1.9–4.7)	8.2	(6.9–9.8)	2.2	(0.3–16)	1.5	0.6[§§]	0.4[§§]
Georgia	11.8	(10.3–13.5)	11.9	(10.5–13.5)	7.1	(5.5–9.2)	15.9	(11.9–21.1)	1.0	1.7[§§]	1.7[§§]
Maryland	12.9	(11.4–14.7)	11.7	(9.3–14.9)	5.9	(3–11.9)	8.2	(4.6–14.4)	1.1	2.2[††]	2.0
Missouri	14.6	(12.9–16.5)	9.3	(7.1–12)	9.0	(4.5–18)	9.8	(4.9–19.6)	1.6[§§]	1.6	1.0
New Jersey	21.0	(16.5–26.8)	20.6	(14.7–29)	20.0	(14.7–27.2)	3.1	(0.4–22)	1.0	1.0	1.0
North Carolina	14.6	(13.1–16.4)	15.4	(13.1–18.1)	7.6	(5.6–10.5)	11.8	(7.2–19.3)	1.0	1.9[§§]	2.0[§§]
Pennsylvania	14.3	(11.4–17.9)	12.7	(10.6–15.2)	9.1	(6.3–13.2)	8.4	(4.4–16.2)	1.1	1.6[††]	1.4
South Carolina	10.2	(8.6–12.2)	9.9	(8.1–12.1)	7.0	(3.6–13.5)	—	—	1.0	1.5	1.4
Utah	40.0	(28.9–55.5)	25.9	(8.3–80.2)	4.4	(1.7–11.8)	—	—	1.5	9.0[§§]	5.8[††]
Wisconsin	8.6	(7.5–9.9)	5.0	(3.5–7.2)	3.8	(2.4–6.1)	2.4	(0.8–7.4)	1.7[§§]	2.3[§§]	1.3
Total	**12.0**	**(11.5–12.5)**	**10.2**	**(9.5–10.9)**	**7.9**	**(7.2–8.6)**	**9.7**	**(8.1–11.6)**	**1.2[§§]**	**1.5[§§]**	**1.3[§§]**

Abbreviations: CI = confidence interval; API = Asian/Pacific Islander.

[*] Per 1,000 children aged 8 years.

[†] All children are included in the total regardless of race or ethnicity. Overall prevalence also includes children for whom race/ethnicity was unknown.

[§] All sites identified statistically significantly higher prevalence among males compared with females (p<0.01).

[¶] Colorado health and education source type surveillance area.

[**] Expanded Colorado health source type only surveillance area.

[††] Prevalence ratio statistically significant at p<0.05.

[§§] Prevalence ratio statistically significant at p<0.01.

[¶¶] No children identified in this group.

Previously Documented ASD Classification

Among all children meeting the ASD surveillance case definition, approximately 79% had a previously documented ASD classification (range: 67% [Colorado]–87% [Pennsylvania and Wisconsin]). The median age of earliest known ASD diagnosis documented in children's records (Table 3) varied by diagnostic subtype (Autistic Disorder: 48 months; ASD/PDD: 53 months; Asperger Disorder: 75 months). Of the 2,627 children with a diagnostic subtype on record, 516 (20%) had different subtypes noted across multiple evaluations, suggesting instability in the initial subtype diagnosed for approximately one in five children. The age of earliest known diagnosis for all subtypes combined is not reported because of substantial variability in the median age at the earliest known ASD diagnosis by subtype, the proportion of children within each subtype category across the different ADDM sites, and the subtype noted across multiple evaluations for each child.

Table 3. Median age (in months) of earliest known autism spectrum disorder (ASD) diagnosis among children identified with autism spectrum disorders by age 8 years, and number and proportion within each diagnostic subtype — Autism and Developmental Disabilities Monitoring Network, 14 sites, United States, 2008

Site	Autistic disorder			ASD/PDD			Asperger disorder			Any specific ASD diagnosis	
	Median age	No.	%	Median age	No.	%	Median age	No.	%	No.	%
Alabama	48	48	42	62	57	50	82	—*	9	115	66
Arizona	56	182	63	54	84	29	76	24	8	290	57
Arkansas	55	—	39	46	18	50	88	—	11	36	69
Colorado†	52	26	46	54	23	40	79	—	14	57	63
Florida	36	64	44	43	73	50	59	—	7	147	70
Georgia	53	188	50	54	150	40	72	37	10	375	62
Maryland	59	98	40	67	127	52	79	21	9	246	73
Missouri	58	65	24	39	186	67	75	26	9	277	78
New Jersey	38	19	19	51	70	71	66	—	9	98	68
North Carolina	39	187	54	55	128	37	79	30	9	345	66
Pennsylvania	43	73	35	59	117	57	70	17	8	207	85
South Carolina	46	102	56	58	67	37	81	—	7	181	69
Utah	52	—	42	52	—	45	68	—	13	31	69
Wisconsin	46	79	36	52	116	52	74	27	12	222	83
Total	**48**	**1,158**	**44**	**53**	**1,230**	**47**	**75**	**239**	**9**	**2,627**	**69**

Abbreviation: PDD = pervasive developmental disorder – not otherwise specified.

* Data not reported because N<15.

† Colorado health and education source type surveillance area.

Special Education Eligibility

Sites with access to education records collected information about the eligibility categories under which special education services were received in public schools (Table 4). Wide variation existed in the proportion of children with a primary eligibility category of autism (range: 39% [Colorado]–72% [North Carolina]). In Colorado, autism is a subcategory of physical disability, so the primary eligibility might have been documented as autism or physical disability, depending on the school district. Other common special education eligibilities included intellectual disability, health or physical disability, speech and language impairment, and specific learning disability, with these proportions also varying by site.

Intellectual Ability

Data on intellectual ability are reported for the seven sites having information available for at least 70% of children who met the ASD case definition (Figure 2). When data from these seven sites were combined, 38% of children with ASDs were classified in the range of intellectual disability (i.e., IQ ≤70 or an examiner's statement of intellectual disability), 24% in the borderline range (IQ 71–85), and 38% had IQ scores >85 or an examiner's statement of average or above-average intellectual ability. The proportion of children classified in the range of intellectual disability ranged from 13% in Utah to 54% in South Carolina. The two sites with the highest proportions of children classified above the range of intellectual disability (IQ >70) were Utah (87%) and New Jersey (73%). In all seven sites reporting data on intellectual ability, a higher proportion of females with ASDs had intellectual disability compared with males, although the proportions differed significantly (52% for females and 35% for males; $p<0.01$) in only one site (North Carolina). When data from these seven sites were combined, 150 (46%) of 328 females with ASDs had IQ scores or examiners' statements indicating intellectual disability compared with 608 (37%) of 1,653 males.

Evaluation of Missing Records and Expanded ICD-9 Codes

Underascertainment of ASDs because of missing records varied by site. The majority of sites estimated that the total number of children identified with ASDs might potentially have increased <5% had all records been located for review. However, it is estimated that ASD prevalence would have been 9% higher in Utah, 13% higher in Pennsylvania, 16% higher in Alabama and Maryland, and 26% higher in Florida.

Among the 12 sites reviewing records based on an expanded list of ICD-9 codes, five sites did not identify any children with ASDs solely on the basis of the expanded code list, whereas six sites identified approximately 1% or fewer, and Arkansas identified approximately 4% of the total number of children with ASDs solely on the basis of the expanded code list.

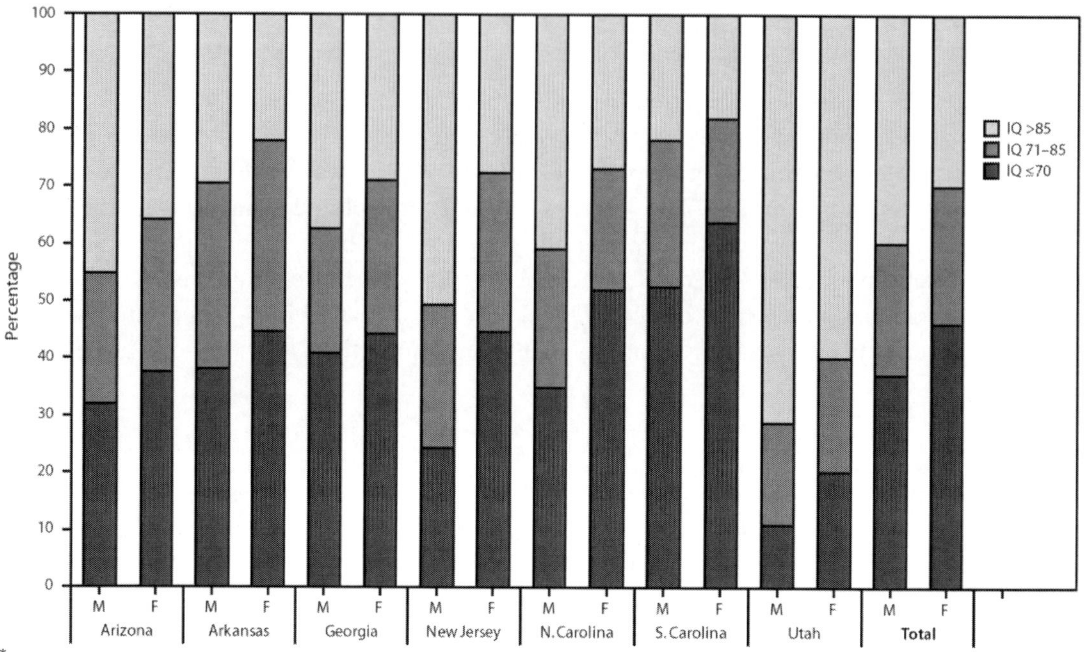

* N=1,981

† Includes sites having information on intellectual ability available for at least 70% of children who met the ASD case definition.

Figure 2. Most recent intelligence quotient (IQ) as of age 8 years among children identified with autism spectrum disorders (ASDs) for whom psychometric test data were available,* by site and sex — Autism and Developmental Disabilities Monitoring Network, seven sites,† United States, 2008.

Comparison between 2006 and 2008 Prevalence Estimates

Of the 11 sites completing both the 2006 and 2008 surveillance years, seven sites identified a higher prevalence of ASDs in 2008 compared with 2006, whereas three sites identified a similar prevalence in both years, and one site identified a lower prevalence in 2008 compared with 2006 (Table 5). Combining data from all 11 sites, estimated ASD prevalence increased 23% during 2006 to 2008 (9.0–11.0 per 1,000), ranging from -20% in Alabama (6.0–4.8 per 1,000) to +80% in Florida (4.0–7.2 per 1,000). The percentage increase in estimated ASD prevalence was similar for males (23%; 14.5–17.9 per 1,000) and for females (21%; 3.2–3.8 per 1,000). Six sites identified an increased prevalence among males in 2008, and the remaining five sites identified a similar prevalence among males in 2006 compared with 2008. Only three sites identified an increase in prevalence among females, while seven sites identified similar prevalence among females in 2006 and 2008, and one site identified a lower ASD prevalence among females in 2008 compared with 2006.

Table 4. Number and percentage of children aged 8 years identified with autism spectrum disorders (ASDs) for whom special education data were available, by site and primary special education eligibility category — Autism and Developmental Disabilities Monitoring Network, nine sites with access to education records, United States, 2008

Special education category*	Arizona %	Arkansas %	Colorado† %	Georgia %	Maryland %	New Jersey %	North Carolina %	South Carolina %	Utah %
Autism	50.4	53.6	39.0§	67.3	63.1	43.2	71.8	50.7	48.6
Emotional disturbance	7.1	0	2.6	3.1	3.9	2.2	2.2	1.5	14.3
Specific learning disability	10.6	0	0	4.0	7.1	10.1	6.4	5.4	8.6
Speech or language impairment	12.1	17.9	19.5	1.1	8.9	11.5	1.8	9.9	11.4
Hearing or visual impairment	0.2	3.6	0	0	0	0.7	0	1.0	0
Health or physical disability	6.2	14.3	27.3§	4.9	7.8	19.4	7.5	13.8	0
Multiple disabilities	1.3	3.6	7.8	0	2.8	7.9	2.2	0.5	2.9
Intellectual disability	11.9	7.1	3.9	4.9	2.5	4.3	5.3	14.8	11.4
Developmental delay/ preschool	0	0	0	14.8	3.9	0.7	2.7	2.5	2.9
Total no. of ASD cases	**507**	**52**	**91**	**601**	**336**	**145**	**525**	**264**	**45**
(No./%¶)	**(480/94.7)**	**(28/53.8)**	**(77/84.6)**	**(554/92.2)**	**(282/83.9)**	**(139/95.9)**	**(451/85.9)**	**(203/76.9)**	**(35/77.8)**

* Some state-specific categories were recoded or combined to match current U.S. Department of Education categories.

† Colorado health and education source type surveillance area.

§ Autism is a subcategory of physical disability in Colorado. The primary eligibility might have been documented as autism or physical disability, depending on the school district.

¶ Number and percentage receiving special education services during 2008.

Table 5. Estimated prevalence of autism spectrum disorders (ASDs) per 1,000 children aged 8 years, by sex and race/ethnicity — comparison of select earlier surveillance years to 2008, with rate ratio and percentage of prevalence change[*] — Autism and Developmental Disabilities Monitoring Network, 14 sites, United States, 2002, 2006, and 2008

	Alabama	Arizona	Arkansas	Colorado	Florida	Georgia	Maryland	Missouri	New Jersey	North Carolina	Pennsylvania	South Carolina	Utah	Wisconsin	All sites combined
Total ASD															
2002	**3.3**	**7.9**	**10.6**	**6.2**	**—[†]**	**7.5**	**7.0**	**7.2**	**11.1**	**6.6**	**5.2**	**6.1**	**8.3**	**5.1**	**6.4**
2008	**4.8**	**15.6**	**10.5**	**11.8**	**—**	**11.9**	**12.1**	**13.9**	**20.3**	**12.7**	**13.3**	**11.1**	**21.2**	**7.8**	**11.4**
Rate ratio	**1.5[§]**	**2.0[§]**	**1.0**	**1.9[§]**	**—**	**1.6[§]**	**1.7[§]**	**1.9[§]**	**1.8[§]**	**1.9 [§]**	**2.6[§]**	**1.8 [§]**	**2.6[§]**	**1.5[§]**	**1.8[§]**
(95% CI)	**(1.3–1.7)**	**(1.9–2.1)**	**(0.6–1.4)**	**(1.5–2.3)**	**—**	**(1.5–1.7)**	**(1.5–1.9)**	**(1.7–2.1)**	**(1.5–2.1)**	**(1.7–2.1)**	**(2.4–2.8)**	**(1.6–2)**	**(2.1–3.1)**	**(1.3–1.7)**	**(1.7–1.9)**
% change	**45.6**	**97.1**	**-0.3**	**88.8**	**—**	**58.3**	**74.1**	**92.7**	**83.4**	**93.6**	**156.1**	**83.0**	**157.0**	**51.7**	**78.5**
2006	**6.0**	**15.8**	**—**	**7.4**	**4.0**	**10.1**	**9.1**	**12.1**	**—**	**10.2**	**8.4**	**8.8**	**—**	**7.7**	**9.0**
2008	**4.8**	**15.6**	**—**	**11.8**	**7.2**	**11.9**	**12.4**	**13.9**	**—**	**12.4**	**13.3**	**11.1**	**—**	**7.8**	**11.0**
Rate ratio	**0.8[¶]**	**1.0**	**—**	**1.6[§]**	**1.8[§]**	**1.2[§]**	**1.4[§]**	**1.1**	**—**	**1.2[¶]**	**1.6[§]**	**1.3[¶]**	**—**	**1.0**	**1.2[§]**
(95% CI)	**(0.6–1)**	**(0.9–1.1)**	**—**	**(1.3–1.9)**	**(1.6–2)**	**(1.1–1.3)**	**(1.2–1.6)**	**(0.9–1.3)**	**—**	**(1–1.4)**	**(1.4–1.8)**	**(1.1–1.5)**	**—**	**(0.8–1.2)**	**(1.1–1.3)**
% change	**-20.4**	**-1.8**	**—**	**60.1**	**79.8**	**18.0**	**36.7**	**14.9**	**—**	**21.0**	**58.6**	**26.0**	**—**	**0.8**	**22.6**
Male															
2002	5.0	12.9	17.4	10.8	—	12.3	10.6	11.2	18.2	10.8	8.5	9.3	15.6	7.8	**10.2**
2008	8.1	25.1	17.5	20.1	—	19.6	20.2	21.6	33.9	20.6	22.2	18.3	31.7	11.7	**18.6**
Rate ratio	1.6[§]	2[§]	1.0	1.9[§]	—	1.6[§]	1.9[§]	1.9[§]	1.9[§]	1.9[§]	2.6[§]	2.0[§]	2.0[¶]	1.5[§]	**1.8[§]**
(95% CI)	(1.3–1.9)	(1.8–2.2)	(0.6–1.4)	(1.5–2.3)	—	(1.5–1.7)	(1.7–2.1)	(1.7–2.1)	(1.6–2.2)	(1.7–2.1)	(2.4–2.8)	(1.8–2.2)	(1.4–2.6)	(1.3–1.7)	**(1.7–1.9)**
% change	61.5	95.3	0.5	86.2	—	59.7	90.9	93.6	86.2	91.7	160.0	97.7	103.3	49.4	**81.6**
2006	9.0	24.5	—	11.3	6.9	16.5	15.5	19.3	—	16.8	13.2	14.6	—	13.0	**14.5**
2008	8.1	25.1	—	20.1	11.3	19.6	20.6	21.6	—	19.9	22.2	18.3	—	11.7	**17.9**
Rate ratio	0.9	1.0	—	1.8[§]	1.6[§]	1.2[¶]	1.3[§]	1.1	—	1.2	1.7[§]	1.3[¶]	—	0.9	**1.2[§]**

	Alabama	**Arizona**	**Arkansas**	**Colorado**	**Florida**	**Georgia**	**Maryland**	**Missouri**	**New Jersey**	**North Carolina**	**Pennsylvania**	**South Carolina**	**Utah**	**Wisconsin**	**All sites combined**
(95% CI)	(0.7–1.1)	(0.9–1.1)	—	(1.4–2.2)	(1.4–1.8)	(1.1–1.3)	(1.1–1.5)	(0.9–1.3)	—	(1–1.4)	(1.5–1.9)	(1.1–1.5)	—	(0.7–1.1)	**(1.1–1.3)**
% change	-9.5	2.4	—	77.2	62.7	18.6	32.4	12.4	—	18.2	67.8	25.8	—	–9.7	**23.0**
Female															
2002	1.4	2.7	3.7	1.4	—	2.6	3.2	3.0	3.5	2.1	1.8	2.8	0.9	2.3	**2.4**
2008	1.1	5.4	3.6	2.9	—	3.8	3.6	5.9	5.7	4.6	4.3	3.5	11.7	3.7	**4.0**
Rate ratio	0.8	2.0[§]	1.0	2.1	—	1.4[¶]	1.1	1.9[§]	1.6	2.2[§]	2.4[§]	1.3	12.7[¶]	1.6[¶]	**1.6[§]**
(95% CI)	(0.2–1.4)	(1.6–2.4)	(0.1–1.9)	(1–3.2)	—	(1.1–1.7)	(0.6–1.6)	(1.5–2.3)	(0.9–2.3)	(1.7–2.7)	(1.9–2.9)	(0.8–1.8)	(10.7–14.7)	(1.2–2)	**(1.5–1.7)**
% change	-18.7	102.6	-2.7	110.0	—	44.6	13.2	93.4	62.8	115.1	138.0	28.4	1168.5	61.9	**63.2**
2006	2.8	6.4	—	3.3	0.9	3.4	2.4	4.8	—	3.4	3.3	2.6	—	2.3	**3.2**
2008	1.1	5.4	—	2.9	2.9	3.8	3.9	5.9	—	4.6	4.3	3.5	—	3.7	**3.8**
Rate ratio	0.4[§]	0.8	—	0.9	3.1[§]	1.1	1.6[¶]	1.2	—	1.4	1.3	1.4	—	1.6[¶]	**1.2[§]**
(95% CI)	(0.1–0.9)	(0.5–1.1)	—	(0.1–1.7)	(2.5–3.7)	(0.8–1.4)	(1.2–2)	(0.9–1.5)	—	(1–1.8)	(0.8–1.8)	(0.9–1.9)	—	(1.2–2)	**(1.1–1.3)**
% change	-60.1	-15.6	—	-10.9	212.0	11.9	63.7	23.8	—	37.4	28.3	34.7	—	59.1	**20.8**
White, non-Hispanic															
2002	3.3	9.9	10.5	6.7	—	8.8	7.1	7.6	15.1	6.5	7.6	6.1	15.1	5.8	**7.0**
Rate ratio	1.5[§]	2.1[§]	1.3	2.2[§]	—	1.3[§]	1.7[§]	1.9[§]	1.4	2.0[§]	1.9[§]	1.7[§]	2.7[§]	1.5[§]	**1.7[§]**
(95% CI)	(1.2–1.8)	(1.9–2.3)	(0.8–1.8)	(1.8–2.6)	—	(1.1–1.5)	(1.5–1.9)	(1.7–2.1)	(1–1.8)	(1.7–2.3)	(1.5–2.3)	(1.4–2)	(2.1–3.3)	(1.3–1.7)	**(1.6–1.8)**
2008	5.0	20.7	13.5	14.8	—	11.8	12.1	14.6	20.4	12.7	14.3	10.2	40.0	8.6	**11.9**
% change	54.0	109.3	28.2	122.4	—	34.2	71.0	91.6	35.3	96.0	87.5	69.0	165.5	47.8	**69.5**
2006	5.8	18.3	—	6.6	3.3	12.0	9.2	13.7	—	12.0	10.3	7.3	—	8.7	**10.0**
2008	5.0	20.7	—	14.8	4.6	11.8	12.9	14.6	—	12.2	14.3	10.2	—	8.6	**11.5**
Rate ratio	0.9	1.1	—	2.2[§]	1.4	1.0	1.4[§]	1.1	—	1.0	1.4	1.4[¶]	—	1.0	**1.2[§]**

Table 5. (Continued)

	Alabama	Arizona	Arkansas	Colorado	Florida	Georgia	Maryland	Missouri	New Jersey	North Carolina	Pennsylvania	South Carolina	Utah	Wisconsin	All sites combined
(95% CI)	(0.7–1.1)	(0.9–1.3)	—	(1.7–2.7)	(0.9–1.9)	(0.8–1.2)	(1.2–1.6)	(0.9–1.3)	—	(0.8–1.2)	(1–1.8)	(1.1–1.7)	—	(0.8–1.2)	**(1.1–1.3)**
% change	-13.3	13.1	—	123.1	39.0	–2.0	40.3	6.7	—	1.7	38.2	40.9	—	–1.3	**15.6**
Black, non-Hispanic															
2002	3.4	7.0	9.6	5.6	—	6.7	6.7	4.7	6.4	7.2	4.1	5.5	0	3.6	**5.5**
2008	4.0	16.1	7.1	10.5	—	11.9	12.6	9.3	20.6	14.2	12.7	9.9	25.9	5.0	**10.5**
Rate ratio	1.2	2.3¶	0.7	1.9	—	1.8§	1.9§	2.0§	3.2§	2.0§	3.1§	1.8§	NA**	1.4	**1.9§**
(95% CI)	(0.7–1.7)	(1.6–3)	(0.1–1.4)	(0.8–3.0)	—	(1.6–2)	(1.5–2.3)	(1.6–2.4)	(2.5–3.9)	(1.6–2.4)	(2.8–3.4)	(1.5–2.1)	NA	(0.9–1.9)	**(1.8–2.0)**
% change	17.8	128.7	-26.2	88.6	—	77.9	87.2	97.6	222.3	98.3	207.3	79.2	NA	37.2	**91.1**
2006	6.7	16.8	—	12.1	1.5	9.3	7.8	5.1	—	7.4	7.4	7.4	—	3.7	**7.0**
2008	4.0	16.1	—	10.5	3.0	11.9	11.7	9.3	—	14.2	12.7	9.9	—	5.0	**10.0**
Rate ratio	0.6¶	1.0	—	0.9	2.0	1.3¶	1.5¶	1.8§	—	1.9§	1.7§	1.3	—	1.4	**1.4§**
(95% CI)	(0.2–1)	(0.5–1.5)	—	(0.1–1.7)	(1.2–2.8)	(1.1–1.5)	(1.1–1.9)	(1.4–2.2)	—	(1.5–2.3)	(1.4–2)	(1–1.6)	—	(0.8–2)	**(1.3–1.5)**
% change	-40.6	-4.5	—	-13.7	96.1	27.8	50.8	80.9	—	91.2	72.4	34.7	—	36.4	**42.1**
Hispanic															
2002	1.9	4.4	5.6	2.8	—	4.6	0	1.6	6.4	4.2	4.6	4.3	0	0.3	**3.7**
2008	1.4	8.9	10.1	6.7	—	7.1	4.3	9.0	20.1	6.9	9.1	7.0	4.4	3.8	**7.7**
Rate ratio	0.8	2.0§	1.8	2.4	—	1.5	NA	5.5	3.1§	1.7	2.0¶	1.6	NA	13.2¶	**2.1§**
(95% CI)	(0.1–2.6)	(1.7–2.3)	(0.5–4.1)	(1.3–3.5)	—	(1.0–2.0)	NA	(3.4–7.6)	(2.4–3.8)	(0.9–2.5)	(1.4–2.6)	(0.3–2.9)	NA	(11.2–15.0)	**(1.9–2.3)**
% change	-26.3	102.3	80.4	139.3	—	54.3	NA	462.5	214.1	64.3	97.8	62.8	NA	1,166.7	**109.2**
2006	0.6	11.4	—	4.4	4.9	4.8	6.2	2.6	—	5.9	7.7	4.7	—	1.7	**6.1**
2008	1.4	8.9	—	6.7	8.2	7.1	5.9	9.0	—	6.7	9.1	7.0	—	3.8	**7.9**

	Alabama	Arizona	Arkansas	Colorado	Florida	Georgia	Maryland	Missouri	New Jersey	North Carolina	Pennsylvania	South Carolina	Utah	Wisconsin	**All sites combined**
Rate ratio	2.3	0.8¶	—	1.5	1.7§	1.5	1.0	3.5	—	1.1	1.2	1.5	—	2.2	**1.3§**
(95% CI)	(0.1–4.6)	(0.6–1)	—	(0.6–2.4)	(1.4–2)	(1.1–1.9)	(0.1–2)	(2–5)	—	(0.5–1.7)	(0.6–1.8)	(0.4–2.6)	—	(1.3–3.1)	**(1.2–1.4)**
% change	132.8	-21.7	—	53.8	67.8	48.1	-3.9	246.7	—	12.3	18.7	47.7	—	122.8	**29.1**
IQ < 70															
2002	—	2.8	3.5	—	—	3.4	—	—	3.7	3.0	—	3.3	1.8	—	**3.2**
2008	—	4.9	3.6	—	—	4.6	—	—	4.9	4.1	—	5.1	2.4	—	**4.6**
Rate ratio	—	1.7§	1.0	—	—	1.3§	—	—	1.3	1.4¶	—	1.6§	1.3	—	**1.5§**
(95% CI)	—	(1.4–2)	(0.3–1.7)	—	—	(1.1–1.5)	—	—	(0.8–1.8)	(1.1–1.7)	—	(1.3–1.9)	(0.1–2.6)	—	**(1.4–1.6)**
% change	—	73.2	3.4	—	—	33.7	—	—	33.9	39.1	—	56.6	29.0	—	**45.4**
2006	—	5.9	—	—	—	3.5	—	—	—	3.8	—	3.9	—	—	**4.2**
2008	—	4.9	—	—	—	4.6	—	—	—	4.1	—	5.1	—	—	**4.7**
Rate ratio	—	0.8	—	—	—	1.3§	—	—	—	1.1	—	1.3	—	—	**1.1**
(95% CI)	—	(0.6–1.0)	—	—	—	(1.1–1.5)	—	—	—	(0.8–1.4)	—	(1–1.6)	—	—	**(1.0–1.2)**
% change	—	-17.8	—	—	—	32.6	—	—	—	6.8	—	31.5	—	—	**11.9**
IQ = 71–85															
2002	—	1.6	3.3	—	—	1.3	—	—	1.9	1.4	—	0.7	0	—	**1.4**
2008	—	3.5	3.0	—	—	2.5	—	—	4.4	3.3	—	2.3	3.3	—	**2.9**
Rate ratio	—	2.2§	0.9	—	—	2.0§	—	—	2.4§	2.3§	—	3.6§	NA	—	**2.2§**
(95% CI)	—	(1.9–2.5)	(0.2–1.6)	—	—	(1.7–2.3)	—	—	(1.7–3.1)	(1.9–2.7)	—	(3–4.2)	NA	—	**(2.0–2.4)**
% change	—	119.6	-8.2	—	—	96.9	—	—	135.1	130.5	—	255.4	NA	—	**116.8**
2006	—	3.3	—	—	—	2.1	—	—	—	1.9	—	1.6	—	—	**2.3**
2008	—	3.5	—	—	—	2.5	—	—	—	3.2	—	2.3	—	—	**2.8**

Table 5. (Continued)

	Alabama	Arizona	Arkansas	Colorado	Florida	Georgia	Maryland	Missouri	New Jersey	North Carolina	Pennsylvania	South Carolina	Utah	Wisconsin	All sites combined
Rate ratio	—	1.0	—	—	—	1.2	—	—	—	1.7 §	—	1.5	—	—	**1.2 §**
(95% CI)	—	(0.7–1.3)	—	—	—	(0.9–1.5)	—	—	—	(1.3–2.1)	—	(1.1–1.9)	—	—	**(1.0–1.4)**
% change	—	3.9	—	—	—	20.8	—	—	—	66.5	—	47.1	—	—	**21.7**
IQ >85															
2002	—	2.9	3.5	—	—	2.3	—	—	3.4	1.9	—	1.7	4.1	—	**2.4**
2008	—	6.5	2.6	—	—	4.0	—	—	8.3	4.8	—	2.0	12.3	—	**4.7**
Rate ratio	—	2.3§	0.7	—	—	1.7§	—	—	2.4§	2.5§	—	1.2	3.0§	—	**1.9§**
(95% CI)	—	(2.1–2.5)	(0.1–1.4)	—	—	(1.5–1.9)	—	—	(1.9–2.9)	(2.1–2.9)	—	(0.8–1.6)	(2.2–3.8)	—	**(1.8–2.0)**
% change	—	127.3	-25.3	—	—	75.2	—	—	142.5	152.1	—	16.1	196.6	—	**92.9**
2006	—	5.5	—	—	—	3.7	—	—	—	4.1	—	2.1	—	—	**3.9**
2008	—	6.5	—	—	—	4.0	—	—	—	4.6	—	2.0	—	—	**4.4**
Rate ratio	—	1.2	—	—	—	1.1	—	—	—	1.1	—	1.0	—	—	**1.1**
(95% CI)	—	(1.0–1.4)	—	—	—	(0.9–1.3)	—	—	—	(0.8–1.4)	—	(0.6–1.4)	—	—	**(1.0–1.2)**
% change	—	18.4	—	—	—	8.6	—	—	—	13.1	—	-4.3	—	—	**12.8**

Abbreviations: CI = confidence interval; NA = not available.

* Rate ratios and percentage change calculated with 2008 as the numerator and either 2002 or 2006 as the denominator.

† Data not reported.

§ Rate ratio statistically significant at p<0.01.

¶ Rate ratio statistically significant at p<0.05.

** A change cannot be calculated because the denominators are zero.

Changes in estimated ASD prevalence during 2006–2008 also varied by race within individual ADDM sites and when combining data from all sites. The combined estimates indicated a 16% increase in ASD prevalence among non-Hispanic white children (10.0–11.5 per 1,000), a 42% increase among non-Hispanic black children (7.0–10.0 per 1,000), and a 29% increase among Hispanic children (6.1–7.9 per 1,000). The percentage increase was statistically significant for all three racial/ethnic groups. Alabama identified a lower prevalence among non-Hispanic black children in 2008, and Arizona identified a lower prevalence among Hispanic children in 2008 compared with 2006 results.

In the four sites with IQ test data available on at least 70% of children with ASDs in both the 2006 and 2008 surveillance years, the estimated prevalence of ASD with intellectual disability increased 12% on average (4.2–4.7 per 1,000), while the prevalence of ASD with borderline intellectual ability increased 22% (2.3–2.8 per 1,000), and the prevalence of ASD with average or above-average intellectual ability increased 13% (3.9–4.4 per 1,000).

Comparison between 2002 and 2008 Prevalence Estimates

Thirteen ADDM sites completed both the 2002 and 2008 surveillance years, with all but one (Arkansas) identifying a significantly higher prevalence of ASDs in 2008 compared with 2002 (Table 5). When data from all sites were combined, ASD prevalence estimates among children aged 8 years increased 78% during 2002–2008 (from 6.4 to 11.4 per 1,000). The combined increase across all sites was 82% for males (10.2–18.6 per 1,000) and 63% for females (2.4–4.0 per 1,000) during this 6-year period. The combined estimates indicated a 70% increase among non-Hispanic white children (7.0–11.9 per 1,000), a 91% increase among non-Hispanic black children (5.5–10.5 per 1,000), and a 110% increase among Hispanic children (3.7–7.7 per 1,000) during 2002–2008.

In the seven sites with IQ test data available on at least 70% of children with ASDs in both the 2002 and 2008 surveillance years, estimated prevalence of ASD with intellectual disability increased 45% on average (3.2–4.6 per 1,000), while the estimated prevalence of ASD with borderline intellectual ability increased 117% (1.4–2.9 per 1,000), and the estimated prevalence of ASD with average or above-average intellectual ability increased 93% (2.4–4.7 per 1,000).

When data from all 13 sites participating in the 2002 and 2008 surveillance years were combined, the proportion of children meeting the ASD surveillance case definition who had a comprehensive evaluation completed by age 36 months increased over time, from 32% for children born in 1994 to 41% for children born in 2000 (i.e., children identified in the 2002 and 2008 surveillance years, respectively). During this time, the proportion with an earliest known ASD diagnosis by age 36 months increased from 12% for children born in 1994 to 18% for children born in 2000.

Previously Documented ASD Classification: 2002, 2006, and 2008

The proportion of children meeting the ASD surveillance case definition who had a documented ASD classification in their records increased over time in seven of the 10 sites completing all 3 surveillance years (Figure 3). For these 10 ADDM sites combined, and restricting analysis to residents of the core surveillance areas that were common across all 3 surveillance years, the proportion of surveillance cases with a previous ASD classification increased from 72% in 2002 to 77% in 2006 and to 79% in 2008.

DISCUSSION

The results provided in this report suggest that three topics require further exploration. First, estimated ASD prevalence continues to rise in most ADDM Network sites, indicating an expanded need for programs serving children with ASDs. Second, a wide range of ASD prevalence was estimated across ADDM Network sites. Finally, estimated prevalence varied widely by sex and race/ethnicity. To address such wide variation in ASD prevalence estimates (over time, across sites, and between sex and racial/ethnic groups) a number of factors should be considered, primarily those focusing on ascertainment.

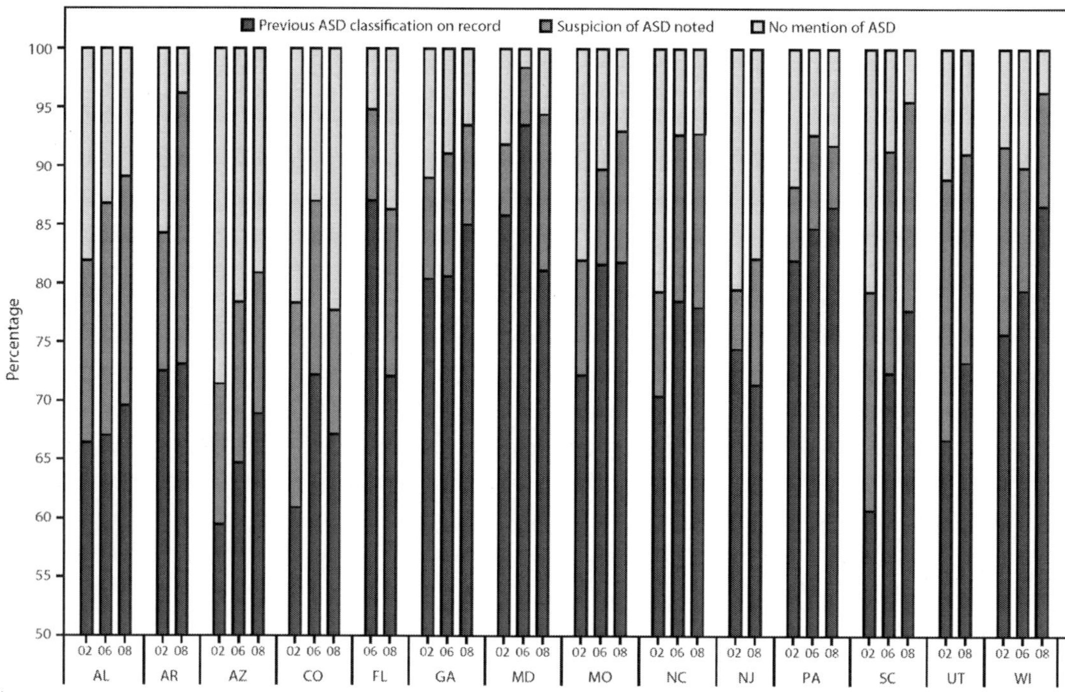

* N = 2,682
† N = 2,757
§ N = 3,820

Figure 3. Proportion of children identified with autism spectrum disorders (ASDs) by previous ASD classification on record as of age 8 years, by state and year — Autism and Developmental Disabilities Monitoring Network, United States, 14 sites, 2002,* 2006,† and 2008§.

Temporal Changes in ASD Prevalence

While ASD prevalence estimates in the overall population increased 23% for the 2-year period 2006–2008, and 78% during the 6-year period 2002–2008, the largest increases over time were noted among Hispanic children and non-Hispanic black children and among children without co-occurring intellectual disability. Better identification in these specific groups explains only part of the overall increase, however, as estimated ASD prevalence increased in all groups when data were stratified by sex, race/ethnicity, and intellectual ability. Previous reports from the ADDM Network have discussed underascertainment in racial and ethnic minority groups, and ADDM data have revealed ASD as one of the few developmental disabilities for which a positive correlation exists between socioeconomic status (SES) and identified prevalence of the condition [18]. Further investigation is needed to better understand potential ascertainment bias and disparities by race/ethnicity and SES in access to diagnostic and treatment services for children with ASDs. If these gaps are decreasing, continued ASD prevalence increases might be expected overall and among specific groups.

Children meeting the surveillance case definition for ASD are not required to have an existing ASD diagnosis or classification on record, but examiners' diagnostic impressions do factor prominently in ascertainment methods and can influence temporal changes in ASD prevalence. Approximately 79% of all children meeting the surveillance case definition in 2008 had a documented ASD classification in their records, the highest proportion ever reported for any ADDM Network surveillance year. This offers evidence that providers in these communities are increasingly more likely to document the presence of ASDs and facilitate access to services that are specific to the needs of children with ASDs. Also, the proportion of children with an earliest known ASD diagnosis by age 36 months increased over time. However, 21% of the children meeting the ASD surveillance case definition do not have any documented ASD classification in their records, and those who do are not being identified early enough. In areas where autism-specific interventions are available to children who qualify on the basis of diagnosis, early screening and diagnosis improves access to services during the most critical developmental periods. Limitations in the data and report findings in terms of the earliest "known" diagnosis suggest that the diagnostic information obtained from evaluation records might not capture the exact age of each child's earliest diagnosis. Given this and the instability of diagnostic subtypes over time, the median age of earliest known diagnosis for any specific ASD should be interpreted cautiously. Nonetheless, the data indicate that many children with ASDs do not receive a diagnosis until they reach preschool or kindergarten age, missing opportunities for earlier therapies that potentially could improve communication and socialization while these skills are developing. Because the data for this report were collected on children born during 1994–2000, future reports from the ADDM Network might demonstrate greater progress in early identification stemming from policy changes initiated in recent years, including state-based insurance reform and the expansion of services for children with ASDs occurring in many states.

Variation in ASD Prevalence by Site, Sex, and Race/Ethnicity

For the 2008 surveillance year, a wider range of site-specific ASD prevalence estimates was identified than in previous ADDM Network surveillance years. Variation in estimated ASD prevalence was associated primarily with sites having access to education records and also appeared to be associated with improved identification among children without intellectual disability. On average, estimated ASD prevalence was significantly higher in ADDM sites that had access to education sources compared with sites that relied solely on health sources to identify cases, and ASD prevalence in the one Colorado county where project staff had access to both health and education sources was almost twice as high as in the six counties where only health records were accessed. Such differences cannot be attributed solely to source access, as other factors (e.g., demographic differences and service availability) also might have influenced these findings. In general, however, having access to education records continues to be associated with higher identified ASD prevalence when comparing across or within most ADDM Network sites.

The two sites with the highest ASD prevalence estimates in 2008 (Utah and New Jersey) identified higher proportions of children with IQ >70 compared with any site participating in 2008 or previous ADDM Network surveillance years. Among the seven sites reporting data on intellectual ability, ASD prevalence was typically higher in sites having a greater percentage of children with IQ > 70 (Figure 4). Because testing practices and other factors that influence these findings might vary across sites, further analysis is needed to understand this pattern in 2008 and earlier ADDM surveillance years.

The availability of children's records also was identified as a potential source of underascertainment and variation in ASD prevalence estimates among sites. When a sensitivity evaluation algorithm was applied to counts of records that could not be located for review, estimated ASD prevalence in some sites might have been much higher if all children's records had been available for review. In other sites, however, the impact of missing records was considered negligible, so record availability likely accounted for at least some of the variation across sites. Because nearly half of the missing records in Florida were from a program serving children aged birth to 3 years, 26% is considered a liberal estimate, and the actual yield from these early childhood records might have been smaller. In Alabama, the vast majority of missing records was from facilities that were in the process of converting from paper to electronic records or had storage limitations during the period of data collection, so the large number of missing records might have had a one-time effect on the 2008 surveillance data for this site.

The estimated prevalence of ASDs was significantly higher among boys (one in 54) than among girls (one in 252), with a male-to-female RR of 4.6 for all sites combined. Although the ADDM site with the highest ASD prevalence had the lowest male-to-female ratio while the site with the lowest ASD prevalence had the highest male-to-female ratio, improved identification among females compared with males did not appear to be associated with between-site differences in overall ASD prevalence. Much wider variation existed in sites' prevalence estimates for males than for females.

ASD prevalence estimates also varied widely by race/ethnicity across and within most sites, with only one site (New Jersey) identifying approximately the same ASD prevalence among non-Hispanic white, non-Hispanic black, and Hispanic children. Most ADDM Network sites continue to identify higher ASD prevalence estimates among non-Hispanic white children compared with other racial/ethnic groups, and with no clearly documented differences between these groups in known risk factors for ASDs, disparities in prevalence estimates suggest underascertainment among Hispanic and non-Hispanic black children. However, these disparities in identification appear to be diminishing in many sites, and further work is needed to evaluate how identification among certain racial/ethnic populations is associated with differences in ASD prevalence between sites and over time.

Limitations

The data provided in this report are subject to at least two limitations. First, increases in awareness and access to services have improved the ability of the ADDM Network to identify children with ASD over time, and this likely contributes to the increase in estimated prevalence. The proportion of the increase that is attributable to such changes in case ascertainment or attributable to a true increase in prevalence of ASD symptoms cannot be determined. Ongoing monitoring is an important tool to learn why more children are being identified with ASDs and can provide important clues in the search for risk factors.

Second, the surveillance areas were not selected to be representative of the United States as a whole, nor were they selected to be representative of the states in which they are located. Limitations regarding population size, surveillance areas, and the consistency of these attributes were considered when analysts evaluated comparisons across multiple time points. Although the two ADDM sites reporting the highest prevalence estimates in 2008 also reported among the highest prevalence estimates in 2002, the most recent results from New Jersey and Utah are based on subregions of their 2002 surveillance areas, with smaller populations compared with those areas and with most other ADDM sites. The estimated prevalence in these subregions possibly was influenced by factors unique to these smaller communities and might not reflect the number and characteristics of children with ASDs in the larger areas covered by these ADDM sites in 2002. Similarly, five other ADDM sites covered different surveillance areas in 2008 compared with 2002 and/or 2006. Although comparisons with earlier surveillance years were carefully restricted to comparable surveillance areas, caution is advised when interpreting results. For example, the addition of one North Carolina county in 2008 resulted in a nearly 15% increase in the overall prevalence of ASDs in that site compared with their findings when this new county was excluded from the prevalence estimate. Although this county was excluded from calculations when the 2008 results were compared with those from earlier surveillance years, the impact of this single county highlights the relative differences across subregions of any given ADDM site.

Future Analyses to Address Limitations

For differences in ASD prevalence, across sites and within subregions of each site to be understood better, further exploration of geographic variation in multiple contextual and potential risk factors is needed. This involves in-depth analysis of known characteristics in the population of children identified with ASDs (e.g., intellectual ability, SES, and birth characteristics), as well as geographic differences affecting the population as a whole. These results point to a need for geospatial analyses of both physical and social environments, including occupational and socioeconomic characteristics of the population, state policy differences potentially affecting access to services (e.g., insurance reform, per capita educational spending, and immigration policy), and geographic differences in environmental exposures that potentially might affect neurodevelopment.

Another important consideration for future analyses is the changing clinical definition of ASDs over time. Although the ADDM methods have always been based on the DSM-IV-TR [1] diagnostic criteria, proposed changes to the definition of Autism Spectrum Disorder in the forthcoming revised Diagnostic and Statistical Manual of Mental Disorders (DSM-5) might affect prevalence estimates and complicate temporal comparisons [19]. The proposed revised diagnostic criteria for Autism Spectrum Disorder would combine three subgroups currently under the DSM-IV-TR heading of Pervasive Developmental Disorders into one category and might require a child to display more pronounced symptoms to receive a diagnosis. Because the ADDM methods include information on a broad range of symptoms, the ADDM Network is well-positioned to adopt the proposed DSM-5 definition into its ongoing study and, at the same time, obtain comparison estimates based on the DSM-IV-TR definition. CDC and ADDM Network investigators are exploring the data to understand how the proposed changes might affect the current prevalence estimates and will continue to prioritize these comparisons so as to understand trends better over time. This information is crucial to increasing knowledge of this complex spectrum of behaviors.

Ongoing Efforts

Although multiple factors influence the identification of children with ASDs and differences in prevalence estimates across sites, the data provided in this report indicate the need for further exploration of possible associations between overall ASD prevalence and improved identification among children without intellectual disability, children in all racial/ethnic populations, and both males and females, including potential interactions between these factors. ADDM Network investigators continue to explore a broad variety of potential risk and ascertainment factors to understand differences in ASD prevalence estimates between sites and over time.

With 5 surveillance years completed to date, and data collection underway for the 2010 surveillance year, the ADDM Network has compiled extensive data on the prevalence and characteristics of ASDs and other developmental disabilities. These data cover large populations for obtaining prevalence estimates and provide depth and breadth of information on topics not captured in national health surveys. The ADDM record-review methodology enables reporting of data on intellectual ability, specific ASD subtype diagnosis and educational classification, within- and between-state comparisons, and linkage to other datasets for exploration of potential risk factors such as birth characteristics and socioeconomic disparities as well as examination of health services utilization. Currently, the ADDM Network is collecting information on children who were aged 8 years in 2010 and for the first time also is monitoring ASDs among children aged 4 years. In 2012, ADDM sites will begin collecting information for the 2012 surveillance year.

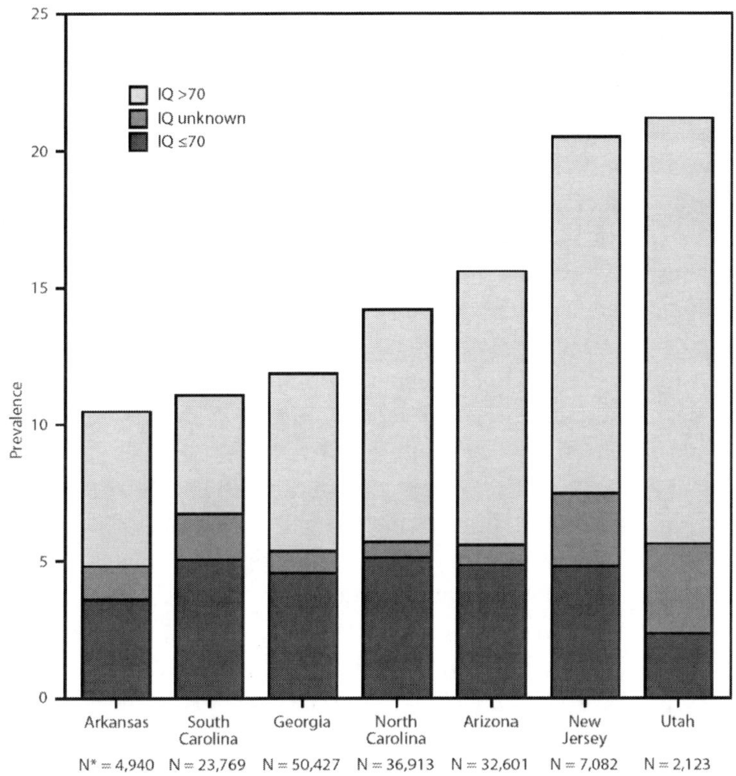

* Includes sites having information on IQ score available for at least 70% of children who met the ASD case definition.

† Total population aged 8 years.

Figure 4. Variation in estimated prevalence (per 1,000 population) of autism spectrum disorders (ASDs) among children aged 8 years, by Intelligence Quotient (IQ) score — Autism and Developmental Disabilities Monitoring Network, seven sites,* United States, 2008.

CONCLUSION

ASDs continue to be an important public health concern. The findings provided in this report confirm that prevalence estimates of ASD continue to increase in the majority of ADDM Network communities, and ongoing public health surveillance is needed to quantify and understand these changes over time. Further work is needed to evaluate multiple factors affecting ASD prevalence over time. ADDM Network investigators continue to explore these factors in multiple ways, with a focus on understanding disparities in the identification of ASDs among certain subgroups and evaluating temporal changes in the prevalence of ASDs. CDC also is engaged with other federal, state, and private partners in a coordinated response to identify risk factors for ASDs and meet the needs of persons with ASDs and their families. Additional information http://www.cdc.gov/autism is available at http://www.cdc.gov/autism.

ACKNOWLEDGMENTS

Data in this report were provided by ADDM Network Surveillance Year 2008 investigators: Martha Wingate, DrPH, Beverly Mulvihill, PhD, University of Alabama at Birmingham; Russell S. Kirby, PhD, University of South Florida, Tampa; Sydney Pettygrove, PhD, Chris Cunniff, MD, F. John Meaney, PhD, University of Arizona, Tucson; Eldon Schulz, MD, University of Arkansas for Medical Sciences, Little Rock; Lisa Miller, MD, Colorado Department of Public Health and Environment, Denver; Cordelia Robinson, PhD, University of Colorado at Denver and Health Sciences Center; Gina Quintana, Colorado Department of Education, Denver; Marygrace Yale Kaiser, PhD, University of Miami, Coral Gables, Florida; Li-Ching Lee, PhD, Johns Hopkins University, Rebecca Landa, PhD, Kennedy Krieger Institute, Baltimore, Maryland; Craig Newschaffer, PhD, Drexel University, Philadelphia, Pennsylvania; John Constantino, MD, Robert Fitzgerald, MPH, Washington University in St. Louis, Missouri; Walter Zahorodny, PhD, University of Medicine and Dentistry of New Jersey, Newark; Julie Daniels, PhD, University of North Carolina, Chapel Hill; Ellen Giarelli, EdD, Drexel University, Philadelphia, Pennsylvania; Jennifer Pinto-Martin, PhD, University of Pennsylvania; Susan E. Levy, MD, The Children's Hospital of Philadelphia, Pennsylvania; Joyce Nicholas, PhD, Jane Charles, MD, Medical University of South Carolina, Charleston; Judith Zimmerman, PhD, University of Utah, Salt Lake City; Matthew J. Maenner, PhD, Maureen Durkin, PhD, DrPH, University of Wisconsin, Madison; Catherine Rice, PhD, Jon Baio, EdS, Kim Van Naarden Braun, PhD, Keydra Phillips, MPH, Nancy Doernberg, Marshalyn Yeargin-Allsopp, MD, Division of Birth Defects and Developmental Disabilities, National Center on Birth Defects and Developmental Disabilities, CDC.

Data collection was coordinated at each site by ADDM Network project coordinators: Anita Washington, MPH, Yasmeen Williams, MPH, Kwin Jolly, MS, Research Triangle Institute, Atlanta, Georgia; Neva Garner, University of Alabama at Birmingham; Kristen Clancy Mancilla, University of Arizona, Tucson; Allison Hudson, University of Arkansas for Medical Sciences, Little Rock; Andria Ratchford, MSPH, Colorado Department of Public Health and Environment, Denver; Yolanda Castillo, MBA, Colorado Department of Education, Denver; Claudia Rojas, Yanin Hernandez, University of Miami, Coral Gables, Florida; Kara Humes, Rebecca Harrington, MPH, Johns Hopkins University, Baltimore, Maryland; Rob Fitzgerald, MPH, Washington University in St. Louis, Missouri; Josephine Shenouda, MS, University of Medicine and Dentistry of New Jersey, Newark; Paula Bell, University of North Carolina, Chapel Hill; Rachel Reis, University of Pennsylvania, Philadelphia; Lydia King, PhD, Medical University of South Carolina, Charleston; Amanda Bakian, PhD, Amy Henderson, University of Utah, Salt Lake City; Carrie Arneson, MS, University of Wisconsin, Madison; Susan Graham Schwartz, MSPH, CDC. Additional assistance was provided by project staff including data abstractors, clinician reviewers, epidemiologists, and data management/programming support. Ongoing ADDM Network support was provided by Joanne Wojcik, Victoria Wright, National Center on Birth Defects and Developmental Disabilities, CDC, Rita Lance, Northrop Grumman, contractor to CDC.

REFERENCES

[1] American Psychiatric Association. *Diagnostic and statistical manual of mental disorders*. 4th ed. Washington, DC: American Psychiatric Association; 2000.

[2] Rice, CE; Baio, J; Van Naarden Braun, K; Doernberg, N; Meaney, FJ; Kirby, RS; for the ADDM Network. A public health collaboration for the surveillance of autism spectrum disorders. *Paediatr Perinat Epidemiol* 2007; 21, 179–90.

[3] CDC. *Prevalence of autism spectrum disorders—Autism and Developmental Disabilities Monitoring Network, six sites, United States, 2000*. MMWR 2007; 56(No. SS-1), 1–11.

[4] CDC. *Prevalence of autism spectrum disorders—Autism and Developmental Disabilities Monitoring Network, 14 sites, United States, 2002*. MMWR 2007; 56(No. SS-1), 12–28.

[5] CDC. *Prevalence of autism spectrum disorders—Autism and Developmental Disabilities Monitoring Network, United States, 2006*. MMWR 2009; 58(No. SS-10).

[6] Kogan, MD; Blumberg, SJ; Schieve, LA; et al. *Prevalence of parent-reported diagnosis of autism spectrum disorder among children in the U.S.*, 2007. Pediatrics 2009; 124, 1395–403.

[7] Boyle, CA; Boulet, S; Schieve, LA; et al. *Trends in the prevalence of developmental disabilities in U.S. children*, 1997–2008. Pediatrics 2011; 127, 1034–42.

[8] Baron-Cohen, S; Scott, FJ; Allison, C; et al. Prevalence of autism-spectrum conditions: UK school-based population study. *Br J Psychiatry* 2009; 194, 500–9.

[9] Fombonne, E. Estimated prevalence of autism spectrum conditions in Cambridgeshire is over 1%. *Evid Based Ment Health* 2010; 13, 32.

[10] Kim, YS; Leventhal, BL; Koh, YJ; F, et al. Prevalence of autism spectrum disorders in a total population sample. *Am J Psychiatry* 2011; 168, 904–12.

[11] HR 4365, 106th Cong, 1999–2000. *Children's Health Act of 2000*. Available at http://www.govtrack.us/congress/bill.xpd?bill=h106-4365. Accessed March 14, 2012.

[12] Yeargin-Allsopp, M; Rice, C; Karapurkar, T; Doernberg, N; Boyle, C; Murphy, C. *Prevalence of autism in a US metropolitan area*. JAMA 2003; 289, 49–55.

[13] Van Naarden Braun, K; Pettygrove, S; Daniels, J; et al. Evaluation of a methodology for a collaborative multiple source surveillance network for autism spectrum disorders—Autism and Developmental Disabilities Monitoring Network, 14 sites, United States, 2002. MMWR 2007; 56(No. SS-1), 29–40.

[14] US Department of Health and Human Services. *Code of Federal Regulations*. Title 45. Public Welfare CFR 46. Available at http://www.hhs.gov/ohrp/humansubjects/guidance/45cfr46.html. Accessed March 14, 2012.

[15] CDC. Estimates of the July 1, 2000–July 1, 2009, *United States resident population from the vintage 2009 postcensal series by year, county, age, sex, race, and Hispanic origin*. Available at http://www.cdc.gov/nchs/ nvss/bridged_race/data_documentation.htm#vintage2009. Accessed March 14, 2012.

[16] US Department of Education. *Common core of data*. Available at http://nces.ed.gov/ccd/bat. Accessed March 14, 2012.

[17] Lazarus, C; Autry, A; Baio, J; Avchen, RN; Van Naarden Braun, K. Impact of postcensal versus intercensal population estimates on prevalence of selected developmental disabilities—metropolitan Atlanta, Georgia, 1991–1996. *Am J Ment Retard* 2007; 112, 462–6.

[18] Durkin, MS; Maenner, MJ; Meaney, FJ; et al. Socioeconomic inequality in the prevalence of autism spectrum disorder: evidence from a U.S. cross-sectional study. *PLoS One* 2010; 5, e11551.

[19] American Psychiatric Association. *DSM-5 development: autism spectrum disorder*. Available at http://www.dsm5.org/Proposed Revisions/Pages/proposedrevision.aspx?rid =94. Accessed March 14, 2012.

In: Autism Spectrum Disorders ISBN 978-1-62257-076-8
Editors: Gregory L. Campbell and Anthony O. Phillips ©2012 Nova Science Publishers, Inc.

Chapter 4

THE NEW GENETICS OF AUTISM: WHY ENVIRONMENT MATTERS*

U. S. Department of Health and Human Services

[Last week] the CDC reported a 78 percent increase in autism prevalence since 2002. This week's autism news is about genetics—*three papers in Nature* describe new genes associated with autism. For many people, these two stories seem contradictory or, at best, unrelated. Increasing prevalence suggests environmental factors like chemicals and microbes changing over the past decade, whereas genes change over generations. Why is anyone looking for genetic causes when there is such a rapid increase in prevalence? Shouldn't every research dollar be invested in finding the environmental culprit rather than searching for rare gene variants?

The simple answer is that *some* autism is genetic. Autism, like *schizophrenia* and *mood disorders*, includes many syndromes. Indeed, we should probably speak of the "autisms." Some of these autisms are single gene disorders, such as *Fragile X*, *tuberous sclerosis*, and Rett *syndrome*. While these rare genetic disorders account for less than 5 percent of children within the autism spectrum, children with any of these disorders are at high risk for autism, roughly a 30-fold higher risk than the general population and higher than any of the other known risk factors. Recent genomics research has discovered that many children diagnosed within the autism spectrum have other genetic mutations that have not yet been designated as named syndromes. Each of these mutations is rare, but in aggregate they may account for 10 - 20 percent or more of what we have been calling the autisms.[1]

The new papers published today in Nature use an approach called whole exome sequencing, mapping every base of DNA across the exome—the 1.5 percent of the genome known to code for protein. The three research groups are members of the Autism Sequencing Consortium (ASC), an international team of autism genetics researchers. All three look for *de novo* or spontaneous mutations, changes in DNA sequence that are not found in either parent. Recent sequencing studies in the general population have demonstrated that each of us diverges genomically from our parents — the process of reproduction introduces variation

* This is an edited, reformatted and augmented version of the National Institute of Mental Health, dated April 04, 2012.

even beyond the random mixture of the genomes we inherit from mom and dad. People with autism and schizophrenia are far more likely to have large *de novo* copy number variants, sometimes a million bases of DNA that are abnormally duplicated or deleted and not found in either parent.

These new papers go beyond the previous discovery of *de novo* copy number variants to identify de novo single base changes associated with autism. This is tough sailing because there are so many of these changes in all of us and most of these single base changes have no impact. These studies tried to improve the odds of success by focusing on individuals from families with no one else affected (these are called "simplex" families), and sometimes comparing the individual with autism to a sibling without autism. The results are intriguing.

There is no breakthrough or single gene that is a major new cause of autism. But the role of genetics becomes even more evident when these single base changes are considered. For instance, an individual with autism is nearly 6-fold more likely to have a functional variant in genes expressed in the brain. Sanders et al. estimate as many as 14 percent of affected individuals have such a risk variant.[2] This 14 percent is in addition to the 10–20 percent with a large copy number variant or identified genetic syndrome. O'Roak et al. find that 39 percent of these variants are related to a specific biochemical pathway, important for brain signaling.[3] And Neale et al., while cautioning that the net effect of all of these changes still leave much of the risk for autism unexplained, note the roles of a few specific genes as genuine risk factors.[4]

Stepping back from this flood of genomic information, what is most important? First, these reports along with previous publications confirm that genetic risk is both complex and substantial. While individual genes appear to confer limited risk, the aggregate effect of spontaneous coding mutations across the genome is now estimated to increase the risk of autism by 5–20-fold.[4] Complex genetics does not mean modest effects.

Second, the kinds of small and large genetic changes associated with autism are common in everyone. Risk is conferred not by the size of the mutation or the number of mutations (we all have many) but by the location. Increasingly, we see that interference with the genes involved in development of synapses confer risk; a similar change upstream or downstream does not.

A third point takes us back to the questions we started with. It is important to understand that *de novo* mutations may represent environmental effects. In other words, environmental factors can cause changes in our DNA that can raise the risk for autism and other disorders. One of these papers reports that spontaneous changes are four times more likely to show up in paternally inherited DNA and are correlated with paternal age.[2] The father's germline, his sperm cells, turn over throughout the lifespan. Presumably, with advancing paternal age, there are a greater number of spontaneous mutations and a greater likelihood that some of these will affect risk genes. Environmental factors and exposures can cause sperm cells to develop mutations that are not found in the father's somatic, or body cell, DNA, but these new, spontaneous mutations can be passed to the next generation, raising the risk for developing autism. In the initial report of the relationship between autism and paternal age, boys with autism were 6-fold more likely to have a father in his 40s vs his 20s. In girls with autism, this difference went up to 17-fold.[5] Paternal age has, of course, increased in the past few decades. This does not explain the increasing prevalence of autism, but it may contribute.

Is autism genetic or environmental? These new studies suggest it can be both. Genetics will not identify the environmental factors, but it may reveal some of the many syndromes within the autism spectrum (as in other neurodevelopmental disorders), it can define risk (as in other medical disorders), and it should yield clues to the biology of autism (revealing potential targets for new treatments). These three new papers on spontaneous mutations are an important milestone in a long journey. In parallel we need to find environmental factors, recognizing that there will be many causes for the autisms and many roads to find them.

Finally, an unavoidable insight from these new papers is that autism even when genetic may be spontaneous and not inherited in the sense that one or both parents carry some reduced form of the syndrome. Perhaps this insight will finally reduce the "blame the parents" legacy perpetuated for too long in the absence of scientific evidence.

References

[1] Geschwind, DH. Genetics of autism spectrum disorders. *Trends Cogn Sci.* 2011 Sep; 15(9), 409-16. Epub 2011 Aug 18. PubMed PMID: 21855394.1

[2] Sanders, SJ; Murtha, MT; Gupta, AR; Murdoch, JD; Raubeson, MJ; Willsey, AJ; Ercan-Sencicek, AG; DiLullo, NM; Parikshak, NN; Stein, JL; Walker, MF; Ober, GT; Teran, NA; Song, Y; El-Fishawy, P; Murtha, RC; Choi, M; Overton, JD; Bjornson, RD; Carriero, NJ; Meyer, KA; Bilguvar, K; Mane, SM; Sestan, N; Lifton, RP; Günel, M; Roeder, K; Geschwind, DH; Devlin, B; State, MW. *De novo mutations revealed by whole-exome sequencing are strongly associated with autism.* April 5, 2012. Nature.

[3] O'Roak, BJ; Vives, L; Girirajan, S; Karakoc, E; Krumm, N; Coe, BP; Levy, R; Ko, A; Lee, C; Smith, JD; Turner, EH; Stanaway, IB; Vernot, B; Malig, M; Baker, C; Reilly, B; Akey, JM; Borenstein, E; Rieder, MJ; Nickerson, DA; Bernier, R; Shendure, J; Eichler, EE. Sporadic autism exomes reveal a highly interconnected protein network of de novo mutations. *Nature.* April 5, 2012.

[4] Neale, BM; Kou, Y; Liu, L; Ma'ayan, A; Samocha, KE; Sabo, A; Lin, CF; Stevens, C; Wang, LS; Makarov, V; Polak, P; Yoon, S; Maguire, J; Crawford, EL; Campbell, NG; Geller, ET; Valladares, O; Schafer, C; Liu, H; Zhao, T; Cai, G; Lihm, J; Dannenfelser, R; Jabado, O; Peralta, Z; Nagaswamy, U; Muzny, D; Reid, JG; Newsham, I; Wu, Y; Lewis, L; Han, Y; Voight, BF; Lim, E; Rossin, E; Kirby, A; Flannick, J; Fromer, M; Shair, K; Fennell, T; Garimella, K; Banks, E; Poplin, R; Gabriel, S; DePristo, M; Wimbish, JR; Boone, BE; Levy, SE; Betancur, C; Sunyaev, S; Boerwinkle, E; Buxbaum, JD; Cook, EH; Devlin, B; Gibbs, RA; Roeder, K; Schellenberg, GD; Sutcliffe, JS; Daly, MJ. Patterns and rates of exonic de novo mutations in autism spectrum disorders. *Nature.* April 5, 2012.

[5] Reichenberg, A; Gross, R; Weiser, M; Bresnahan, M; Silverman, J; Harlap, S; Rabinowitz, J; Shulman, C; Malaspina, D; Lubin, G; Knobler, HY; Davidson, M; Susser, E. Advancing paternal age and autism. *Arch Gen Psychiatry.* 2006 Sep; 63(9), 1026-32. PubMed PMID: 16953005.

In: Autism Spectrum Disorders ISBN 978-1-62257-076-8
Editors: Gregory L. Campbell and Anthony O. Phillips

Chapter 5

2011 Strategic Plan for Autism Spectrum Disorder Research*

Interagency Autism Coordinating Committee

Introduction

Two decades ago, autism was a little-known, uncommon disorder. Today, autism is more common in the United States than childhood cancer, juvenile diabetes, and pediatric AIDS combined, and the increasing numbers of children being diagnosed with autism has created a national health emergency. In a speech at the National Institutes of Health on September 30, 2009, President Obama specifically cited autism, along with cancer and heart disease, as one of three health conditions targeted for major scientific research investment through the American Recovery and Reinvestment Act. The President expressed his hope that research into genetic and environmental factors would result in strides in early intervention, treatments, and therapies to help people affected by autism achieve their fullest potential.

Autism is now recognized as a group of syndromes denoted as autism spectrum disorder (ASD). The most recent Centers for Disease Control and Prevention (CDC) prevalence estimates of ASD for children are 1 in 110 (CDC, 2009). These estimates, more than tenfold higher than two decades ago, raise several urgent questions: Why has there been such an increase in prevalence? What can be done to reverse this alarming trend? How can we improve the outcomes of people already affected, including youth and adults?

Approaches to ASD diagnosis have evolved as more has been learned about the disorder. Currently, ASD is diagnosed on a combination of behavioral characteristics of impairment in verbal and nonverbal communication skills and social interactions, and restricted, repetitive, and stereotyped patterns of behavior. These characteristics can range in impact from mild to significantly disabling. Adequately addressing these conditions requires sophisticated

* This is an edited, reformatted and augmented version of the Department of Health and Human Services Interagency Autism Coordinating Committee, dated January, 2011.

educational and therapeutic approaches. Some people with ASD also have a range of medical conditions including, but not limited to: motor and sensory impairments, seizures, immunological and metabolic abnormalities, sleep problems, and gastrointestinal symptoms.

The cost of ASD to affected people, families, and society is enormous. A great majority of adults with ASD struggle with ongoing and mostly unmet needs for employment, housing, services, and supports. Compounding these stressors, families of a child with autism typically lose income, sometimes as a result of one parent leaving the workforce in order to care for and meet the special health and educational needs of the child (Montes & Halterman, 2008). The cost to society of ASD is currently estimated to be $35 billion to $90 billion annually, the higher estimate being comparable to Alzheimer's disease (Ganz, 2007; Knapp, Romeo & Beechum, 2009). Although research on ASD has expanded over the past decade, there remains an urgent need for increased research support.

It is imperative that resources be devoted to research commensurate with the public health need. Specifically, we need research that deepens our understanding of ASD, including the mechanisms by which complex genetic and environmental factors play a role in its causation; development of improved ASD diagnostic approaches and treatments; and science to enhance the level of services and supports available to people with ASD, their families, and caregivers. With current scientific knowledge and tools, we have unprecedented potential for discoveries that will improve the quality of life for people with ASD.

In response to the heightened societal concern over ASD, Congress passed the Combating Autism Act (CAA) of 2006 (P.L. 109-416). Through this Act, Congress intended to rapidly increase, accelerate the pace, and improve coordination of scientific discovery in ASD research. The CAA requires the Interagency Autism Coordinating Committee (IACC) to develop and annually update a Strategic Plan for ASD research, including proposed budgetary requirements.

Driven by both the sense of urgency and a spirit of collaboration, the IACC developed an initial Strategic Plan for ASD Research in 2009 and revised it in 2010 and 2011 in accordance with the CAA. The Plan and its revisions were developed through extensive and iterative input from the public and members of the academic and advocacy communities.

In developing and revising the Strategic Plan, the IACC:

- Gathered ideas for research opportunities and objectives from a diverse group of stakeholders through convened working groups, public comments, and formal requests for information (RFIs).
- Convened town hall meetings in 2008 and 2009 to gather public input.
- Convened scientific workshops in 2008 and 2009 to obtain input from subject matter experts in autism research.
- Convened a services workshop in 2010 to obtain input from subject matter experts in services and policy.
- Conducted an annual analysis of the ASD research portfolio spanning both Federal and private funders of ASD research, identifying research investments, opportunities, gaps, and progress.
- Reviewed the biomedical and services research literature for significant advances in the field and annually published an IACC Summary of Advances in ASD Research.

The Strategic Plan incorporates this array of input in two main sections. First, the foundation of the Plan—vision, mission, core values, and crosscutting themes—is described. The remainder of the Plan is organized around seven critical questions asked by people and families living with ASD:

- **When should I be concerned?**
- **How can I understand what is happening?**
- **What caused this to happen and can it be prevented?**
- **Which treatments and interventions will help?**
- **Where can I turn for services?**
- **What does the future hold, particularly for adults?**
- **What other infrastructure and surveillance needs must be met?**

Each question is followed by a brief discussion of what we currently know and need from research, an aspirational goal, research opportunities and objectives, and progress toward accomplishing research objectives. This framework was chosen by the IACC to emphasize the need for consumer-focused research that addresses the most pressing questions of people and families living with ASD, and to link these questions to specific research efforts.

Vision Statement

The Strategic Plan will accelerate and inspire research that will profoundly improve the health and well-being of every person on the autism spectrum across the lifespan. The Plan will set the standard for public-private coordination and community engagement.

Mission Statement

The purpose of the Strategic Plan is to focus, coordinate, and accelerate high-quality research and scientific discovery in partnership with stakeholders to answer the urgent questions and needs of people on the autism spectrum and their families.

Core Values

The IACC adopted these core values and emphasized their importance for the Strategic Plan development and implementation:

Sense of Urgency: We will focus on what steps we can take to respond rapidly and efficiently to the needs and challenges of people and families affected by ASD.

Excellence: We will pursue innovative basic and clinical research of the highest quality to protect the safety of and to advance the interests of people affected by ASD.

Spirit of Collaboration: We will treat others with respect, listen to diverse views with open minds, discuss submitted public comments, and foster discussions where participants can comfortably offer opposing opinions.

Consumer Focus: We will focus on making a difference in the lives of people affected by ASD, including people with ASD, their families, medical practitioners, educators, and scientists. It is important to consider the impact of research on the human rights, dignity, and quality of life of people with ASD, from prenatal development forward.

Partnerships in Action: We will value cross-disciplinary approaches, data sharing, teamwork, and partnerships with clearly defined roles and responsibilities.

Accountability: We will develop SMART (Specific, Measurable, Achievable, Realistic, and Time-bound) research objectives aligned with funding priorities and develop systems for evaluation, assessing impact, and course corrections.

Crosscutting Themes

The Strategic Plan for ASD Research is designed to highlight the most promising research ideas, while appreciating the inherent unpredictability of research. These ideas form the basis for the research opportunities and objectives of the Strategic Plan. In the process of gathering ideas from ASD stakeholders for this Plan, certain themes emerged repeatedly. These themes are highlighted here to emphasize their importance across the framework.

Heterogeneity: Although certain core features are present at varying degrees among all people with ASD—i.e., social impairments, communication difficulties, and stereotyped behaviors—considerable heterogeneity exists as well. In the context of ASD, the term "heterogeneity" refers to the range of and variability in severity of behavioral and medical conditions and symptoms that may comprise the disorder.

There is little reason to assume that this spectrum identifies a single disorder. Rather, the spectrum encompasses a range of disorders. The heterogeneity of ASD poses both challenges and opportunities to researchers: Challenges because there are likely to be many different causal factors and trajectories for ASD subtypes, and opportunities because recognition of the variety of ASD phenotypes can lead to more appropriate diagnosis, more precisely targeted treatments, and increased public awareness about the diversity inherent in ASD. Heterogeneity has a profound impact on the priorities and tactics of ASD research, because any given study either must focus on a particular focal point on the spectrum, or must be sufficiently complex and resourced to encompass a broader range along the spectrum.

Acknowledging heterogeneity also has implications for intervention. With multiple causes and symptoms, there likely will be multiple ways and approaches to intervene (e.g., medical, behavioral, nutritional). In so doing, the ASD field will be more strategically positioned to determine what works best for which people.

Co-Occurring Conditions: Although autism is currently defined by abnormal behavior, several medical symptoms frequently occur in autism and are an additional source of disability. It is unknown whether these medical symptoms are a primary aspect of some forms of autism or whether they are secondary features. In this document, they will be referred to as co-occurring medical conditions, recognizing that future research may reveal that some of these features could be integral to the behavioral syndrome. In a recent report from the Autism Treatment Network, a program funded by Autism Speaks in part through grants from the Health Resources and Services Administration (HRSA) and the National Institute of Mental Health (NIMH), 50% of children with ASD reported experiencing gastrointestinal problems and 65% reported sleep disturbances (Autism Speaks, 2010). Other health issues identified included food sensitivities, anxiety, depression, and seizures. Based on the literature, it is estimated that 22 to 38% of children with ASD experience seizures (Danielsson, 2005; Mouridsen, 2011). These co-occurring conditions, if not treated, can limit a person's ability to benefit fully from educational and behavioral interventions and fully participate in community life. And too often these conditions may not be treated. For example, nonverbal individuals may be unable to voice their health concerns, or clinicians may assume that these co-occurring symptoms are an inherent part of ASD. Research to understand the scope and cause of health conditions for those with ASD, along with the development of multidisciplinary health assessments and effective treatment guidelines, can immediately improve the quality of life for individuals with ASD and their families.

Prevention: It is critical for research to identify the methods and approaches that can be used to prevent the challenges and disabilities of ASD. Additionally, if one views ASD as a biological disorder triggered in genetically susceptible people by environmental factors, then prevention can include prevention of new cases of ASD through the identification and elimination of environmental causes. What is essential for ASD research is to develop the state of knowledge to a level similar to what is now available in fields such as cardiology. No longer do we need to wait for someone to suffer a heart attack before providing life-saving treatments. Rather, early interventions are applied upon the detection of risk factors so as to preempt these more serious consequences. Having sound research on the risk factors and the environmental triggers for ASD ultimately may allow us to achieve the goal of prevention: preventing the development of the disorder in some people at risk or reducing the degree of severity in those affected.

Earlier Detection: ASD is considered a developmental brain disorder that is currently diagnosed by the observation of core behavioral symptoms. As with many neurodevelopmental disorders, brain dysfunction may precede abnormal behavior by months or even years. However, without biomarkers to detect either people with ASD or at risk for ASD during pre- or neonatal periods, diagnosis must rely on behavioral observations long after birth. As a result, intervention efforts may miss a critical developmental window. Until recently, most children with ASD in the United States did not receive a diagnosis until school age, and diagnosis was further delayed among disadvantaged or rural populations (Mandell et al., 2007). It is critical that the field enhance methods for detecting ASD earlier in life and across diverse populations in order to bring about earlier intervention. Furthermore, a recurrent theme expressed during the scientific workshops for the Plan was the need for biomarkers to identify ASD risk before the behavioral manifestations and the delayed developmental trajectory are established.

Lifespan Perspective: Historically, ASD has been characterized as a disorder of childhood. Although most people with ASD will not outgrow their diagnosis, their symptoms will change in form and severity over time. There was great support during the development of this Plan for more research on ASD in older people, especially the need for practical strategies for increasing the quality of life and functioning of adolescents and adults with ASD. As people with ASD advocate for themselves and expand our knowledge of their experiences and needs, they become partners in the research effort.

Self-Determination: People with ASD can, with educational supports and accommodations, acquire skills to lead self-determined lives. Wehmeyer et al. (2010) define self-determined behavior as human behavior that is caused (i.e., determined) by the person as opposed to being caused by someone or something else. People leading self-determined lives make or cause things to happen, acting based on their own will, preferences, choices, and interests, instead of being coerced or forced to act in certain ways by others or circumstances (Wehmeyer et al., 2010). It is essential that ASD-related research incorporate and promote principles of self-determination. In addition, research is needed to help people with ASD incorporate principles of self-determination in their daily living.

Data Sharing: Data sharing allows researchers to (a) validate the research results of other investigators, (b) pool standardized information collected by many different researchers to facilitate rapid progress, and (c) use data collected by others to explore hypotheses not considered by the original investigators. The expectations for data sharing have increased with the recognition that larger samples are needed to answer many research questions and with the sense of urgency for making progress. Databases for neuroimaging scans and genomic sequence are already proving important for ASD research. Wide adoption of a standardized data sharing system like the National Database for Autism Research (NDAR) can provide the necessary infrastructure to combine important research participant data and thereby propel ASD research forward.

Resources: In addition to data sharing, research often depends on the availability and quality of research resources, such as access to scientific instruments and repositories of biospecimens. An important resource, paradoxically, is the identification, assessment, and collection of biospecimens from people who do not have the disorder, as a basis for comparison. Such comparison groups serve a critical role in interpreting ASD research and findings. Moreover, human resources such as adequate numbers of well-trained researchers and administrators are vital to these efforts. This need cannot be understated. Attracting a cadre of rigorously trained researchers, including those outside the ASD research field, will foster innovative ideas and interdisciplinary approaches.

Public-Private Partnerships: A strength of current ASD research is the degree of private involvement and investment in research funding from advocacy groups and committed stakeholders. In addition, the amount of research money awarded by the U.S. government for ASD research has grown rapidly over the past 10 years. There is currently a great willingness on the part of government agencies and private organizations to collaborate on the development and implementation of the Strategic Plan for ASD Research. In fact, the Strategic Plan is built on the premise that the public and private sectors will work collaboratively to better leverage resources to advance the research opportunities and objectives and to prevent unnecessary duplication of research efforts. The existence of such partnerships is a critical component in ensuring the success of the Plan.

Community Engagement in ASD Research: People with ASD, their families, their practitioners, their caregivers, and advocacy organizations have vital roles to play in shaping, participating in, and disseminating research. Their insights and perspectives are needed in order for interventions and services to be developed that will have maximal impact and have the strongest evidence and means for real-world uptake and utilization. The inclusion of stakeholders is also essential to ensure that the personal experiences of people with ASD and their families are reflected in scientific considerations, investment strategy, and research focus. Strategies are needed to increase community engagement in an effort to incorporate the firsthand experience of people with ASD, their families, and their caregivers into the Plan. Community engagement in study design, implementation, and analysis will maximize both the effectiveness and the relevance of new research. Community-based participatory research (CBPR) or participatory action research (PAR) models represent an important avenue to solicit the needed perspectives of people with ASD and their family members in autism research and should be adopted whenever possible.

Ethical, Legal, and Social Implications of Autism Research: As more progress is made in the autism research arena, new ethical, legal, and social implications of ASD research will need to be considered and taken into account by researchers and consumers of research findings. In particular, autism research including studies of genetics, diagnostic screening, and interventions pose unique ethical risks that require consideration both within research projects focused on other questions and in efforts dedicated specifically to exploring these ethical challenges and the appropriate responses to them. As such efforts are undertaken, it is critically important to include people with ASD, family members of individuals on the autism spectrum, and other stakeholder groups within the discussion.

1. When Should I be Concerned?

- **What are the early signs of ASD?**
- **Are there typical characteristics that are part of an ASD diagnosis?**
- **How do variations in symptoms and severity create challenges in early diagnosis of ASD?**

What Do We Know?

A child's caregivers are often first to identify the signs of ASD. In the classic case, there may be delays or plateaus in a child's attainment of developmental milestones, such as the use of gestures, responding to name, or the onset of speech and pretend play. In other cases, the first signs of ASD occur in young children who appear to regress after they seem to have been developing normally. Current diagnostic criteria and classifications of ASD represent progress in identifying a core set of developmental symptoms that, in the past, might have been attributed to other disorders because of more narrowly defined ASD evaluation criteria.

The diagnosis of ASD can be reliably made by age 3, because the core symptoms emerge by that time. However, most children eventually diagnosed with ASD exhibit signs of abnormal development well before the age of 2. Recent studies of children at high risk because of the presence of a sibling with ASD suggest that many cases of autism can be detected by 12 months of age using simple behavioral tests, such as response to calling the child's name or ease of engaging the child in jointly looking at an object (Landa, Holman & Garrett-Mayer, 2007). Nevertheless, the median age of earliest ASD diagnosis is 4½ years of age (CDC, 2009). A number of screening tools have been developed for detecting autism for children of varied ages and different levels of clinical variability. There are tools available for parents and caregivers, including a video glossary of early "red flags" of ASD in young children developed to help families and professionals learn how to identify subtle differences in development that may indicate areas of concern (Wetherby et al., 2007). In terms of diagnosis, there is emerging evidence that tools can be developed with sufficiently high sensitivity and specificity to support epidemiologic and risk factor studies.

Nationwide, there has been an effort to improve early identification of children with ASD to improve their functioning and outcomes. A recently published randomized, controlled trial demonstrated how a comprehensive developmental behavioral intervention for toddlers with ASD led to improvements in cognitive and adaptive behavior, thereby emphasizing the importance of early identification of and intervention for young children with ASD (Dawson et al., 2010). Various public campaigns, including the CDC's "Learn the Signs. Act Early," have been initiated in recent years to raise awareness about the importance of early identification of developmental delays, including those associated with ASD. The American Academy of Pediatrics (AAP) recommends screening children for ASD at 18 and 24 months with a standardized screening tool (Council on Children with Disabilities, 2006).

What Do We Need?

Most cases of autism and related disorders are not diagnosed until after a child's third birthday and sometimes not until adulthood, yet early intervention can have a critical influence on the future course of ASD. Moreover, many children from culturally, linguistically, and other diverse groups may have limited access to assessment services, leading to delays in diagnosis (Mandell et al., 2007). Several issues have limited the use of early interventions. It remains difficult to diagnose ASD in very young children because there is considerable healthy variation in the age at which infants and toddlers reach typical developmental milestones (e.g., speech), and delays do not always indicate the presence of a disorder. The diagnosis of ASD in a person of any age is currently based on behavioral and cognitive signs reflecting abnormal brain development, but not on detection of brain or other biological differences that may be present before the emergence of the behavioral or cognitive signs. The discovery of reliable biomarkers could potentially identify people with ASD, or infants who will subsequently develop or are already developing subtle signs of ASD.

Children with ASD develop along different trajectories. Some show abnormal behavior soon after birth; some develop normally for the first year or longer and then regress; while others appear to later improve significantly. Greater clarity is needed in identifying these different trajectories, and greater consistency is needed in applying their definitions. Health care and other early care and education providers may not have received training in recognizing the early warning signs of ASD. Pediatricians may not have received training on using existing screening tools at well checkups as recommended by the American Academy of Pediatrics (Council on Children with Disabilities, 2006). And some caregivers may be unaware of the early warning signs of ASD or where to access services, leading to delays in diagnosis.

Although families are eager for guidance, more research is needed to better answer the question of when developmental variation should become cause for concern. Studies that test both new and current diagnostic and screening methods and that integrate both developmental and biologic approaches in community-based settings are needed. In particular, studies need to be designed to validate methods in underrepresented minorities and disadvantaged populations. Such studies could increase the understanding of barriers to diagnosis and access to services. Taken together, earlier identification, coupled with increased access to interventions and services, could reduce disparities in health care and service provision and ultimately improve outcomes for people with ASD.

Scientific studies of ASD require the reliable diagnosis of participants, but this can be a time-consuming and labor-intensive process. Therefore, streamlined diagnostic approaches that facilitate the enrollment of research participants are needed. Researchers also need ASD measures that are easy to administer and are sensitive to changes in clinical status. With regard to heterogeneity, identifying characteristics that are specific to certain ASD subpopulations could potentially identify neurobiological and genetic markers and improve our understanding of more global causal and intervention mechanisms.

2011 Addendum to Question 1: When Should I be Concerned?

What Is New in This Research Area, and What Have We Learned This Past Year?

The prevalence of autism continues to rise, according to the most recent data gathered by the Autism and Developmental Disabilities Monitoring (ADDM) Network, supported by the Centers for Disease Control and Prevention (CDC), indicating that nearly 1% of children in the United States have an ASD diagnosis. This reflects an increase of 57% over a four-year period. Importantly, the mean age at diagnosis did not change significantly over this time period, with most children not diagnosed until age 3 to 5 years (Wiggins, Baio & Rice, 2006; CDC, 2009). A second study from the large National Survey of Children's Health, sponsored by the Health Resources and Services Administration (HRSA), used very different study methods from those used in the ADDM project, but also reported an ASD prevalence rate of approximately 1% in children (Kogan et al., 2009).

Research from three important studies over the past year has pointed to the importance of factors that place children at increased risk for ASD. Findings indicate the role of underlying genetic disorders and prenatal risk factors that may warrant screening and early follow-up, and in some instances more specific medical workup. First, an evidence-based review of a large clinical series of people with ASD and with other developmental disorders concluded that using chromosomal microarray resulted in considerably higher diagnostic sensitivity for genetic testing than did G-banded karyotyping, particularly for submicroscopic deletions and duplications (Miller et al., 2010). Second, a study by Johnson et al. found that very preterm birth (<26 weeks gestational age) was associated with a much higher risk of developing ASD, with a prevalence of 8% diagnosed by age 11. While early gestational age has been identified as a risk factor for ASD, previous studies have lacked the power to examine children born at such vulnerable gestational ages. A third study of 7.9 million children in California showed that older fathers and mothers were more likely to have a child with autism as compared with younger parents (Grether et al., 2009). Evidence is also accumulating on the developmental trajectory for autism. A 2010 prospective study showed little deviation between children who eventually developed autism and typically developing children up to age 6 months, after which time measurable differences emerged (Ozonoff et al., 2010). Importantly, while a decrease in developmental trajectory of skills was found in the majority of children, it was not identified by most parents, suggesting current limitations in the use of parent-identified early markers of ASD in the first year of life. Also, Klin et al. found that as compared with typically developing toddlers, toddlers with ASD paid more attention to stimuli in which sound and motion were synchronous. This difference in sensory processing may be connected to the tendency of people with ASD to focus on the mouth rather than the eyes in conversation.

Two important studies highlighted work on the barriers to early screening and diagnosis. Evaluation of the implementation of the AAP recommendations for developmental surveillance was conducted in 17 diverse pediatric practices and demonstrated reasonable success in implementing ongoing screening (85% of practices screened children at recommended screening ages), but also found that pediatric practices experienced challenges in referral for medical subspecialty care and early intervention (King et al., 2010). A second study evaluated the diagnostic sensitivity of the various parent/caregiver autism Level 2 screening scales for children older than 3 years—beyond the AAP-recommended screening ages—and concluded that even in this older age group, while some tests performed well, overall, more scientific evidence is needed for these instruments (Norris & Lecavalier, 2010).

What Gaps Have Emerged since Last Year?

Recent data show that girls are diagnosed with ASD at a later age than are boys (Giarelli et al., 2010; Shattuck et al., 2009). Examination of the 2009 IACC ASD Research Portfolio

Analysis shows that studies in girls and minority racial/ethnic/socioeconomically disadvantaged populations remains a gap area (IACC, 2010). While possible reasons for this disparity—including different clinical manifestations of ASD by gender and cultural differences in accepted or anticipated behaviors in girls relative to boys—are unclear, gender should be included as an important disparity factor in studies examining barriers to early screening and diagnosis.

There are important ethical, legal, and social implications resulting from the study by Miller et al. (2010), particularly relating to screening for genetic and other markers for autism and other developmental disorders. There is a diverse range of opinions in the autism community on early screening for autism, ranging from strong support for developing biologic prenatal screening methods to concerns that such efforts may lead to selected terminations of fetuses showing genetic or other biomarkers of increased risk. It is imperative that autism research proceed with the appropriate precautions and safeguards and that the concerns of the autism community are reflected in this process. At this point, the state of the science is focused on improving early screening in the first years of life to identify risk for ASD in order to initiate early intervention to reduce or prevent the development of disabling symptoms and promote positive skill development.

The study by King et al. (2010) highlights the need for a clearer understanding of the challenges and barriers to screening and referral. Studies are needed to determine the factors that lead to implementing screening and referral programs that successfully serve children with ASD and their families. Studies should include factors relating to the clinical practice, availability, and collaboration among community-based services, and information needs of parents, other caregivers, and early educators.

There is a lack of reliable and valid screening and diagnostic tests for use in international, resource-poor settings. Early screening and diagnosis, when coupled with inexpensive, parent-guided interventions, is an important potential prevention strategy in such settings.

Research is needed to identify effective methods for identifying children at higher risk for ASD, such as extremely preterm children and children with a sibling with ASD, in community screening efforts. Although the AAP recommends ongoing developmental and autism-specific screening in the first few years of life, establishing risk profiles indicating the need for heightened monitoring of development among some children warrants investigation as an additional tool to improve early identification.

Aspirational Goal: Children at risk for ASD will be identified through reliable methods before asd behavioral characteristics fully manifest.

Research Opportunities

- Valid and reliable ASD screening instruments and approaches, including general developmental screening instruments for use in community settings to identify a wide range of people, including younger children, adolescents, adults, people with co-occurring medical conditions, and people with subtle characteristics, who require diagnostic evaluation.

- Sensitive and efficient clinical diagnostic tools for diagnosing ASD in widely diverse populations, including underrepresented racial and ethnic groups, females, younger and older age groups, and people with co-occurring medical conditions.
- ASD measures that are easy to administer and sensitive to incremental changes in both core and associated ASD characteristics. Such measures can be used to help track the clinical course of people with ASD, monitor responses to interventions, and provide information about the broader autism phenotype.
- Detailed criteria for specific ASD subtypes in order to better describe the variations in characteristics and severity and study how these variations relate to underlying pathology, intervention strategies, and outcomes.
- ASD subpopulations and associated biobehavioral markers that provide early indication of ASD risk and opportunities for appropriate early intervention.
- Protocols for genetic testing in routine clinical practice in order to identify people at risk for ASD. Identification of people with genetic variations associated with ASD will facilitate intensive studies of ASD subpopulations with shared genetic risk factors to characterize common phenotypic and biological features.
- Inclusion of ethical considerations into the diagnosis and screening processes, including consideration of the implications of genetic testing.
- Addressing barriers to the use of screening and diagnostic tools in minority populations and in community settings, including training programs for professionals.

Short-Term Objectives

2009	**A.** Develop, with existing tools, at least one efficient diagnostic instrument (i.e., briefer, less time intensive) that is valid in diverse populations for use in large-scale studies by 2011. *IACC Recommended Budget: $5,300,000 over 2 years.*
2009 Revised in 2010 & 2011	**B.** Validate and improve the sensitivity and specificity of new or existing screening and diagnostic tools, including comparative studies of general developmental screening versus autism-specific screening tools, in both high-risk and population-based samples, including those from resource-poor international settings and those that are diverse in terms of age, socio-economic status, race, ethnicity, gender, characteristics of ASD, and general level of functioning by 2012. *IACC Recommended Budget: $5,400,000 over 3 years.*
2010 Revised in 2011	**C.** Conduct at least three studies to identify reasons for the health disparities in accessing early screening and diagnosis services, including identification of barriers to implementation of and access to screening, diagnosis, referral, and early intervention services among diverse populations, as defined by socioeconomic status, race, ethnicity, and

gender of the child, by 2012. *IACC Recommended Budget: $2,000,000 over 2 years.*

2010 **D.** Conduct at least two studies to understand the impact of early diagnosis on choice of intervention and outcomes by 2015. *IACC Recommended Budget: $6,000,000 over 5 years.*

2011 **E.** Conduct at least one study to determine the positive predictive value and clinical utility (e.g., prediction of co-occurring conditions, family planning) of chromosomal microarray genetic testing for detecting genetic diagnoses for ASD in a clinical setting by 2012. *IACC Recommended Budget: $9,600,000 over 5 years.*

2011 **F.** Convene a workshop to examine the ethical, legal, and social implications of ASD research by 2011. The workshop should define possible approaches for conducting future studies of ethical, legal, and social implications of ASD research, taking into consideration how these types of issues have been approached in related medical conditions. *IACC Recommended Budget: $35,000 over 1 year.*

Note: Dates that appear next to the objectives indicate the year that the objective was added to the Strategic Plan. If the objective was revised in subsequent editions of the Plan, the revision date is also noted.

Long-Term Objectives

2009 Revised in 2010& 2011 **A.** Identify behavioral and biological markers that separately, or in combination, accurately identify, before age 2, one or more subtypes of children at risk for developing ASD, and evaluate whether these risk markers or profiles can improve early identification through heightened developmental monitoring and screening by 2014. *IACC Recommended Budget: $33,300,000 over 5 years.*

2009 **B.** Develop at least five measures of behavioral and/or biological heterogeneity in children or adults with ASD, beyond variation in intellectual disability, that clearly relate to etiology and risk, treatment response, and/or outcome by 2015. *IACC Recommended Budget: $71,100,000 over 5 years.*

2009 Revised in 2010 **C.** Identify and develop measures to assess at least three "continuous dimensions" (e.g., social reciprocity, communication disorders, and repetitive/restrictive behaviors) of ASD symptoms and severity that can be used by practitioners and/or families to assess response to intervention for people with ASD across the lifespan by 2016. *IACC Recommended Budget: $18,500,000 over 5 years.*

Note: Dates that appear next to the objectives indicate the year that the objective was added to the Strategic Plan. If the objective was revised in subsequent editions of the Plan, the revision date is also noted.

2. How Can I Understand What Is Happening?

- **What is happening early in development?**
- **Are there known biological differences that help explain ASD symptoms?**
- **Can subgroups of people with ASD help us understand the etiology of ASD symptoms?**

What Do We Know?

Researchers, clinicians, and families have long posed questions about the possible biological bases of ASD. Clinicians classify ASD as a developmental brain disorder based on the behavioral features required for diagnosis. Little evidence exists, however, for a specific neurological abnormality beyond reports of an exuberant and transient pattern of brain or head growth (Akshoomoff, Pierce & Courchesne, 2002; Dawson et al., 2007; Hazlett et al., 2005). While much of the current science suggests that the behavioral features of ASD result from atypical brain structure, wiring, or connections, there is no proven neural variance associated with ASD. Nevertheless, there are some promising leads, and projects are under way that have the potential to provide biological signatures of some forms of ASD.

The development of sophisticated imaging methods has enabled researchers to accurately visualize many aspects of brain structure and functioning. For example, many children and adults with ASD perceive and analyze the visual information conveyed by facial expression differently than do other people (Spezio et al., 2007). Other researchers have employed magnetic resonance imaging (MRI) methods to investigate differences in brain anatomy between people with and without ASD, and have found differences in the density of white and gray matter, in some cases linked to specific symptoms of ASD (Craig et al., 2007).

Subsets of people with ASD have been reported to have experienced regression (i.e., the loss of previously acquired language, social, and developmental skills). The phenomenon is poorly understood and may co-occur with medical conditions common to people with ASD, such as epilepsy. Recent studies have sought to understand the relationship between regressive symptoms, co-occurring disorders such as epilepsy, and the etiology of ASD.

Regression is not unique to people with ASD, and the loss of language skills (acute language regression) can occur in people without the disorder. In one study, researchers found that children with acute language regression (who did not have ASD) were more likely to have associated seizures or epilepsy than were children with regressive autism (which includes language regression, as well as the loss of other social and developmental skills). This suggests that there are different subtypes of language regression and may help to understand the phenomenon and its relationship to ASD (McVicar et al., 2005).

Currently, the frequency of language regression is unknown in either children with ASD or the general population. Previous studies of regression have been hampered by delayed referral for evaluation after the onset of regressive symptoms (McVicar et al., 2005).

A few hypotheses regarding how disruptions of the immune system might contribute to ASD and other neurodevelopmental disorders have emerged in recent years. Some recent findings suggest that the immune system differences of parents and their children may affect early brain development and the onset and fluctuation of symptoms in some children with ASD (Pardo, Vargas & Zimmerman, 2005). For example, some research indicates that maternal autoantibodies directed at fetal brain tissue could interfere with normal brain development (Braunschweig et al., 2008). While such medical symptoms may not be entirely specific to ASD, treating them may have significant impact on quality of life, symptom severity, and level of functioning.

Better understanding of the biology of genes linked to ASD and their functions can also provide insight. Recent studies have shown that the MECP2 gene (mutations in which can cause Rett syndrome) is involved in forming connections at the synapse. Genes regulated by the fragile X syndrome gene, FMR1, also directly affect synapse function by controlling signaling of the neurotransmitter glutamate. In addition, a 2008 study found that the two genes that cause tuberous sclerosis complex (TSC) impair the formation of axons. Recently, several groups reported remarkable success with targeted therapies in animal models of these disorders, showing the ability to reverse the underlying neuroanatomical and even behavioral deficits in the adult (Dolen et al., 2007; Ehninger et al., 2008; Guy et al., 2007). Understanding how MECP2, TS1, FMR1, TSC1 and TS2/TSC2 regulate the growth and function of neurons may help scientists understand related disorders such as autism.

What Do We Need?

Exploring the biological bases of ASD requires access to biospecimens of people with and without ASD. Some progress has been made to establish the necessary infrastructure for the collection and preservation of postmortem tissue from people with ASD. Nevertheless, the tissues currently available are insufficient for the needs of researchers. Educational campaigns, through contact with health care providers and the internet, may be useful to increase public awareness. New technology is expanding biological research beyond postmortem tissue. For example, it is now possible to create pluripotent stem cells from skin fibroblasts of individual patients to create neuronal cell lines for study.

One of the greatest barriers to progress in determining the biological bases of ASD has been the heterogeneity of the spectrum. A clear need exists to advance understanding of the many phenotypes of ASD, including studies that link genotype to phenotype, investigations of natural and treated history, analyses of genetic interaction with environmental exposures, and studies of co-occurring behavioral and medical conditions. Different autism phenotypes may have different etiologies. There is a need to combine genotyping and functional analysis to better understand the contribution of specific genotypes with functional or structural subtypes. To determine the earliest discernable onset of ASD, experts have expressed the need for an intensive, multidisciplinary study starting at early ages that examines biomedical, neurodevelopmental, and behavioral trajectories of children with ASD. A parallel multidisciplinary analysis of typically developing children and children with non-ASD developmental disorders would be especially enlightening, as limited normative information is currently available. An evaluation of differences in the interplay of biology and environmental exposures for children with and without ASD is also needed. Understanding early trajectories may lead to targeted interventions aimed at mitigating behavioral and medical challenges and improving outcomes through adulthood.

Another understudied arena of ASD research is gender differences. Many studies of autism preferentially enroll males, who, due to a 4:1 increased prevalence, are easier to recruit. Without additional information about the biological features of ASD in females, it remains unclear whether the course of ASD is similar and whether currently used interventions are appropriate for females. It is critical to determine how sex is related to etiology, protective factors, diagnosis, and trajectory. In addition, many studies of autism preferentially enroll higher-functioning individuals who do not have cognitive impairment, because of their ability to cooperate and participate in study-related tasks. However, these individuals represent only a subset of all individuals with autism, and lessons learned from them may or may not be generalizable to all individuals with ASD. Priority must be made to develop studies looking at the underlying etiology of nonverbal individuals and to understand the impact of and etiology of co-occurring language and cognitive impairment.

2011 Addendum to Question 2: How Can I Understand What Is Happening?

What Is New in This Research Area, and What Have We Learned This Past Year?

Over the past year, a group of notable studies advanced what is known about the underlying biology of ASD with respect to neuropathology, symptoms, and cellular metabolism/signaling. In recent years, researchers have noted abnormalities in brain growth, structure, and connectivity in ASD, and numerous 2010 studies strengthen the idea that the brains of people with ASD develop and connect in atypical ways (Anderson et al., 2010; Groen et al., 2010; Lai et al., 2010, Qiu et al., 2010; von dem Hagen et al., 2010).

Researchers published results of the first longitudinal study of early brain growth in toddlers aged 1½ to 5 (Schumann et al., 2010). They found evidence of cerebral gray and white matter overgrowth in all regions by age 2 ½. After correcting for age and gender, they found that almost all brain regions developed at an abnormal rate in ASD and that this trend was more pronounced in girls. Other studies uncovered differences in the volume and structure of the brain's white matter, the component of the brain that carries signals from one region to another and that allows communication between the two hemispheres (Kumar et al., 2010; Zikopoulos & Barbas, 2010). It was recently discovered that such structural abnormalities are found not only in children with ASD, but their unaffected siblings as well (Barnea-Goraly, Lotspeich & Reiss, 2010). New advances in the use of magnetic resonance imaging (MRI) suggest that structural differences in the cortex of the brain could be used as a potential biomarker for ASD (Ecker, 2010).

Important research advances continue to improve the understanding of how changes in the brain might lead to unique characteristics of ASD. Researchers have recently found abnormalities in underlying neural circuits linked to characteristic traits such as atypical eye gaze and difficulties processing visual information, facial expressions, and biological motion

(Akechi et al., 2010; Brieber et al., 2010; Dinstein et al., 2010; Dziobek et al., 2010; Kikuchi et al., 2010; Kliemann et al., 2010; Koh, Milne & Dobkins, 2010; Loth, Gomez & Happe, 2010; New et al., 2010). A recent study of biological motion perception suggests that the distinct brain response in ASD may provide a neural endophenotype for the disorder (Kaiser et al., 2010a; Kaiser et al., 2010b). Another notable study is the first to identify a specific gene that can be associated with a neural endophenotype of ASD (Scott-van Zeeland et al., 2010). Using brain imaging, researchers found that variations in the known risk gene CNTNAP2 are associated with differences in functional connectivity in the frontal cortex and can predict performance on a rewards task.

In addition, the Committee has noted the importance of a consensus report about evaluation, diagnosis, and treatment of gastrointestinal disorders in children with ASD in the journal Pediatrics (Buie et al., 2010b). While the panel concluded that it was too early to make evidence-based recommendations, the consensus expert opinion was that people with ASD deserve the same thoroughness and standard of care in treating gastrointestinal symptoms as all patients, and that problem behaviors in ASD may stem from gastrointestinal problems. Of note, a study conducted in Minnesota found that children with ASD did not experience any greater frequency of gastrointestinal symptoms than the general population (Ibrahim et al., 2009). The Committee has also discussed reports of ASD symptoms diminishing during periods of fever and noted that this phenomenon, described in a 2009 review article (Mehler & Purpura, 2009) and discussed at a 2010 Simons Foundation conference (Simons Foundation, 2010) warrants further study.

Committee members have pointed to the new focus on metabolic and immune system interactions in ASD through studies of immune molecules, mitochondria, oxidative stress, and viral infections. In 2010, a team of researchers examined oxidative stress in Egyptian children with autism (Mostafa, et al., 2010). They found oxidative stress in close to 90% of these children and that this was related to an index of autoimmunity. They suggest that oxidative stress may play a role in autoimmunity, and that this represents a potential treatment target. In other notable work, a literature review suggests that extant energy metabolism deficits in ASD are not systematically related to specific genetic or genomic defects (Palmieri & Persico, 2010).

Researchers also examined gray matter from postmortem brains of individuals with ASD and found increased levels of oxidized mitochondrial proteins in more than half of subjects that were related to high calcium levels (Palmieri et al., 2010). They concluded that interactions between the mitochondrial aspartate/glutamate carrier gene and altered calcium homeostasis may play a role in autism.

Researchers are continuing to study how neuroimmune abnormalities may be associated with ASD. In a 2010 study, researchers investigated activation in microglia, cells that offer the first line of immune defense in the central nervous system. Marked activation was observed in 5 of the 13 people with ASD included in the study (Morgan et al., 2010). There is also evidence that autoimmune factors may play a role. A study of 690,000 Danish children found that those with ASD were significantly more likely to have families with a history of rheumatoid arthritis, Type 1 diabetes, or celiac disease (Atladóttir et al., 2009).

Another notable study in 2010 explored how vertical viral transmission, or the transmission of a virus from mother to child just before or after birth, may play a role in the development of ASD (Lintas et al., 2010), and a study of urinary porphyrin excretion found elevated levels in children with ASD when compared to their typically developing peers, indicating a potentially unusual pattern of metabolism (Woods et al., 2010). In addition, recent progress has been made in the development of mouse models of autism (Silverman et al., 2010; Hamilton et al., 2011). These studies and others highlight the importance of continuing to investigate multiple potential pathways and develop improved model systems to better understand the complexity of ASD.

The Committee highlighted the newly emerging area of metabolomics, which in well-controlled studies may provide a way to examine genotype- phenotype relationships. The Committee also noted the importance of staying abreast of research from other fields that may be helpful in identifying "endophenotypes" in autism. Endophenotypes are partial/constituent phenotypes that may be more highly linked to specific genetic causes, which may not be appreciated in studies that combine all symptom profiles. Endophenotypes may aggregate in families and be amenable to deep sequencing genetic studies to identify genetic underpinnings. They also can be common to multiple neurodevelopmental disorders and offer leverage for understanding similarities and differences between different forms of developmental psychopathology.

Public comment received by the Committee in the past year points to the need for continued study of regressive autism and females with ASD. In addition, new concerns were raised about the relationship between ASD and epilepsy, liver issues, and other diseases. The relationship between inflammation in expectant mothers and ASD, as well as the association of ASD with apraxia of speech, were also identified as potential issues for further examination.

Several implementation-related issues were raised by the Committee. These include the need to add rapidly emerging findings related to cell metabolism, signaling, neuroimaging, genetics, epigenetics, and co-existing medical conditions into existing databases designed to phenotype the "autisms." Finally, the Committee emphasized the urgent need to accelerate translation of research findings to clinical practice.

What Progress Is Being Made in Fulfilling Objectives?

As exemplified by the progress in the literature and funding as documented by the 2009 IACC ASD Research Portfolio Analysis, autism research is proceeding at a brisk pace (IACC, 2010). There are many promising studies of the neural correlates of autism-related symptoms that have yet to be classified.

Aspirational Goal: Discover how ASD affects development, which will lead to targeted and Personalized Interventions.

Research Opportunities

- Multidisciplinary, longitudinal, biobehavioral studies of children, youths, and adults beginning during infancy that characterize neurodevelopmental and medical developmental trajectories across the multiple axes of ASD phenotype and identify

ASD risk factors, subgroups, co-occurring symptoms, and potential biological targets for intervention. Such studies could include:
  - High-risk siblings of children, youths, and adults with ASD, children without a family history of ASD, and typically developing children; and
  - Multidisciplinary assessments of brain imaging, metabolic and immunity markers, microbiomics, metabolomics, electrophysiology, and behavior. *(Revised 2011)*
- Research on females with ASD to better characterize clinical, biological, and protective features.
- Human and animal studies that examine immune, infectious, and environmental factors in the occurrence of ASD.
- Research on the unique strengths and abilities of people with ASD with evaluation of functional and biological mechanisms behind social, linguistic, and cognitive profiles.
- Research on individuals with ASD who are nonverbal and/or cognitively impaired.
- Research targeting the underlying biology of co-occurring syndromes and co-occurring conditions.
- Prospective research on children with autistic regression, including potential underlying genetic and other risk factors, such as seizures and epilepsy. *(Revised 2011)*

Short-Term Objectives

2009 Revised in 2011	**A.** Support at least four research projects to identify mechanisms of fever, metabolic and/or immune system interactions with the central nervous system that may influence ASD during prenatal-postnatal life by 2010. *IACC Recommended Budget: $9,800,000 over 4 years. (Fever studies to be started by 2012)*
2009 Revised in 2010	**B.** Launch three studies that specifically focus on the neurodevelopment of females with ASD, spanning basic to clinical research on sex differences by 2011. *IACC Recommended Budget: $8,900,000 over 5 years.*
2009	**C.** Identify ways to increase awareness among the autism spectrum community of the potential value of brain and tissue donation to further basic research by 2011. *IACC Recommended Budget: $1,400,000 over 2 years.*
2010	**D.** Launch three studies that target improved understanding of the underlying biological pathways of genetic conditions related to autism (e.g., fragile X, Rett syndrome, tuberous sclerosis complex) and how these conditions inform risk assessment and individualized intervention by 2012. *IACC Recommended Budget: $9,000,000 over 5 years.*
2010 Revised in 2011	**E.** Launch three studies that target the underlying biological mechanisms of co-occurring conditions with autism, including seizures/epilepsy, sleep disorders, wandering/elopement behavior, and familial autoimmune

disorders, by 2012. *IACC Recommended Budget: $9,000,000 over 5 years.*

2010 G. Support five studies that associate specific genotypes with functional or structural phenotypes, including behavioral and medical phenotypes (e.g., nonverbal individuals with ASD and those with cognitive impairments) by 2015. *IACC Recommended Budget: $22,600,000 over 5 years.*

Note: Dates that appear next to the objectives indicate the year that the objective was added to the Strategic Plan. If the objective was revised in subsequent editions of the Plan, the revision date is also noted.

Long-Term Objectives

2009 **A.** Complete a large-scale, multidisciplinary, collaborative project that longitudinally and comprehensively examines how the biological, clinical, and developmental profiles of individuals, with a special emphasis on females, youths, and adults with ASD, change over time as compared to typically developing people by 2020. *IACC Recommended Budget: $126,200,000 over 12 years.*

2010 **B.** Launch at least three studies that evaluate the applicability of ASD phenotype and/or biological signature findings for performing diagnosis, risk assessment, or clinical intervention by 2015. *IACC Recommended Budget: $7,200,000 over 5 years.*

Note: Dates that appear next to the objectives indicate the year that the objective was added to the Strategic Plan. If the objective was revised in subsequent editions of the Plan, the revision date is also noted.

3. What Caused This to Happen and Can It be Prevented?

- **Is there something in my genetic or family history that poses a risk for ASD?**
- **What environmental exposures pose risks for the development of ASD?**
- **How might genetics and the environment interact to influence the occurrence of ASD?**

What Do We Know?

As with many complex disorders, causation is generally thought to involve some forms of genetic risk interacting with some forms of non-genetic environmental exposure. The balance of genetic risk and environmental exposure likely varies across the spectrum of ASD. The greatly increased concordance of strictly defined autism in monozygotic (identical) twins (70 - 90%) compared to dizygotic (fraternal) twins (0 - 10%) argues for the importance of genetic factors (Bailey et al., 1995; Steffenburg et al., 1989). Moreover, there are subpopulations of those diagnosed with ASD who have a known genetic mutation, often associated with a genetic disorder, such as fragile X syndrome, Rett syndrome, or tuberous sclerosis complex, the understanding of which has led to identification of possible pharmaceutical interventions. In many cases, the same genetic variation does not result in an ASD phenotype, suggesting possible genetic or environmental modifiers that could be important intervention targets. Using new technology that reveals gaps and extra copies in DNA sequences, researchers have found that some people with ASD have deletions and duplications of genetic material not found in their parents' DNA (Sebat et al., 2007). Recent genetics research has identified common genetic variations (e.g., Wang et al., 2009; Weiss et al., 2009), changes in chromosomal structure in specific genomic regions, (Marshall et al., 2008; Kumar et al., 2008; Weiss et al., 2008) and rare mutations in genes all associated with synaptic connectivity (Alarçon et al., 2008; Bakkaloglu et al., 2008; Durand et al., 2007; Jamain et al., 2003; Laumonnier et al., 2004; Strauss et al., 2006). Some of these findings have contributed to new hypotheses about the inheritance of ASD. In families with just one affected member, spontaneous deletions and duplications may be causal factors of ASD. However, what causes these spontaneous deletions and duplications is not clear and could be due to environmental exposures.

Taken together, rare genetic mutations, chromosomal abnormalities, and sub-microscopic deletions and duplications of genetic material are involved in at least 10% of ASD cases, yet individually each abnormality is found in no more than about 1 to 2% of cases (Abrahams & Geschwind, 2008). Since common genetic variations confer only a modest increase in risk, this suggests that the genetic factors in ASD may involve many different genes and interactions between genes and environment. Possible models include: many additional rare genetic mutations to be discovered; multiple common genetic variations each conferring a small increased risk; and many forms of ASD with different genetic contributions, both common and rare, in the population. There is growing recognition that the same genetic contributions can lead to a wide variety of different phenotypes across individuals. As one good example, deletions and duplications in chromosomal region 16p11 have been associated with a broad range of phenotypes, including disorders outside the autism spectrum. The factors responsible for this variability in disease phenotypes remain to be defined.

Researchers are working to better understand the interaction of genetic vulnerability with developmental experiences, such as a specific environmental exposure. While gene-environment interactions have been hypothesized to play a role in many medical disorders, these interactions have been difficult to prove or disprove beyond statistical tests showing that some genetic subgroups have a greater response to some environmental factors. Epigenetics is one mechanism by which it is thought that environmental factors may be influencing gene expression, and now molecular tools are allowing researchers to gain insight into epigenetic phenomena that may be contributing to a variety of disorders, including ASD (Baccarelli & Bollati, 2009; Nagarajan et al., 2008).

While genetics maps the sequence of DNA, epigenetics maps the modifications of the structure of DNA due to proteins or other factors that bind to the DNA helix. DNA is essentially linear text that gets "read" into RNA that in turn codes for proteins. Epigenetic modifications do not change the text, but they highlight or redact large sections of text, changing how it is read. Epigenetic modifications consist of biochemical "tags" that attach to the DNA in different places, leading to the "silencing" or "activation" of genes. The pattern of epigenetic silencing or activation of genes can differ between genders, between species or between generations, and can change during specific time windows in development or in response to environmental cues. It is thought that the addition or removal of epigenetic tags from DNA is one mechanism by which developmental experience (e.g., exposure to physical or emotional stimuli) can cause long-term biological and behavioral effects. In 2009, the first maps of the human epigenome provided the first comprehensive look at where and how nature and nurture may interact (Lister et al., 2009).

Progress in identifying environmental factors that increase autism risk has been made recently (Eskenazi et al., 2007; Palmer et al., 2006; Palmer, Blanchard & Wood, 2009; Rauh et al., 2006; Roberts et al., 2007; Windham et al., 2006), although this area of research has received less scientific attention and far fewer research dollars than genetic risk factors. Environmental factors may be pertinent not only to brain development, but also to chronic systemic features of at least some subgroups of ASD. An Institute of Medicine (IOM) workshop held in 2007 summarized what is known and what is needed in this field (Forum on Neuroscience and Nervous System Disorders, Institute of Medicine, 2008). Numerous epidemiological studies have found no relationship between ASD and vaccines containing the mercury based preservative thimerosal (Immunization Safety Review Committee, 2004). These data, as well as subsequent research, indicate that the link between autism and vaccines is unsupported by the epidemiological research literature. However, the IOM report acknowledged that the existing population-based studies were limited in their ability to detect small susceptible subpopulations that could be more genetically vulnerable to environmental exposures.

Of note, the Committee receives many public comments that reflect concerns about vaccines as a potential environmental factor in autism. Some members of the public are convinced that the current data are sufficient to demonstrate that vaccines do not play a causal role in autism and argue against using limited autism research funds to do additional vaccine studies when many other scientific avenues remain to be explored. At the same time, those who believe that prior studies of the possible role of vaccines in ASD have been insufficient argue that investigation of a possible vaccine/ASD link should be a high priority for research (e.g., a large-scale study comparing vaccinated and unvaccinated groups). A third view urges shifting focus away from vaccines and onto much-needed attention toward the development of effective treatments, services, and supports for those with ASD.

In addition, a number of other environmental factors are being explored through research because they are known or suspected to influence early development of the brain and nervous system. Recent studies suggest that factors such as parental age and exposure to infections, toxins, and other biological agents may confer environmental risk. These findings require further investigation and testing, some of which is ongoing through the CDC's Centers for Autism and Developmental Disabilities Research and Epidemiology (CADDRE) and Study to Explore Early Development (SEED) programs, as well as through several NIH-funded studies, including the Norwegian Autism Birth Cohort (ABC) study, the Childhood Autism Risks from Genetics and the Environment (CHARGE) study, the Early Autism Risk Longitudinal Investigation (EARLI) study, and the Centers for Children's Environmental Health and Disease Prevention, which is supported collaboratively by the National Institute of Environmental Health Sciences (NIEHS) and the Environmental Protection Agency (EPA).

What Do We Need?

Although most scientists believe that risk factors for ASD are both genetic and environmental, there is considerable debate about whether potential environmental causes, genetic precursors, or interactions between genes and environmental factors should be the highest priority for research aimed at identifying the causes of ASD. To date, few studies have ruled in or ruled out specific environmental factors. There are reports of associations of ASD with exposure to medications, maternal antibodies, toxicants, and infections prenatally or postnatally; however, these observations need to be the subject of additional study. It is still not known whether any specific factor is necessary or sufficient to cause ASD. Similar to other disease areas, advancing research on the potential role of environmental factors requires resources and the attraction of scientific expertise. Bringing this to bear on autism will help define the environmental factors to study, as well as the best approach for staging studies to examine environmental factors, interaction between factors, and between individual susceptibility and various environmental factors.

For example, some researchers believe that it is important to study a large number of exposures, or classes of exposure, that are known to affect brain development. Others support more tightly focused studies of one exposure or a limited number of exposures, with greatest biologic plausibility for interacting with known or suspected biologic or genetic ASD risk factors. In addition, it is also important to design studies that assess environmental exposure during the most relevant exposure windows: pregnancy and early development. In doing this research, it will be important for the field to develop sound standards for identifying and claiming that environmental factors contribute to ASD, as it is for genetics.

Research studies on risk factors can be pursued through several means. Smaller, focused studies are needed for hypothesis testing and to provide insight for replication studies. Similar to other health outcomes research for relatively rare conditions, case-control studies can be an effective first line of inquiry. The NIH-supported CHARGE and CDC-supported CADDRE/SEED studies are good examples of this approach, in which environmental exposures and biological pathways, along with genetics, are being examined. Other existing cohorts could also be identified and used for epigenomic as well as traditional genomic and environmental studies.

To address public concerns regarding a possible vaccine/ASD link, it will be important for the IACC to continue to coordinate with the National Vaccine Advisory Committee (NVAC), a Federal advisory committee chartered to advise and make recommendations regarding the National Vaccine Program.

Epigenomics provides a ready mechanism for understanding how genes and environment may act jointly to affect autism risk. Studies are needed to investigate whether candidate environmental exposures alter epigenetic mechanisms that modify the expression of suspected autism susceptibility genes or genomic regions. Such studies should incorporate examination of time or stage of development as an important factor determining the impact of environmental agents on epigenetic programming. Finally, studies are needed to understand how changes in epigenetic tags in response to environmental stimuli could lead to specific phenotypic characteristics associated with autism.

Another approach for studying risk factors for ASD requires large sample sizes to disentangle the many possible genetic and environmental factors that contribute to and help explain ASD and the frequently co-occurring conditions. For other complex disorders, large DNA collections (i.e., >20,000 samples) have been necessary to detect the full genetic risk architecture. There are no genetic repositories of this size for ASD. Similarly, large birth cohort studies, in which biological samples have been collected throughout pregnancy and early postnatal life, may be essential for detecting the interplay of environmental exposures and genetic factors that lead to ASD. As a complement to these large-scale studies, research on critical subpopulations that may be at higher risk could provide leverage in identifying genetic and environmental risk factors.

2011 Addendum to Question 3: What Caused This to Happen and Can It be Prevented?

What Is New in This Research Area, and What Have We Learned This Past Year?

A variety of discoveries have advanced knowledge of the biological underpinnings of autism. It was previously found that, among individuals with ASD, copy number variants, which are submicroscopic deletions and duplications in the genome occur more frequently in areas containing ASD risk genes (Cook & Scherer, 2008; Sebat et al., 2007; Weiss et al., 2008). A 2010 study showed that some of these copy number variants involved genes previously found to be associated with autism and some involved new rare mutations (Pinto et al., 2010). In addition, it was reported that neurodevelopmental disorders are more common in infants born prematurely and that preterm infants are at increased risk of developing autism (Johnson et al., 2010b). A study of blood mercury levels in 452 children in the NIH-funded Childhood Autism Risk from Genetics and the Environment (CHARGE) study showed that total mercury in blood was neither elevated nor reduced in preschool children with ASD (Hertz-Picciotto et al., 2010). In a separate study, no link was found between the exposure to thimerosal, a mercury-containing preservative used in vaccines, and increased risk for ASD (Price et al., 2010).

New data based on the Autism Speaks–supported Autism Treatment Network (ATN) patient registry and studies of high-risk infants indicate that autism is associated with high rates of several medical conditions, including gastrointestinal dysfunction, sleep disturbance, psychiatric conditions, and seizures (Presentation to IACC on the Autism Treatment Network, 2010). These co-occurring conditions are poorly studied, yet investigating them may reveal unexpected clues to environmental risk factors. For example, nonmotor features associated with Parkinson's disease (e.g., gastrointestinal problems, olfactory deficits, autonomic abnormalities) have yielded information about Parkinson's disease etiology and can serve as harbingers of the condition (Tolosa et al., 2009).

On September 8, 2010, NIEHS and Autism Speaks co-sponsored a meeting of scientists from both inside and outside the field of autism to identify novel opportunities and mechanisms to accelerate research on environmental factors and autism (Agenda from Autism and the Environment Workshop, 2010). Environmental factors considered included all factors affecting health that are external to the individual (such as physical, biological, chemical, dietary, social, and cultural), as well as the non-genetic characteristics of an individual (such as age, nutritional status, physical functioning, and medical history). As noted during the meeting, understanding environmental influences to autism will require both agnostic, discovery-based science as well as hypothesis-driven science in parallel. The set of recommendations developed from the meeting cite the need for strong interdisciplinary teams to move findings back and forth from clinical and epidemiologic settings to mechanistic studies. Research needs and opportunities identified included expansion of epidemiology investigations to capitalize on existing resources, development of a range of model systems that can address the complexity of autism, exploration of bioinformatics and screening approaches to identify environmental chemicals of interest, increased emphasis on neuropathology, enhancement of capacity for measurement of environmental compounds, harmonization of exposure assessment instruments, and mechanisms for expanding the workforce.

Technical advances in the past year increase traction for finding genetic and environmental risk factors. Novel bioinformatics platforms can be used to map genes to specific signaling pathways and to explore what environmental exposures are most likely to influence those pathways. Toxicogenomics data such as those produced by the EPA's National Center for Computational Toxicology could be mined to determine which environmental compounds act on the genes of interest. An important finding this year revealed the extent of "parent of origin" effects—i.e., for many genetic variations, risk depends on whether this variation was inherited from the maternal or paternal genome. And recent studies have revealed the importance of epigenetic mechanisms in disease etiology, bringing together genetic and environmental factors for the first time.

Information on the utility of induced pluripotent stem (iPS) cells and mesenchymal stem cells for exploring the biological bases of ASD is rapidly developing, pointing to the opportunity to use these tools as molecular assays for understanding genetic variation as well as for translational toxicology. Although research this year revealed several differences between these iPS cells, which can be easily and non-invasively derived from a person's skin cells, and embryonic stem cells, iPS cells continue to be one of the most promising new frontiers for understanding risk for ASD.

In a 2009 report by the National Vaccine Advisory Committee (NVAC), it was recommended that, in the context of immunization research, the ASD clinical subset of particular interest is regressive autism (National Vaccine Advisory Committee, 2009). Although the NVAC stressed that the temporal occurrence of this regression and the immunization schedule is not evidence of a causal relationship, regressive autism warrants further research in rigorously defined subsets of ASD. The NVAC noted that studies in this subpopulation might involve comparison of immune cytokine profiles between regressive and non-regressive ASD to screen for differential immune system profiles, or prospective immunization responsive profiling in siblings of children with regressive ASD. In addition, the NVAC recommended that studies assess whether adverse events following immunization (e.g., fever and seizures) correlate with risk of ASD, and that immune response profiles be examined in ASD cases with a history of adverse events following immunization.

The 2009 IACC ASD Research Portfolio Analysis indicated that about one-third of autism research studies funded by the Federal government and private organizations corresponded to risk factors/Strategic Plan Question 3, with the majority of this funding directed toward the identification of genetic risk factors and less funding and attention toward environmental research (IACC, 2010). This analysis suggests that environmental research is an understudied area that has been given insufficient attention and requires a heightened priority. Based on this, the Committee made several specific recommendations for research objectives and needed resources, which are reflected in the new objectives added to the Plan in 2011.

What Gap Areas Have Emerged since Last Year?

Suitable model systems and those that offer better high-throughput capabilities for the study of environmental risk factors and their interaction with genetic susceptibility are needed. For example, models such as *Drosophila melanogaster* (fruit flies) and *Danio rerio* (zebrafish) have been extremely useful in identifying environmental contributors to other conditions, such as Parkinson's and Alzheimer's disease. The genetics and biology of synapse formation and function are increasingly well understood, underscoring the potential utility of vertebrate and invertebrate models for exploring how environmental exposure can affect brain function at the cellular and molecular levels.

Expansion and integration of epidemiological studies using different designs and types of data are needed. Combining data from multiple studies will be necessary to enhance statistical power, requiring standardization of protocols, instrument development, and data harmonization methods. This should also include standardized protocols on biological specimen collection, storage, and analysis. International studies offer unique opportunities to examine populations with different genetic and environmental exposure backgrounds. It would be helpful to create an autism "atlas" to examine differences in autism prevalence as a function of geography. Such analysis has proved useful in both cancer and asthma research.

There is a need for greater collaboration between genetic and environmental science investigators. Studies collecting genetic information should include data on environmental exposures and vice versa; large data sets are needed to allow mapping of detailed genetic, environment, and phenotypic information, including co-occurring medical conditions, inflammatory markers, pattern of onset, developmental course, and family history.

To accelerate our understanding of the role of epigenetics in autism etiology, further development and application of sensitive assays to measure DNA methylation, histone modification, and other epigenetic marks are needed. Studies are also needed to examine how exposures may act on maternal or paternal genomes via epigenetic mechanisms to influence risk for ASD.

The lack of adequate postmortem brain tissue continues to be a major barrier to progress in understanding the neurobiology of ASD, including the potential influence of environmental factors on the functional pathways involved in ASD.

Efforts to increase analytical capacity and core facilities are needed. For example, adding an environmental, immune, or animal models core to an already existing multidisciplinary team that studies autism would be beneficial. Access to these core facilities and services could encourage individual scientists to expand the scope of their studies to address environmental hypotheses.

Aspirational Gpoal: Causes of ASD will be discovered that inform prognosis and treatments and lead to Prevention/Preemption of the challenges and disabilities of ASD.

Research Opportunities

- Genetic and epigenetic variations in ASD and the symptom profiles associated with these variations.
- Environmental influences in ASD and the symptom profiles associated with these influences.
- Family studies of the broader autism phenotype that can inform and define the heritability of ASD.
- Studies in simplex families that inform and define de novo genetic differences and focus on what role the environment might play in inducing these differences.
- Standardized methods for collecting and storing biospecimen resources from well-characterized people with ASD as well as a comparison group for use in biologic, environmental, and genetic studies of ASD.
- Case-control studies of unique subpopulations of people with ASD that identify novel risk factors.
- Monitor the scientific literature regarding possible associations of vaccines and other environmental factors (e.g., ultrasound, pesticides, pollutants) with ASD to identify emerging opportunities for research and indicated studies.
- Better understanding environmental and biological risk factors during prenatal and early postnatal development in "at risk" samples.
- Cross-disciplinary collaborative efforts to identify and analyze biological mechanisms that underlie the interplay of genetic and environmental factors relevant to the risk and development of ASD, including co-occurring conditions.
- Convene ASD researchers on a regular basis to develop strategies and approaches for improving data standards and sharing, understanding gene-environment interactions, improving the speed of replication of findings, and enhancing the translation of research on potential causative factors to prevention and treatment studies.
- Measures of key exposures for use in population- and clinic-based studies and standards for sample collection, storage, and analysis of biological materials.
- Studies of behavioral, developmental, and medical variations across those with ASD who share common genetic factors.
- Studies of clinically meaningful subgroups to examine common genetic and environmental factors, as well as unique epigenomic signatures.

Short-Term Objectives

2009 Revised **A.** Coordinate and implement the inclusion of approximately 20,000 subjects for genome-wide association studies, as well as a sample of 1,200 for in 2010 sequencing studies to examine more than 50 candidate genes by 2011. Studies should investigate factors contributing to phenotypic variation across individuals who share an identified genetic variant and stratify subjects according to behavioral, cognitive, and clinical features. *IACC Recommended Budget: $43,700,000 over 4 years.*

2009 B. Within the highest-priority categories of exposures for ASD, identify and standardize at least three measures for identifying markers of environmental exposure in biospecimens by 2011. *IACC Recommended Budget: $3,500,000 over 3 years.*

2009 C. Initiate efforts to expand existing large case-control and other studies to enhance capabilities for targeted gene-environment research by 2011. *IACC Recommended Budget: $27,800,000 over 5 years.*

2009 D. Enhance existing case-control studies to enroll racially and ethnically diverse populations affected by ASD by 2011. *IACC Recommended Budget: $3,300,000 over 5 years.*

2010 E. Support at least two studies to determine if there are subpopulations that are more susceptible to environmental exposures (e.g., immune challenges related to infections, vaccinations, or underlying autoimmune problems) by 2012. *IACC Recommended Budget: $8,000,000 over 2 years.*

2010 F. Initiate studies on at least 10 environmental factors identified in the recommendations from the 2007 IOM report "Autism and the Environment: Challenges and Opportunities for Research" as potential causes of ASD by 2012. *IACC Recommended Budget: $56,000,000 over 2 years.*

2011 **G.** Convene a workshop that explores the usefulness of bioinformatic approaches to identify environmental risks for ASD by 2011. *IACC Recommended Budget: $35,000 over 1 year.*

2011 **H.** Support at least three studies of special populations or use existing databases to inform our understanding of environmental risk factors for ASD in pregnancy and the early postnatal period by 2012. Such studies could include:

- Comparisons of populations differing in geography, gender, ethnic background, exposure history (e.g., prematurity, maternal infection, nutritional deficiencies, toxins), and migration patterns; and
- Comparisons of phenotype (e.g., cytokine profiles), in children with and without a history of autistic regression, adverse events following immunization (such as fever and seizures), and mitochondrial impairment. These studies may also include comparisons of phenotype between children with regressive ASD and their siblings.

Emphasis on environmental factors that influence prenatal and early postnatal development is particularly of high priority. Epidemiological studies should pay special attention to include racially and ethnically diverse populations. *IACC Recommended Budget: $12,000,000 over 5 years.*

2011 **I.** Support at least two studies that examine potential differences in the microbiome of individuals with ASD versus comparison groups by 2012. *IACC Recommended Budget: $1,000,000 over 2 years.*

2011 **J.** Support at least three studies that focus on the role of epigenetics in the etiology of ASD, including studies that include assays to measure DNA methylations and histone modifications and those exploring how exposures may act on maternal or paternal genomes via epigenetic mechanisms to alter gene expression, by 2012. *IACC Recommended Budget: $20,000,000 over 5 years.*

2011 **K.** Support two studies and a workshop that facilitate the development of vertebrate and invertebrate model systems for the exploration of environmental risks and their interaction with gender and genetic susceptibilities for ASD by 2012. *IACC Recommended Budget: $1,535,000 over 3 years.*

Note: Dates that appear next to the objectives indicate the year that the objective was added to the Strategic Plan. If the objective was revised in subsequent editions of the Plan, the revision date is also noted.

Long-Term Objectives

2009 **A.** Conduct a multi-site study of the subsequent pregnancies of 1,000 women with a child with ASD to assess the impact of environmental factors in a period most relevant to the progression of ASD by 2014. *IACC Recommended Budget: $11,100,000 over 5 years.*

2009 **B.** Identify genetic risk factors in at least 50% of people with ASD by 2014. *IACC Recommended Budget: $33,900,000 over 6 years.*

2009 **C.** Determine the effect of at least five environmental factors on the risk for subtypes of ASD in the prenatal and early postnatal period of development by 2015. *IACC Recommended Budget: $25,100,000 over 7 years.*

2009 **D.** Support ancillary studies within one or more large-scale, population-based surveillance and epidemiological studies, including U.S. populations, to collect data on environmental factors during preconception, and during prenatal and early postnatal development, as well as genetic data, that could be pooled (as needed) to analyze targets for potential gene/environment interactions by 2015. *IACC Recommended Budget: $44,400,000 over 5 years.*

Note: Dates that appear next to the objectives indicate the year that the objective was added to the Strategic Plan. If the objective was revised in subsequent editions of the Plan, the revision date is also noted.

4. Which Treatments and Interventions Will Help?

- **When should treatments or interventions be started?**
- **What are the medical issues I need to know about?**
- **How do I know that treatments are both safe and effective?**

What Do We Know?

Although autism is defined and diagnosed by deficits in core behaviors, accumulating evidence suggests that the breadth of this disorder extends well beyond the behavioral diagnosis. There is increasing recognition that the multiple systemic issues in children with ASD may influence vulnerability, onset, and severity of symptoms and behaviors. The systemic component of autism supports the possibility that both the core behaviors and medical issues have a convergent mechanistic basis that, if identified, could provide new insights into treatment targets, candidate genes, and strategies for prevention.

A wide range of treatment and intervention options are available for children and adults with ASD that can target core symptoms, ameliorate associated symptoms, and prevent further disability. For example, interventions such as speech therapy facilitate language development, pragmatic communication, and social interaction. Occupational therapy can improve functioning in everyday activities (e.g., eating, bathing, and learning) as well as sensory integration. Both types of therapy can promote the development of life skills, which help people with ASD to gain more independence. People with ASD can benefit from adaptive technologies, such as the use of keyboards and computers that promote expressive communication skills, and visual representation tools such as the Picture Exchange Communication System (PECS) that assist those with little or no language to communicate more effectively. For preschool and school-age children, public school systems and private schools can provide essential interventions including curricula that are individualized to the child, testing for cognitive and academic strengths and weaknesses, and special education services with lower teacher-to-student ratios, to name a few. For all of these interventions, there is a range of improvement, with some people making profound gains and others showing little response. We do not know how to predict which people will benefit from any of the available treatments.

Of the numerous behavioral interventions currently in use, little scientific evidence from randomized controlled trials (RCTs) supports their efficacy. Behavioral therapies, such as applied behavior analysis (ABA) based therapies, which use the principles of reinforcement and repetition, have been used since the 1960s and have been studied most extensively. Controlled trials have shown ABA to be effective for improving social skills and language when provided for at least 25 to 40 hours per week for 2 years (Lord & McGee, 2001). Efficacy is greatest when behavioral interventions are used early, but improved skills have been reported with adolescents and adults (McClannahan, MacDuff & Krantz, 2002; Weiss & Harris, 2001).

Medications to improve some of the symptoms associated with autism have been studied. However, thus far, no medication has been shown in controlled trials to enhance social behavior or communication. In 2006, risperidone became the first Food and Drug Administration (FDA) approved pharmacologic therapy for certain symptoms of autism. First introduced in 1993 as a medication used to treat symptoms of schizophrenia, risperidone has now been shown to be effective as a treatment of irritability and aggression seen in some children with ASD (McDougle et al., 2005). Selective serotonin reuptake inhibitors have had mixed results in decreasing certain repetitive and stereotyped behaviors (Kolevzon, Mathewson & Hollander, 2006; King et al., 2009). Other biological and pharmacological treatments that have been investigated in small studies and may warrant fuller attention include omega-3 fatty acids, memantine, oxytocin, and pioglitazone (Amminger et al., 2007; Chez et al., 2007; Hollander et al., 2007; Boris et al., 2007).

There are other treatments in wide use that have not been studied in randomized controlled trials. These include nutritional supplements and diets (e.g., probiotics, mitochondrial cocktails, CoQ10, carnitine, and gluten-casein free diets), and chelation. One such treatment, the neuropeptide secretin, that had been reported to improve symptoms of ASD, was studied in a placebo-controlled trial and found to be ineffective (Esch & Carr, 2004). Some parents and therapists suggest that these treatments are effective, that recovery is possible, and that further studies are needed. Others are concerned that these treatments involve more than minimal risks and urge caution before recommending large-scale studies.

What Do We Need?

Safe and effective interventions are needed across the lifespan, from early development shortly after the detection of risk or diagnosis through childhood, school age, adolescent, adult, and senior phases of life. Going forward, research needs to be balanced between two poles. On the one hand, there is a need for novel, targeted interventions based on an understanding of the molecular mechanisms of ASD. These interventions, analogous to ongoing efforts in cancer and cardiovascular research, will require a successful commitment to earlier elements of this Strategic Plan. On the other hand, there is a need for rigorous studies to develop and safely test the efficacy of current interventions, identifying which elements are most effective in reducing or ameliorating symptoms for which people. Intervention research should collect information about the mode of delivery, intensity, duration, and dose, as well as unique characteristics of the people with ASD (e.g., behavioral, biological, genetic) in an effort to develop more personalized interventions, treatments, services, and supports, and to help inform basic research about additional targets for study. This research will require large-scale multidisciplinary randomized controlled trials.

The identification of biomarkers—for instance in plasma, saliva, cerebrospinal fluid (CSF), or tissue—is necessary to provide insights into targeted treatment strategies designed to improve or reverse autistic symptoms, as well as insights into preventive measures. Further, if biomarkers present in children with ASD are found to be present in infants and toddlers at high risk of developing autism, then targeted intervention strategies to normalize these biomarkers could be tested for the potential to arrest or reverse the symptoms and progression of autism.

Decision makers (people with ASD, families, clinicians, and payors) frequently lack critical information about which treatment is best for an individual person. While there are many interventions in wide use, the field lacks comparative studies of their value or how these various interventions should be staged or combined. Comparative effectiveness research yields information from head-to-head comparisons of interventions or policies that, when combined with a personalized approach, can inform decision makers about health care choices. This approach, already helpful for cardiovascular and cancer research, needs to be developed to inform ASD interventions.

Special attention is needed on treatment of co-occurring medical conditions, developing pharmacological treatments, and testing interventions that are in wide use (e.g., nutritional supplements), but for which little rigorous efficacy data exist (Levy & Hyman, 2003). Co-occurring conditions, such as gastrointestinal symptoms and sleep disorders, may influence the effectiveness of interventions designed to affect the core symptoms of ASD. Similarly, interventions that focus on co-occurring conditions may also affect or reduce core symptoms. Animal models and/or cell lines relevant to autism are needed to develop new or test existing pharmacological agents for ASD, understand the mechanisms of action, and serve as a first-step in testing drug safety. Such model systems research may be crucial in leveraging the pharmaceutical industry to develop medications that target the core symptoms of ASD.

While some people with ASD have been reported to show marked improvement, little is known about the characteristics of these people or the types of interventions they have received that may help to explain these changes. Studies of these people may provide an opportunity for discovering important clues with regard to risk factors and intervention strategies for specific ASD subgroups.

2011 Addendum to Question 4: Which Treatments and Interventions Will Help?

What Is New in This Research Area, and What Have We Learned This Past Year?

Several notable studies and reviews on the efficacy of specific interventions for improving outcomes of individuals with ASD were published in 2010. These include a study showing that medications such as risperidone are most effective for reducing irritability and aggression when they are combined with intensive behavioral intervention (Frazier et al., 2010). A study of psychotropic medication use over time in youth and adults with ASD showed an increasingly high likelihood of staying medicated across the life course (Esbensen et al., 2009).

Recent research also supports the benefits of social skills training for people with ASD. A 2010 study showed improved levels of social interaction and peer relationships (Frankel et al., 2010), while a randomized controlled trial (RCT) evaluating a social skills group intervention found improvements in social behavior for children with ASD who had high cognitive ability (Derosier et al., 2010).

In other notable work conducted in 2010, a systematic review concluded that modified cognitive behavioral interventions are efficacious for reducing anxiety in individuals with Asperger syndrome (Lang et al., 2010). In addition, a RCT of a caregiver-mediated joint engagement intervention for toddlers showed positive results; it represents the first controlled data to suggest that short-term parent-mediated intervention can be efficacious for improving joint attention and functional play acts with maintenance of skills one year post-intervention (Kasari et al., 2010).

An environmental scan study, supported by the Centers for Medicare & Medicaid Services (CMS), examined interventions for children, youth, and adults with ASD (Young et al., 2010). The scan included services addressing the core impairments associated with ASD, as well as other support services, such as behavioral interventions, peer training, and supported employment. For children, 15 interventions met the "evidence-based" criteria established, while the other 16 interventions studied met only the criteria for emerging or unestablished interventions. Far less evidence was available on services and supports for transitioning youth and adults, underscoring the need for more research in this area.

In the area of early behavioral interventions, a randomized controlled trial demonstrated the efficacy of a comprehensive early intensive behavioral intervention, based on the Early Start Denver Model, which integrates developmental approaches with principles of applied behavioral analysis (ABA) for improving IQ, language, and adaptive behavior and reducing severity of autism diagnosis in toddlers with ASD (Dawson et al., 2010). In addition, three reviews of the effectiveness of early intensive behavioral intervention based on ABA were published. The Institute of Education Sciences reviewed findings specific to the Lovaas model of ABA, concluding that this model has been shown to have potentially positive effects on cognitive development but had no discernable effect on communication/ language competencies, social-emotional development and behavior, or functional abilities (Institute of Education Sciences, 2010). In the Annual Review of Clinical Psychology, Vismara and Rogers (2010) concluded that both comprehensive and targeted early intervention programs based on ABA are effective for improving communication, social skills, and management of behavioral challenges.

Finally, results of a meta-analysis showed that long-term, comprehensive ABA interventions for children with ASD lead to medium to large positive effects in intellectual functioning, language development, acquisition of daily living skills, and social functioning (Virues-Ortega, 2010). Effects for language-related outcomes (e.g., IQ, receptive and expressive language, communication) were more robust than nonverbal IQ, social functioning, and daily living skills.

What Gap Areas Have Emerged since Last Year?

Recent data indicate that several rare and highly penetrant gene variants and copy-number variations (e.g., NLGN3, NLGN4, NRXN1, SHANK2, SHANK3, PTCHD1, maternally inherited 15q11-q13, among others) are involved in ASD (Pinto et al., 2010). There is a need for translational research that can take advantage of these new genetic findings to (1) identify subgroups of individuals with ASD who respond well to specific medications and intervention approaches, (2) inform which molecular signaling pathways are affected in ASD, (3) develop animal models to explore the downstream effects of these genetic variants on brain function, and (4) discover targets for development of therapeutics. In order to develop effective medical and behavioral interventions, there is a continuing need for autism intervention networks that can provide platforms for conducting clinical trials and comparative effectiveness research using genetic and other biomarkers for specific subtypes, other individual characteristics, and their relationship to response to specific treatments for people with ASD.

In a 2010 presentation to the IACC, data were presented from the Autism Speaks–supported Autism Treatment Network (ATN), a system of 14 academic health centers throughout the United States and Canada that provide care to more than 5,000 individuals with ASD, which showed that 65% of individuals with ASD experience sleep disturbances and 14% of those with sleep problems also have seizures (Presentation to the IACC on the Autism Treatment Network, 2010). Gastrointestinal problems were also reported in 50%, and those with gastrointestinal problems were more likely to have sleep disturbances, behavioral problems, and a lower health-related quality of life. Other health issues identified include seizures, food sensitivities, anxiety, and depression. It is not known whether these medical conditions are a primary aspect of some forms of autism or whether they are secondary features. Recent consensus statements and expert reviews indicate that assessment and treatment of such conditions can lead to improvement in behavior and quality of life (Buie et al., 2010a,b; Coury, 2010) and represent a critical unmet need and great opportunity for improving overall health and quality of life for people with ASD. The existence of co-occurring medical conditions in ASD underscores the importance of identifying subgroups of individuals with specific medical conditions who might respond favorably to a particular targeted treatment. In addition, it will be necessary to develop and test multifaceted treatment approaches (e.g., combined behavioral and medical interventions) that address co-occurring medical conditions.

In April 2010, an NIH-sponsored workshop identified the urgent need for more research on children with ASD who have not developed functional verbal language by 5 years of age (Summary of NIH Workshop on Nonverbal School-Aged Children with Autism, 2010). Among the topics discussed was the development of new intervention approaches that directly teach spoken communication skills and augmentative and alternative communication (AAC). More research is needed on the efficacy of novel service provision, education, and treatment approaches that facilitate communication skills in people with ASD who are nonverbal and in individuals with challenges in verbal ability, including the need for evidence on the utility of AAC for specific subpopulations of people with ASD. Potential areas of investigation include oral-motor skills, auditory/speech processing, social attention mechanisms, and impairments in intentional communication. In addition, research is needed on ways to improve access to AAC and the most appropriate means of AAC to utilize with specific subpopulations of individuals on the autism spectrum, including both individuals who are nonspeaking and individuals with speech that is partially or periodically limited. Comprehensive studies focusing on both adults and children on the autism spectrum should address the components of the most effective AAC approaches and factors that enhance or moderate improvements in communication, behavior and quality of life as a result of AAC usage.

Additional focus is needed to identify and address health disparities for people with ASD. While attention has been given to closing disparities in access to health care and health outcomes on the basis of race and income, little has been done to close this gap for people with developmental and intellectual disabilities, including autism (Presentation to IACC on the *Eunice Kennedy Shriver* National Institute of Child Health and Human Development Workshop "Disparities in the Identification of Children with ASD," 2010; Videocast of NICHD Workshop on Disparities in Diagnosing ASD). Recent legislative initiatives, including the Children's Health Insurance Program Reauthorization Act (CHIPRA) and the Affordable Care Act support this research, as well as the refinement of quality-of-life measures for children, and the development of quality-of-life measures for adults (CHIPRA, 2009; Patient Protection and Affordable Care Act, 2010). The National Core Indicators (NCI) Project, sponsored by the National Association of State Directors of Developmental Disabilities Services (NASDDDS), has collected some data regarding quality of life specifically for people with ASD enrolled in State programs (National Core Indicators Project website). NCI-participating States are using the data to inform their quality management processes and to improve the delivery of services and supports to people with intellectual disabilities and other developmental disabilities.

Aspirational Goal: Interventions will be developed that are effective for reducing both core and associated symptoms, for building adaptive skills, and for maximizing quality of life and health for people with ASD.

Research Opportounities

- Large-scale studies that directly compare interventions and combinations of interventions (e.g., pharmaceutical, educational, and behavioral interventions) to identify what works best for which people and how much it will cost.
    - Best practice models that are being used in community-based ASD intervention programs.
    - Clinical trials that assess the safety and efficacy of widely used interventions that have not been rigorously studied for use in ASD populations.
    - Studies in diverse populations.
- Interventions that improve functioning and quality of life for people with ASD across the lifespan, including older children, adolescents, and adults with ASD.
- Early interventions that aim to prevent the development of ASD in very young "at-risk" children and reduce family burden.
- Innovative treatments that specifically target core symptom clusters unique to ASD.
- Development of emerging technologies, such as assisted communication, that provide opportunities for people with ASD to become more engaged in the community.
- Animal models and/or cellular lines that can be used to test efficacy and/or safety of ASD interventions and treatments.
- Strategies that facilitate rapid translation of promising basic scientific discoveries and community practices into clinical research and trials.
- Methods of treating coexisting medical or psychiatric conditions and assessment of how such treatments affect ASD symptoms and severity.
- Interventions that may enhance neural plasticity and adaptive brain reorganization in children, adolescents, and adults with ASD, thereby promoting significant improvement of ASD.
- Outcome studies of the effectiveness of behavioral, developmental, and cognitive therapies and approaches.
- Methods for measuring changes in core symptoms of ASD from treatment.
- Dissemination research (coordinated with subsequent objectives) to ensure that evidence-based interventions are implemented in diverse communities with fidelity and efficiency.
- Investigation of the use of medications to control challenging behaviors in people with ASD, particularly adults.

Short-Term Objectives

2009 **A.** Support at least three randomized controlled trials that address co-occurring medical conditions associated with ASD by 2010. *IACC Recommended Budget: $13,400,000 over 3 years.*

2009 **B.** Standardize and validate at least 20 model systems (e.g., cellular and/or animal) that replicate features of ASD and will allow identification of specific molecular targets or neural circuits amenable to existing or new interventions by 2012. *IACC Recommended Budget: $75,000,000 over 5 years.*

2009 **C.** Test safety and efficacy of at least five widely used interventions (e.g., nutrition, medications, assisted technologies, sensory integration, medical procedures) that have not been rigorously studied for use in ASD by 2012. *IACC Recommended Budget: $27,800,000 over 5 years.*

2009 **D.** Complete two multi-site randomized controlled trials of comprehensive early intervention that address core symptoms, family functioning and community involvement by 2013. *IACC Recommended Budget: $16,700,000 over 5 years.*

2010 **E.** Convene a workshop to advance the understanding of clinical subtypes and treatment personalization (i.e., what are the core symptoms to target for treatment studies) by 2011. *IACC Recommended Budget: $50,000.*

2010 **F.** Launch randomized controlled trials of interventions including biological signatures and other measures to predict response, and monitor quality of life and functional outcomes in each of the following groups:

- Five trials in infants and toddlers by 2013. *IACC Recommended Budget: $30,000,000 over 5 years.*
- Three trials in school-aged children and/or adolescents by 2013. *IACC Recommended Budget: $18,000,000 over 5 years.*
- Three trials in adults by 2014. *IACC Recommended Budget: $18,000,000 over 5 years.*

2011 **G.** Support at least five studies on interventions for nonverbal individuals with ASD by 2012. Such studies may include:

- Projects examining service-provision models that enhance access to augmentative and alternative communication (AAC) supports in both classroom and adult service-provision settings, such as residential service-provision and the impact of such access on quality of life, communication, and behavior;
- Studies of novel treatment approaches that facilitate communication skills in individuals who are nonverbal, including the components of effective AAC approaches for specific subpopulations of people with ASD; and
- Studies assessing access and use of AAC for children and adults with ASD who have limited or partially limited speech and the impact on functional outcomes and quality of life.

IACC Recommended Budget: $3,000,000 over 2 years.

2011 **H.** Support at least two studies that focus on research on health promotion and prevention of secondary conditions in people with ASD by 2012. Secondary conditions of interest include weight issues and obesity, injury, and co-occurring psychiatric and medical conditions. *IACC Recommended Budget: $5,000,000 over 3 years.*

Note: Dates that appear next to the objectives indicate the year that the objective was added to the Strategic Plan. If the objective was revised in subsequent editions of the Plan, the revision date is also noted.

Long-Term Objectives

2009 **A.** Complete at least three randomized controlled trials on medications targeting core symptoms in people with ASD of all ages by 2014. *IACC Recommended Budget: $22,200,000 over 5 years.*

2009 **B.** Develop interventions for siblings of people with ASD with the goal of reducing the risk of recurrence by at least 30% by 2014. *IACC Recommended Budget: $6,700,000 over 5 years.*

2010 **C.** Conduct at least one study to evaluate the safety and effectiveness of medications commonly used in the treatment of co-occurring conditions or specific behavioral issues in people with ASD by 2015. *IACC Recommended Budget: $10,000,000 over 5 years.*

2011 **D.** Support at least five community-based studies that assess the effectiveness of interventions and services in broader community settings by 2015. Such studies may include comparative effectiveness research studies that assess the relative effectiveness of:

- Different and/or combined medical, pharmacological, nutritional, behavioral, service-provision, and parent- or caregiver-implemented treatments;
- Scalable early intervention programs for implementation in underserved, low-resource, and low-literacy populations; and
- Studies of widely used community intervention models for which extensive published data are not available.

Outcome measures should include assessment of potential harm as a result of autism treatments, as well as positive outcomes. *IACC Recommended Budget: $37,500,000 over 5 years.*

Note: Dates that appear next to the objectives indicate the year that the objective was added to the Strategic Plan. If the objective was revised in subsequent editions of the Plan, the revision date is also noted.

5. Where Can I Turn for Services?

- **What types of services and supports should I seek, and where can I find them?**
- **What is my State or local government doing to provide services for ASD?**
- **What is the cost of services, and how will it be paid?**

What Do We Know?

To fulfill the mission to "profoundly improve the health and well-being of every person on the autism spectrum across the lifespan," scientific discoveries must be implemented in communities and supported by public policy. The gap between knowledge and action can only be overcome by an aggressive focus on engaging families, people with ASD, and the services community in the research process, disseminating research findings into the community, eliminating barriers to services, and helping people with ASD and their families identify which services are needed.

The communities in which children are diagnosed vary tremendously in their ability to meet the needs of people with ASD (Shattuck & Grosse, 2007). Local school districts vary in their ability to identify and provide appropriate educational and related programs for children with ASD (Mandell & Palmer, 2005; Palmer et al., 2005). States vary in the policies they have developed to organize, finance, and deliver care. The professional infrastructure or capacity is often inadequate to provide timely diagnosis, appropriate care, services, and supports, and assure health and safety.

While remarkable improvements have been made in the past three decades in understanding the best ways to identify, assess, educate, and support people with autism and their families, these improvements rarely enter community practice. In fact, some have suggested that the lag between research and practice is close to 20 years. When services with proven efficacy are implemented in community settings, they often do not result in the same positive outcomes (i.e., they are efficacious in research settings, but not effective in community practice). The reasons for this lag and ways to improve services only recently have become an area of research in autism.

Another important issue for service delivery is that community needs far outpace the state of research. Most autism services research has focused on behavioral interventions for young children. Behavioral interventions for youth and adults, as well as community supports that address quality of life (as opposed to core symptoms) for people with autism and their families have almost no traditional evidence base to support them. Yet these types of services are some of the most requested and most needed. Providers and policy makers must therefore make decisions in the absence of evidence. Local resources, advocacy, and creativity about existing funding streams all may affect what services get funded, by whom, and for whom.

These differences in policies, resources, and organization result in marked differences in the prevalence of ASD across geographic areas, the types of services and support that are received, availability of appropriate lifespan transition opportunities, and the associated costs (Fujiura, Roccoforte & Braddock, 1994; Ganz, 2007; Järbrink, Fombonne & Knapp, 2003; Mandell et al., 2008; Ruble et al., 2005; Stahmer & Mandell, 2007). In general, children with ASD have a much more difficult time accessing appropriate services than children with other special health care needs (Krauss et al., 2003). Data are still lacking on how these differences in policy and infrastructure relate to the differences in services used, and in turn how these differences affect outcomes for children, adults, and families with ASD.

What Do We Need?

People with ASD and their families need assistance navigating complex service systems to find the most appropriate services and supports. Providers and people with ASD and their families need help choosing and implementing evidence-based services that are effective and sustainable. Policy makers and payers for services, including private insurers and school districts, need assistance creating organizational structures and financial incentives so that high-quality interventions are institutionalized. Equally important, services researchers and community organizations must collaborate to quickly and efficiently develop much-needed services and supports for underserved groups among people with ASD, and to test widely used, safe, and promising services that may not have much evidence to support them.

Strategies to educate people with ASD and their families about the best ways to obtain appropriate services and supports should be developed and tested. Methods for simplifying the process by which people access services also are needed, with a focus on improving collaboration across the many agencies that provide services to people with ASD. This is especially important for traditionally underserved groups whose members often are diagnosed late (or not at all), and who are even more likely than other people with ASD to receive inappropriate or inadequate services.

An initial part of this process is the assessment of needs and costs. Services for developmental disorders are financed largely by Federal, State, and local agencies in both the health care and education sectors. Because there are significant regional differences in ASD resources, describing this varied landscape across States and localities in the United States will provide important baseline data for those with ASD so they can appropriately seek services, and policymakers so they can appropriately plan for services. Research can also define the cost-effectiveness of evidence-based practices and thereby provide the data needed by various payers and policymakers.

Observational studies of current practice can play an important role in understanding how best to address questions surrounding services and supports. They can identify malleable barriers and appropriate points of intervention, and provide a baseline against which to measure future progress. Because service systems vary greatly from place to place, these types of studies also can take advantage of the natural experiments that occur as systems struggle to respond to the needs of people with ASD.

Experimental studies are more difficult to design and conduct in this area of science than they are for traditional intervention trials, and yet are key to understanding the best ways to improve community services. Designs such as those used in comparative effectiveness research, where both groups receive intervention (rather than having a "treatment as usual" control), will be critically important to satisfy ethical and practical concerns. Because the unit of analysis for many of these studies is the provider or system, rather than the person with ASD, large-scale network studies and quasi-experimental designs will also yield information.

Families, people with ASD, and communities can be empowered to become partners in research that can in turn inform policy. Research must include services that are built upon principles of self-direction and self-determination and emphasize quality of life across the ASD spectrum. All people with ASD, their families, and others who support them should have the services and supports they need and desire throughout the lifespan to lead productive lives in the community, and to reach their fullest potential.

2011 Addendum to Question 5: Where Can I Turn for Services?

What Is New in This Research Area, and What Have We Learned This Past Year?

Recent legislative initiatives, including the Affordable Care Act passed by Congress in 2010, support research and State and Federal programs that will positively impact health and quality of life for people with ASD. These include expanded opportunities in 2014 for individuals at 133% of the Federal poverty line to access health care; increased attention to health and medical home care coordination; expanded health information technology; a national quality improvement strategy that will develop and refine quality measures; the expansion of Medicaid options to provide home and community-based services (HCBS) through several new venues, including "targeting" to people who do not meet traditional institutional level of care program requirements, and Community First Choice services; the extension of the Centers for Medicare & Medicaid Services' (CMS) Money Follows the Person Rebalancing Demonstration Program; the CLASS Act; increased opportunities surrounding the removal of barriers to providing HCBS; incentives to offer HCBS as an alternative to nursing homes; a new focus on improved coordination for individuals eligible for both the Medicare and Medicaid programs through the Federal Coordinated Health Care Office; and establishment of the Center for Medicare & Medicaid Innovation (Innovation Center website).

The Mental Health Parity and Addiction Equity Act of 2008 (MHPAEA), went into effect in 2010. Details of how parity will be implemented are still being resolved, but the concept of comparable coverage for mental health and substance use disorder benefits and physical health services has broad implications for children and adults with ASD. An interim final rule was published in February 2010 by the Departments of Labor, the Treasury, and Health and Human Services (Federal Register, 2010).

Several recent articles focused on oral health issues, highlighting a need to further investigate the impact of dental treatment on people with ASD throughout the life course. Oral disease is a major health challenge for people with developmental disabilities, including ASD (Altun et al., 2010a,b; Loo, Graham & Hughes, 2009). In 2010 and 2011, many State Medicaid programs that support adults with ASD have or will substantially reduce optional adult dental care services (Smith, Gifford & Ellis, 2010).

A 2010 Swedish study examining risk factors and causes of death in a cohort of 120 people with ASD found that co-occurring disorders (including sudden unexplained death in epilepsy), accidents, and deaths occurred at a rate 5.6 times higher than that of the general population (Gillberg et al., 2010). In addition, information was presented in 2010 to the IACC regarding wandering incidents, some that resulted in death (Presentation to the IACC on

Wandering and ASD, 2010). In response, the IACC formed a Safety Subcommittee to gather information and take appropriate actions to address wandering and other important safety issues that impact the autism community.

What Gap Areas Have Emerged since Last Year?

Access to quality and affordable oral health care services continues to be a challenge for children, youth, and adults with ASD (Government Accountability Office, 2010). In addition, access to psychiatric expertise specific to intellectual and developmental disabilities (ID/DD) and ASD in State mental health systems is poor, overall capacity is lacking, and issues of seclusion and restraint persist (Barry, Huskamp & Goldman, 2010; Munir, 2009; Prouty et al., 2008). There is greater need during a time when disabled family members are remaining at home longer to coordinate community resources, including mental health services.

Aspirational Goal: Communities will access and implement necessary high-quality, evidence-based services and supports that maximize quality of life and health across the lifespan for all people with ASD.

Research Opportunities

- Development and effective dissemination of evidence-based community practices for people with ASD across the spectrum and lifespan.
- Comparative effectiveness studies of services and supports for people with ASD across the spectrum and lifespan.
- Studies that characterize current ASD diagnostic and service utilization patterns in community settings, examine the relationship between the likelihood of a diagnosis and services availability for ASD, and evaluate services and intervention outcomes across the spectrum and lifespan.
- Development of a coordinated, integrated, and comprehensive community-based service delivery system for people with ASD.

Short-Term Objectives

2009 Revised in 2010	A. Support two studies that assess how variations in and access to services affect family functioning in diverse populations, including underserved populations, by 2012. *IACC Recommended Budget: $1,000,000 over 3 years.*
2010	B. Conduct one study to examine how self-directed community-based services and supports impact children, youth, and adults with ASD across the spectrum by 2014. *IACC Recommended Budget: $6,000,000 over 3 years.*
2010 Revised in 2011	C. Implement and evaluate five models of policy and practice-level coordination among State and local agencies to provide integrated and comprehensive community-based supports and services that enhance access to

services and supports, self-determination, economic self-sufficiency, and quality of life for people with ASD across the spectrum and their families, (which may include access to augmentative and alternative communication [AAC] technology), with at least one project aimed at the needs of transitioning youth and at least one study to evaluate a model of policy and practice-level coordination among State and local mental health agencies serving people with ASD, by 2015. *IACC Recommended Budget: $25,000,000 over 5 years.*

2011 D. Support two studies to examine health, safety, and mortality issues for people with ASD by 2012. *IACC Recommended Budget: $4,500,000 over 3 years.*

Note: Dates that appear next to the objectives indicate the year that the objective was added to the Strategic Plan. If the objective was revised in subsequent editions of the Plan, the revision date is also noted.

Long-Term Objectives

2009
Revised in 2010 — **A.** Test four methods to improve dissemination, implementation, and sustainability of evidence-based interventions, services, and supports in diverse community settings by 2013. *IACC Recommended Budget: $7,000,000 over 5 years.*

2009
Revised in 2010 — **B.** Test the efficacy and cost-effectiveness of at least four evidence-based services and supports for people with ASD across the spectrum and of all ages living in community settings by 2015. *IACC Recommended Budget: $16,700,000 over 5 years.*

2010 — **C.** Evaluate new and existing pre-service and in-service training to increase skill levels in service providers, including direct support workers, parents and legal guardians, education staff, and public service workers, to benefit the spectrum of people with ASD to and promote interdisciplinary practice by 2015. *IACC Recommended Budget: $8,000,000 over 5 years.*

2011 — **D.** Evaluate at least two strategies or programs to increase the health and safety of people with ASD that simultaneously consider principles of self-determination and personal autonomy by 2015. *IACC Recommended Budget: $2,000,000 over 2 years.*

2011 — **E.** Support three studies of dental health issues for people with ASD by 2015. This should include:

- One study on the cost-benefit of providing comprehensive dental services, including routine, non-emergency medical and surgical dental services, denture coverage, and sedation dentistry to adults with ASD as compared to emergency and/or no treatment. *IACC Recommended Budget: $900,000 over 3 years.*
- One study focusing on the provision of accessible, person-centered, equitable, effective, safe, and efficient dental services to

people with ASD. *IACC Recommended Budget: $900,000 over 3 years.*

- One study evaluating pre-service and in-service training program to increase skill levels in oral health professionals to benefit people with ASD and promote interdisciplinary practice. *IACC Recommended Budget: $900,000 over 3 years.*

Note: Dates that appear next to the objectives indicate the year that the objective was added to the Strategic Plan. If the objective was revised in subsequent editions of the Plan, the revision date is also noted.

6. What Does the Future Hold, Particularly for Adults?

- **What will my family member be like when he/she gets older?**
- **What is known about adults with ASD, and how can I plan for the future?**
- **How does American society support people with ASD?**

What Do We Know?

An overarching goal of ASD research is to enable people with ASD to lead fulfilling and productive lives in the community. We are in critical need of information about the current landscape of long-term outcomes for all people with ASD across the spectrum. The lack of knowledge about adults with ASD and their lifetime support needs has repeatedly arisen as a critical issue when stakeholders are queried about their most fundamental concerns. Longitudinal studies designed to capture the range of possible outcomes for people with ASD are best suited to inform public policy decision-making, service and support delivery, and funding strategies. It is also important to improve public understanding of ASD in adults, including older adults, so that they may receive support from the communities where they live. Efforts to improve public awareness and community supports help foster acceptance, inclusion, and appreciation of people with ASD.

ASD poses economic and social costs for people with ASD, their families, and society at large. Although ASD symptoms vary greatly in character and severity, autism occurs in all ethnic and socioeconomic groups and affects every age group. Some scientists and economists have estimated that the combined direct and indirect costs to provide lifelong supports for all Americans with ASD exceeds $35 billion, and that each person accrues approximately $2 million to $3 million in costs over his or her lifetime (Ganz, 2007; Knapp, Romeo & Beechum, 2009). Families often report incurring large debts related to medical and educational services not covered through public programs or medical and dental insurance. Many families find the transition from the education system, where services are mostly obligatory, to the developmental disabilities and vocational systems, where services are optional, difficult to understand and manage. This fragmentation of service systems impedes access to services, especially for youth transitioning to adulthood, as well as during other periods of transition. In addition to financial challenges, ASD can lead to emotional hardships for people with ASD and their families throughout life.

What Do We Need?

Although considerable research has focused on the earliest phase of ASD, including early screening, improved diagnostics, and early intervention, far less effort has addressed the adolescent, adult, and older adult phases of life. Minimal guidance exists for people with ASD across the spectrum and their families about the trajectories of ASD across the lifespan. Although the general assumption is that children who possess expressive and receptive language skills and coping strategies and who do not demonstrate significant challenging behaviors can sometimes excel as adults, while children who do not currently possess typical expressive language skills and who engage in significant challenging behavior will grow up to need long-term, 24/7 supports and services, the evidence base for these ideas is lacking. Scientists have not yet identified key prognostic factors or detailed information about how adults across the spectrum with ASD function, where they are, and how they are best supported.

More research is needed to tailor treatments, interventions, and services and supports to the evolving needs of adolescents transitioning to adulthood, and adults across the spectrum with ASD, with an emphasis on principles of self-determination. There is a need to address co-occurring conditions and developmental changes that coincide with transitions such as adolescence to adulthood to better assess functional outcomes and to integrate standardized quality-of-life measures for adults across the spectrum with ASD living in community settings. Factors that contribute to improved quality-of-life and health outcomes in adulthood are virtually unknown.

A number of other areas raise serious concerns. There is little information about the number of adults with ASD within the criminal justice system. Some adults with ASD may not be diagnosed, or may have been misdiagnosed. Although issues surrounding the direct support workforce are well documented, we do not know if they differ with respect to adults with ASD. Community integration and access to individualized, quality adult supports and services are problematic across the United States, and long waiting lists for subsidized community-based services persist. Many services are available only to people who meet institutional level of care requirements. Additionally, there is scant research on the use and safety of psychopharmaceutical medications in adults with ASD.

2011 Addendum to Question 6: What Does The Future Hold, Particularly for Adults?

What Is New in This Research Area, and What Have We Learned This Past Year?

The continuing lack of services research on youth and adults diagnosed with ASD (as well as those who go undiagnosed), public comment received by the IACC in 2010, and the 2008 and 2009 IACC ASD Research Portfolio Analysis reports continue to highlight the urgent need for additional scientific research specific to this group (IACC, 2010a,b). In 2010, several national advocacy organizations devoted private resources to initiatives on adult services that have been brought to the IACC's attention.

In September 2010, the Department of Health and Human Services (HHS) announced a joint grant program administered by the Centers for Medicare & Medicaid Services (CMS) and the Administration on Aging, in part to expand the Aging and Disability Resource Centers to better assist people with disabilities, older adults, and their caregivers (HHS Press Release, 2010). As greater numbers of adults with disabilities, including ASD, access the strengthened infrastructure, more research is needed regarding their support needs. To help define a national research agenda on autism and aging, a privately funded conference, "Autism and Aging," was held in March 2010 that brought experts in the field together to discuss what is currently known on the subject and what future research is needed. Participants identified several priority areas, including the development of diagnostic criteria and instruments for diagnosing and assessing the needs of older adults with ASD. They also cited the need for descriptive studies that examine the symptoms and behaviors, neuropsychiatric features, and related medical conditions in the population, as well as the progression of these characteristics over time (Piven et al., 2010).

Several articles related to transitioning from entitlement-based education services to the adult services system and higher education were published in 2010 (Chappel & Somers, 2010; McDonough & Revell, 2010; Schall & McDonough, 2010; Wehmeyer et al., 2010). These indicated that early collaboration between services system partners greatly increased access to adult services and employment. A small survey of Japanese adults with ASD who did not have intellectual disability suggested that higher levels of education increased the likelihood of obtaining employment, but that education did not improve the likelihood that the job would be retained (Yokotani, 2010). Studies from the United States indicated that the transition from high school may actually have the most negative impact on individuals with higher cognitive levels, who are more likely to lose services (Taylor et al., 2010a,b).

In July 2010, President Obama indicated the Administration's commitment to expand disability employment in the Federal workforce, emphasizing the need for additional research in the area of ASD employment across the spectrum.

In other new research, recent studies examining the role of behaviors and co-occurring conditions in adults with ASD indicated that many people with ASD, especially those with intellectual and developmental disabilities (ID/DD), have ongoing deficits related to independence and quality of life (Chowdhury, Benson & Hillier, 2010; Cohen et al., 2010; Esbensen et al., 2010; Hove & Havik, 2010; Smith & Matson, 2010a,b).

A 2010 article on the prevalence of ASD in Iceland also indicated that ASD may be about 50% underdiagnosed in adults, especially in people who have ID as their primary diagnosis (Saemundsen et al., 2010). This finding is consistent with recent State data specific to ASD from the National Core Indicators Project, sponsored by the National Association of State Directors of Developmental Disabilities Services (NASDDDS) (National Core Indicators Project website).

Finally, an environmental scan of interventions for people with ASD, sponsored by the Centers for Medicare & Medicaid Services, examined interventions for adults with ASD and found effectiveness for only nine interventions for adults (Young et al., 2010). Only a third of the interventions evaluated rated as "evidence-based." The report also highlighted the need for further research on effective community-based services for adults. For example, adults with ASD commonly attend "day programs," but no formal research exists on the practice.

What Gap Areas Have Emerged since Last Year?

Although some minimal improvement is predicted for State budgets in 2011, State and local governments are anticipated to face continuing fiscal constraints (National Governors Association & National Association of State Budget Officers, 2010). Budget cuts, somewhat mitigated by ongoing Federal financial assistance, have resulted in fewer optional services in programs including Medicaid, which provide many poor adults who have ASD with acute care, home- and community-based services, and other supports (Johnson, Oliff & Williams, 2010).

There is little research specific to older adults with autism and their caregivers, although some research from the University Centers for Excellence in Developmental Disabilities (UCEDD) program, supported by the Administration on Developmental Disabilities (ADD) and Administration for Children and Families (ACF), is directed at cross-disability aging issues (Association of University Centers on Disabilities website). Although some research is focused on adults on the ASD spectrum and their families, more is needed, including greater utilization of the participatory action research (PAR) and community-based participatory research (CBPR) models (Viswanathan et al., 2004). The Administration on Developmental Disabilities (ADD) supported development of a PAR Toolkit, which could serve as a potential resource (Oregon Health & Science University, PAR Toolkit).

Aspirational Goal: All people with ASD will have the opportunity to lead self-determined lives in the community of their choice through school, work, community participation, meaningful relationships, and access to necessary and individualized services and supports.

Research Opportunities

- Studies of the scope and impact of the spectrum of ASD in adults, including diagnosis of ASD in adulthood, needs during critical life transitions, and quality of life.
- Longitudinal studies that follow carefully characterized cohorts of the broad spectrum of adults with ASD and their families into adulthood in order to better understand their needs during critical life transitions, and to identify and track risk and protective factors that account for improved quality of life and health outcomes.
- Projects that increase coordination across State and local delivery systems to improve access to services and supports, particularly those that focus on transitioning youth and adults with ASD.

- Improved understanding of the challenges associated with accessing community housing for people with ASD.
- It is important to include people with ASD and their families in the scientific research process. The use of models such as participatory action research (PAR) and community-based participatory research (CBPR) will facilitate full participation by people with disabilities and their family members in the planning, implementation, and evaluation of research. *(Added 2011)*

Short-Term Objectives

2010 **A.** Launch at least two studies to assess and characterize variation in the quality of life for adults on the ASD spectrum as it relates to characteristics of the service delivery system (e.g., safety, integrated employment, post-secondary educational opportunities, community inclusion, self-determination, relationships, and access to health services and community-based services) and determine best practices by 2012. *IACC Recommended Budget: $5,000,000 over 3 years.*

2010 **B.** Evaluate at least one model, at the State and local level, in which existing programs to assist people with disabilities (e.g., Social Security Administration, Rehabilitation Services Administration) meet the needs of transitioning youth and adults with ASD by 2013. *IACC Recommended Budget: $5,000,000 over 3 years.*

2010 **C.** Develop one method to identify adults across the ASD spectrum who may not be diagnosed, or are misdiagnosed, to support service linkage, better understand prevalence, and track outcomes with consideration of ethical issues (insurance, employment, stigma) by 2015. *IACC Recommended Budget: $8,400,000 over 5 years.*

2010 **D.** Conduct at least one study to measure and improve the quality of lifelong supports being delivered in community settings to adults across the spectrum with ASD through provision of specialized training for direct care staff, parents, and legal guardians, including assessment and development of ASD-specific training, if necessary, by 2015. *IACC Recommended Budget: $7,500,000 over 5 years.*

Note: Dates that appear next to the objectives indicate the year that the objective was added to the Strategic Plan. If the objective was revised in subsequent editions of the Plan, the revision date is also noted.

Long-Term Objectives

2010 **A.** Develop at least two individualized community-based interventions that improve quality-of-life or health outcomes for the spectrum of adults with ASD by 2015. *IACC Recommended Budget: $12,900,000 over 5 years*

2010 **B.** Conduct one study that builds on carefully characterized cohorts of children and youth with ASD to determine how interventions, services, and supports delivered during childhood impact adult health and quality of life outcomes by 2015. *IACC Recommended Budget: $5,000,000 over 5 years.*

2010 Revised in 2011 **C.** Conduct comparative effectiveness research that includes a cost-effectiveness component to examine community-based interventions, services, and supports to improve health outcomes and quality of life for adults on the ASD spectrum over age 21 by 2018. Topics should include:

- Community housing for people with ASD;
- Successful life transitions for people with ASD, including from post-secondary education to adult services, employment, sibling relationships, and day programs; and
- Meeting the service and support needs of older adults with ASD.

IACC Recommended Budget: $6,000,000 over 5 years.

2010 **D.** Conduct implementation research to test the results from comparative effectiveness research in real-world settings, including a cost-effectiveness component to improve health outcomes and quality of life for adults over 21 on the ASD spectrum by 2023. *IACC Recommended Budget: $4,000,000 over 5 years.*

Note: Dates that appear next to the objectives indicate the year that the objective was added to the Strategic Plan. If the objective was revised in subsequent editions of the Plan, the revision date is also noted.

7. What Other Infrastructure and Surveillance Needs Must be Met?

- **What infrastructure systems need to be supported, strengthened, or built to support this plan?**
- **How can we ensure that resources and data are shared to support the scientific research process?**
- **How can we ensure that findings are communicated to the public in a responsible and timely manner?**
- **How can we improve autism surveillance efforts?**

What Do We Know, and What Do We Need?

Current infrastructure may be insufficient to adequately support the research programs outlined in this plan. Additional investment in infrastructure is necessary to collect and share data among researchers, to encourage and enable individuals with ASD and their families to participate in research, and to improve the speed with which findings are disseminated and the extent to which findings are translated into practice and policy.

Data Sharing

In 2006, the National Institutes of Health (NIH) launched the National Database for Autism Research (NDAR) to improve sample sizes and enable researchers to share data for increased analyses. The NIH-supported national Autism Centers of Excellence (ACE), as well as the grants funded under the "Research to Address the Heterogeneity in Autism Spectrum Disorders" request for applications as part of the American Recovery and Reinvestment Act (ARRA), receive funding contingent upon acceptable plans and means for data sharing. Incentives are needed, however, to encourage data submission by other researchers. It will also be necessary to link other significant ASD databases with NDAR. In addition, databases that collect information and coordinate recruitment of people with ASD and their families to participate in research studies need to be enhanced and expanded. Programs to support contribution of data for recruitment, health care, education, social services, and administrative databases, like the Interactive Autism Network (IAN), collaboratively supported at the Kennedy Krieger Institute by Autism Speaks, the Simons Foundation, and NIH, should be encouraged. Collecting information about people with ASD will facilitate the study of whether early diagnosis, entry to services, and type of intervention affects the course of ASD over time. Multiple data sources from existing research or service systems (e.g., education, Medicaid) currently operate in isolation. In compiling and sharing data from existing data sources, researchers need to address data standardization as well as important privacy and ethical issues. Methods for merging such databases and linking investigator-recruited samples to these merged databases have been used in other populations and in specific locales with success and need to be further developed.

Biobanking

Many in the field have highlighted the need to establish nationally coordinated strategies for the collection and preservation of postmortem tissue from people both with and without ASD. The existing brain and tissue bank resources must be expanded to meet the high and continuously increasing demand for postmortem tissue by scientific investigators. More well-preserved brains are needed from people at various stages of development, and particularly from those with few co-occurring disorders. Additional matched controls are needed as well to supplement the limited supply in existing repositories.

In addition, it will be necessary to develop methods, standards, and protocols for collecting and storing other biological specimens, such as blood and urine, which might be used to study biological differences or signatures, and skin fibroblasts for creation of pluripotent stem cells.

Surveillance

Autism surveillance provides important estimates on the number of children affected with ASD and helps describe the characteristics of the people with autism spectrum disorders in the general population. Surveillance must be sustained over a period of many years in order to track trends in prevalence estimates over time and is an essential building block for population-based research, providing clues about potential risk factors that warrant further study. Surveillance provides important data regarding early identification of children with autism and informs education and health systems of areas in which programs can be modified to improve early identification and intervention. Surveillance data also provide critically important information for communities to use when planning for services.

In 2007, CDC's Autism and Developmental Disabilities Monitoring (ADDM) Network published the first and most comprehensive summary of autism prevalence estimates in the

United States (CDC, 2007). These data showed that between 1 in 100 to 1 in 300 (with an average of 1 in 150 children) were identified with ASD. In October 2009, investigators from HRSA and CDC reported that ASD occurs in an estimated 1.1% of children 3 to 17 years old, based on parent report during the National Survey of Children's Health (NSCH), sponsored by HRSA (Kogan et al., 2009). Updated estimates from CDC's ADDM Network, published in December 2009, confirmed that approximately 1% of children were identified with an ASD (between 1 in 80 to 1 in 240 children, with an average of 1 in 110) (CDC, 2009). There was an increase of 57% in identified ASD prevalence from 2002 to 2006 in multiple areas of the United States. While these data provide important information for service planning and begin to help us understand that the increases are not fully accounted for by improved identification, many questions related to the multiple causes of ASD increases remain.

There are a number of areas in which prevalence studies could be improved, including the continued estimation and evaluation of prevalence in the same population over time; assessment of ASD prevalence in the context of other neurodevelopmental disorders; further analyses of existing datasets to examine the multiple identification and potential risk factors as they vary by prevalence; collection of data beyond core ASD symptoms, including genetic data and co-occurring medical, dental, and behavioral conditions; and expansion of studies across ages. Supporting international autism surveillance activities, prevalence estimates, and epidemiologic research will also be important, in order to compare prevalence estimates and epidemiologic characteristics across countries.

Communication and Dissemination

Research data regarding autism is now being published at a rapid rate. It is critical that new findings are communicated promptly and appropriately to the public so that research findings can be better translated into practice as appropriate. Effective translation is important so that new findings can be utilized to improve risk assessment and implementation of individualized interventions to reduce the disabling symptoms and promote a positive developmental trajectory as early as possible. Additional attention needs to be paid to improving the communication channels between scientists, practitioners, people with ASD, and their families.

There is also need to build a system for rapid replication of studies concerning key findings. In addition, there is still not agreement about meaningful subtypes or about how to individualize treatment. As more professionals become involved in autism research, there is a need for organized input from established scientists to provide guidance and expertise.

In addition, it will be necessary to identify and address the wide range of ethical and clinical issues related to the diagnosis, assessment, and communication of genetic, environmental, and clinical risk for autism.

Research Workforce Development

In order to accomplish the necessary research in the field of autism, it will also be important to develop an adequate scientific workforce. While much autism research is already under way, there are several areas of research that are new and growing, including interdisciplinary research, where additional researchers will be needed in the coming years. The continued expansion and development of this research workforce will be essential to fulfilling the goals laid out in the IACC Strategic Plan.

2011 ADDENDUM TO QUESTION 7: WHAT OTHER INFRASTRUCTURE AND SURVEILLANCE NEEDS MUST BE MET?

What Is New in This Research Area, and What Have We Learned This Past Year?

Data Sharing

This year, the Autism Informatics Consortium (AIC), collaboratively supported by NIH, Autism Speaks, and the Simons Foundation, was launched with the goal of accelerating scientific discovery by making informatics tools and resources more useful to, and usable by, autism researchers. The consortium is charged with identifying information technology solutions, harmonizing major informatics frameworks, and developing standards in the field for working with research data. The consortium is composed of representatives from both public and private institutions that are responsible for the development of major autism informatics tools and resources. Current members include the Autism Genetic Resource Exchange (AGRE), supported by Autism Speaks; the Interactive Autism Network (IAN) at the Kennedy Krieger Institute, supported by NIH, Autism Speaks, and the Simons Foundation; the Simons Foundation; Prometheus Research, supported by the Simons Foundation Autism Research Initiative (SFARI); and the National Database for Autism Research (NDAR), supported by NIH. The AIC held its first workshop on August 26-27, 2010, at the National Institute of Mental Health (NIMH)/NIH offices in Rockville, MD. In attendance were representatives from 12 major research institutions. The objective of the meeting was to explore short-term (one to two years) and intermediate term (two to five years) priorities for increasing the utility and harmonization of major autism research informatics resources, identify ways to best pursue those priorities, and determine ways to measure progress toward achieving them.

Considerable progress has been made on the input of data to NDAR. Data are now available to researchers from more than 10,000 participants enrolled in studies of ASD. Access to the data is through a NDAR-supported webportal that allows queries from multiple databases simultaneously.

Biobanking

There has been considerable progress in the growth of a number of major biobank repositories.

The Autism Treatment Network (ATN), a program Autism Speaks funded in part through grants from HRSA and NIMH, is a collaboration among 14 academic medical centers that provide clinical services for children with ASD and collect and store common, extensive phenotypic data on children with autism in a central patient registry. The NIMH is supporting ATN efforts to collect DNA, plasma, and urine from 4 of the 14 sites as a beginning step toward establishing a comprehensive biorepository for the ATN. One goal of establishing the repository is to provide a platform for conducting comparative effectiveness research that can utilize biomarkers to predict response to treatments.

The Simons Simplex Collection, supported by the Simons Foundation Autism Research Initiative (SFARI), was established to develop a permanent research repository of detailed phenotypic and genetic information on 3,000 simplex families with a child with an ASD.

Nearly 2,000 families had been enrolled as of November 2010, with the goal of completing enrollment by the summer of 2011 (Fischbach & Lord, 2010).

The Autism Genome Project (AGP), a collaborative effort between Autism Speaks and several other international partners, including the Health Research Board of Ireland, Genome Canada, the United Kingdom's Medical Research Council (MRC) and the Hilibrand Foundation, is focusing on identifying genes associated with the risk for ASD. The AGP consists of 120 scientists from more than 60 institutions representing 11 countries. The biobank now contains 23,101 total samples, including 5,814 probands (individuals who are the first member within their family identified as having an ASD).

The Autism Genetic Resource Exchange (AGRE) is a program of Autism Speaks to advance genetic research in autism spectrum disorders. Genetic biomaterials and clinical data are obtained from multiplex families (i.e., families with more than one member diagnosed with an ASD). The biological samples, along with the accompanying clinical data, are made available to AGRE-approved researchers. There are more than 10,000 samples in the AGRE repository on individuals with ASD and their family members (including 4,240 probands). About half of the samples in AGRE are also represented in the AGP.

Through the Center for Collaborative Genetic Studies on Mental Disorders, the NIMH/NIH supports the NIMH Genetics Repository, a collection of DNA, cell culture lines, and clinical data from individuals with complex mental disorders, including ASD. From these materials, researchers can discover gene variants, epigenetic signals, and biomarkers that identify disease risk, aid in diagnosis, and predict response to treatments. Beginning in 2008 and continuing through 2013, the NIMH is sponsoring the Human Genetics Initiative to expand the number of samples in the NIMH Genetics Repository. The current biobank collection consists of 589 trios (biomaterials from an ASD-affected individual and both parents), 513 partial trios with biomaterials from one parent, and 972 independent cases. In addition, more than 1,400 ASD samples are being processed and are expected to be available shortly. The Human Genetics Initiative works collaboratively with AGRE and offers access to much of the AGRE collection, as well as samples from the NIMH Genetics Repository. In the coming years, NIMH will focus on increasing the number of samples, particularly from parents and first-degree relatives, and linking the ASD-relevant data with the National Database for Autism Research.

The *Eunice Kennedy Shriver* National Institute of Child Health and Human Development (NICHD)/NIH supports the Brain and Tissue Bank for Developmental Disorders program, which collects, stores, and distributes brain and other tissues for biomedical research. The bank was expanded in 2009 and is currently funded through 2014. To date, researchers can request tissue samples donated by about 60 ASD individuals, as well as tissues from autism-related disorders like fragile X (20 cases), tuberous sclerosis complex (33 cases), neurofibromatosis (18 cases), and Rett syndrome (10 cases). The use of this tissue has resulted in 77 scientific papers on autism and 42 papers on the other disorders. While efforts to recruit donors have had a positive impact, there is still a great unmet need for ASD tissue collection and distribution across the ASD research community.

The Autism Tissue Program (ATP), a clinical program of Autism Speaks, is dedicated to supporting scientists worldwide in their efforts to understand autism, autism-related disorders and the human brain. The ATP makes postmortem brain tissue available to as many qualified scientists as possible to advance research on autism and other related neurological conditions. Toward that end, the ATP has acquired 150 whole brain donations from individuals with autism, autism-related disorders, their relatives, and controls, while making all tissue and comprehensive phenotype data available to the research community.

Surveillance

One area that has progressed is the establishment of systems to identify and monitor the prevalence of ASD in the United States. The CDC's ADDM Network (CDC, 2009) and a report from the HRSA-sponsored National Survey of Children's Health (Kogan et al., 2009) reported ASD prevalence of around 1% of children. Of great concern was the average increase of 57% from 2002 to 2006 in 10 areas of the United States covered by the ADDM Network (CDC, 2009). While some of the increase was attributed to improved identification of particular subgroups, such as Hispanic children and children without cognitive impairment, a true increase in risk is also possible. (CDC, 2009) Several other recent studies have also indicated that multiple identification factors contribute to, but do not fully explain, the rising ASD prevalence (Hertz-Picciotto & Delwiche, 2009; Saemundsen et al., 2010; King & Bearman, 2009; Rice et al., 2010; van Meter et al., 2010; Mazumdar et al., 2010). Concerted efforts are now needed to evaluate the reasons behind these changes.

Information and Communication Dissemination

Of particular importance is the rapid translation of research findings as they apply to intervention and the dissemination to families and practitioners in the community in a way that is easy to access and understand. There have been several reviews of intervention quality and effectiveness (Young et al., 2010; Lang et al., 2010), and several States have formed task forces or councils for ASD and other developmental disability (DD) services and have compiled service plans based on the current state of knowledge (Summary of the Massachusetts Act Early State Team Autism Summit).

In October 2010, the Administration on Developmental Disabilities (ADD)/Administration for Children and Families (ACF) awarded The Arc of the United States $1.87 million for fiscal year 2010 to establish a National Resource and Information Center on ASD and other developmental disabilities. The Autism NOW Project is collaborating with several partners, including the Autistic Self Advocacy Network (ASAN), the Autism Society, and several ADD Network entities to engage and leverage a national network of disability, aging, and family organizations. The center will provide high-quality resources and information related to community-based services that support independent living and self-determination, treatment protocols that promote community-based experiences (e.g., education, employment, recreation, transportation, early intervention, and child care), and evidence-based interventions. The intended audience for the center includes people with ASD, family members, service providers, researchers, and the general public. The center will also host a parent-to-parent call-in center for families addressing issues relating to autism and other developmental disabilities. More information about the center can be found at http://www.autismNOW.org.

Research Workforce Development

In 2009, NIH supported 60 trainees (graduate students and postdoctoral fellows) through individual NIH training and fellowship grants to study autism. These are in addition to a large number of trainees supported by NIH in 2009 on more than 200 traditionally funded NIH research project grants focused on autism, as well as more than 100 new autism-related research projects funded under the American Recovery and Reinvestment Act (ARRA). Private research organizations such as Autism Speaks and the Autism Science Foundation also supported several research training awards in 2009 and 2010.

What Gap Areas Have Emerged since Last Year?

Data Sharing

The Autism Informatics Consortium (AIC) identified several short-term and long-term priorities for increasing the utility and harmonization of major autism research informatics resources, identifying ways to best pursue those priorities, and determining ways to measure progress toward achieving them. Examples of gap areas identified include the need for improved options for data federation, query interfaces, and languages; genetic visualization tools; file and data set management; data quality and validation rules and algorithms; data dictionaries and ontologies; standardizing globally unique identifier (GUID) usage; procedures for maintaining phenotype resources with associated biospecimens (i.e., imaging and genetics); defining a core (clinical) phenotype battery; working with publishers of copyrighted assessments; and addressing concerns about intellectual property.

During 2010, the Affordable Care Act was passed with an unprecedented call to transition record keeping to electronic health records (EHRs). The development of EHRs provides an opportunity to consider the use of EHRs for data collection and analyses related to the service needs of people with ASD. Of course, important privacy issues need to be considered and addressed before these types of data could be more routinely collected and utilized as part of EHRs.

Biobanking

In the absence of biological markers, current approaches for stratification of individuals with ASD into clinically meaningful subgroups have relied on behavioral characteristics. However, the variability of behavioral, medical, and developmental concerns that affect individuals with ASD has made it extremely difficult to predict which treatments work best for which individuals. The integration of biologic information into phenotype selection algorithms can help to guide the development and evaluation of more targeted and effective therapeutics and significantly improve the prediction of a therapeutic response. To this end, there is a need for the establishment of a robust network of clinical research sites offering clinical care in real-world settings that can collect and coordinate standardized and comprehensive diagnostic, biological (e.g., genotype), medical, and treatment history data that would provide a platform for conducting comparative effectiveness research and clinical trials of novel autism treatments. Currently, there is a need for high-throughput screening tools to quickly evaluate gene-environment interactions relevant to ASD (e.g., induced pluripotent stem cells). Lack of progress in this area has made identification of potential exposures of interest difficult and driven by anecdotal evidence.

Surveillance

Moving forward, there is a need to maintain the sites so that early prevalence and population characteristics can be compared over time. A particular challenge is keeping consistency in the number of sites with four-year funding cycles and different numbers of sites funded based on availability of funds. In addition, completeness of data collection is hindered in some sites by the lack of access to educational records for surveillance purposes. Despite these challenges, the CDC's ADDM Network has maintained a core of approximately 12 sites with multiple prevalence years completed. There is now a need to go further to understand how multiple identification and potential risk factors have influenced the increasing estimates of ASD prevalence. Further analyses of existing datasets are needed to examine any relationship between changes in ASD prevalence and changes in potential risk factors in the population. Surveillance cohorts also provide the opportunity for communities and policy makers to use these data for resource allocation in addition to characterizing population-based identification patterns and gaps. Surveillance data can also be used to better characterize the population of children identified with an ASD by select characteristics, such as level of cognitive impairment, subtypes as diagnosed by community professionals, diagnostic features, associated conditions, and degree of impairment by clinician rating. Expansion of surveillance efforts are needed to improve early identification and to understand functioning and outcome of individuals with an ASD as adults.

Communication and Information Dissemination

There have been several reviews of intervention quality and effectiveness, and several States or agencies (e.g., Governor's councils, task forces and the Department of Education) have developed plans for ASD and other DD services based on the current state of knowledge. This information and these plans should be easily accessible to other communities. Right now, there are many public and private resources that work to compile services and supports information; however, finding this information can be challenging.

Focusing more on the issue of translating research into practice, the IACC Services Workshop on November 8, 2010, called for research that is meaningful to teachers and family members and conducted in non-clinical settings to better simulate the settings in which children with ASD are being served. This will help to ensure that students with ASD receive high-quality special education services.

The Agency for Healthcare Research and Quality (AHRQ) has ongoing efforts related to translation of research into practice. This work includes identifying sustainable and reproducible strategies (1) to help accelerate the impact of health services research on direct patient care and (2) to improve the outcomes, quality, effectiveness, efficiency, and/or cost-effectiveness of care through partnerships between health care organizations and researchers. To further address the challenges around dissemination of research findings, AHRQ developed a "knowledge transfer framework," which encompasses three major stages:

knowledge creation and distillation; diffusion and dissemination; and end user adoption, implementation, and institutionalization. While this work is not specific to autism, it may provide a useful framework to guide autism research translation efforts.

Research Workforce Development

Ongoing investment in developing research expertise and facilitating careers in autism research is needed, especially in the emerging areas of health services research, translational research, and international collaborative studies. In addition, continued efforts to enhance diversity in the research workforce are needed, including efforts to include people with disabilities and in particular individuals with ASD. Funds from the American Recovery and Reinvestment Act (ARRA) increased investments in ASD research, which contributed to recent expansion of the research workforce (particularly the number of graduate and postdoctoral students working in the field). With ARRA funding ending in 2011 and the potentially constrained fiscal climate anticipated for fiscal years 2011 and 2012, there is growing concern about the ability for both Federal and private entities to support recent gains in the research workforce.

Aspirational Goal: Develop and support infrastructure and surveillance systems that advance the speed, efficacy, and dissemination of autism research.

Short- and Long-Term Objectives

2009 **A.** Conduct a needs assessment to determine how to merge or link administrative and/or surveillance databases that allow for tracking the involvement of people living with ASD in health care, education, and social services by 2009. *IACC Recommended Budget: $520,000 over 1 year.*

2009 Revised in 2011 **B.** Conduct an annual "State of the States" assessment of existing State programs and supports for people and families living with ASD by 2011. *IACC Recommended Budget: $300,000 each year.*

2009 **C.** Develop and have available to the research community means by which to merge or link databases that allow for tracking the involvement of people in ASD research by 2010. *IACC Recommended Budget: $1,300,000 over 2 years.*

2009 **D.** Establish and maintain an international network of biobanks for the collection of brain tissue, fibroblasts for pluripotent stem cells, and other tissue or biological material, by acquisition sites that use standardized protocols for phenotyping, collection, and regulated distribution of limited samples by 2011. *(Revised 2011)*

- This includes support for post-processing of tissue, such as genotyping, RNA expression profiling, and MRI.
- Protocols should be put into place to expand the capacities of ongoing large-scale children's studies to collect and store additional biomaterials, including newborn bloodspots, promoting detection of biological signatures.

- Support should also be provided to develop an international web-based digital brain atlas that would provide high-resolution 3-D images and quantitative anatomical data from tissue of patients with ASD and disease controls across the lifespan, which could serve as an online resource for quantitative morphological studies, by 2014.

IACC Recommended Budget: $82,700,000 over 5 years.

2010 **E.** Begin development of a web-based toolbox to assist researchers in effectively and responsibly disseminating their findings to the community, including people with ASD, their families, and health practitioners, by 2011. *IACC Recommended Budget: $400,000 over 2 years.*

2010 **F.** Create funding mechanisms that encourage rapid replication studies of novel or critical findings by 2011.

2010 **G.** Develop a web-based tool that provides population estimates of ASD prevalence for States based on the most recent prevalence range and average identified by the ADDM Network by 2012. *IACC Recommended Budget: $200,000 over 2 years.*

2010 **H.** Create mechanisms to specifically support the contribution of data from 90% of newly initiated projects to the National Database for Autism Research (NDAR), and link NDAR with other existing data resources, by 2012. *IACC Recommended Budget: $6,800,000 over 2 years.*

2010 **I.** Supplement existing ADDM Network sites to use population-based surveillance data to conduct at least five hypothesis-driven analyses evaluating factors that may contribute to changes in ASD prevalence by 2012. *IACC Recommended Budget: $660,000 over 2 years.*

2010 **J.** Develop the personnel and technical infrastructure to assist States, territories, and other countries that request assistance describing and investigating potential changes in the prevalence of ASD and other developmental disabilities by 2013. *IACC Recommended Budget: $1,650,000 over 3 years.*

2010 **K.** Encourage programs and funding mechanisms that expand the research workforce, enhance interdisciplinary research training, and recruit early-career scientists into the ASD field by 2013. *IACC Recommended Budget: $5,000,000 over 3 years.*

2010 Revised in 2011 **L.** Expand the number of ADDM sites in order to conduct ASD surveillance in children and adults; conduct complementary direct screening to inform completeness of ongoing surveillance; and expand efforts to include autism subtypes by 2015. *IACC Recommended Budget: $16,200,000 over 5 years.*

2010 M. Support 10 "Promising Practices" papers that describe innovative and successful services and supports being implemented in communities that benefit the full spectrum of people with ASD, which can be replicated in other communities, by 2015. *IACC Recommended Budget: $75,000 over 5 years.*

2011 **N.** Enhance networks of clinical research sites offering clinical care in real-world settings that can collect and coordinate standardized and comprehensive diagnostic, biological (e.g., DNA, plasma, fibroblasts, urine), medical, and treatment history data that would provide a platform for conducting comparative effectiveness research and clinical trials of novel autism treatments by 2012. *IACC Recommended Budget: $1,850,000 over 1 year.*

2011 **O.** Create an information resource for ASD researchers (e.g., PhenX Project) to share information to facilitate data sharing and standardization of methods across projects by 2013.

- This includes common protocols, instruments, designs, and other procedural documents and should include updates on new technology and links to information on how to acquire and utilize technology in development.
- This can serve as a bidirectional information reference, with autism research driving the development of new resources and technologies, including new model systems, screening tools, and analytic techniques.

IACC Recommended Budget: $2,000,000 over 2 years.

2011 **P.** Provide resources to centers or facilities that develop promising vertebrate and invertebrate model systems, and make these models more easily available or expand the utility of current model systems, and support new approaches to develop high-throughput screening technologies to evaluate the validity of model systems by 2013. *IACC Recommended Budget: $1,100,000 over 2 years.*

Note: Dates that appear next to the objectives indicate the year that the objective was added to the Strategic Plan. If the objective was revised in subsequent editions of the Plan, the revision date is also noted.

RESEARCH RESOURCES

Below is a list of currently available resources for conducting ASD research. It includes government and nongovernment resources spanning topics such as genetics, bioinformatics, brain and tissue samples, and animal resources, as well as resources related to surveillance, prevalence, and services.

Government Resources

ADDM (Autism and Developmental Disabilities Monitoring) Network

www.cdc.gov/ncbddd/autism/addm.html

A surveillance network that provides data about ASD prevalence and describes the population of children with ASD. Supported by CDC.

AutismNOW: The National Autism Resource and Information Center

www.autismNOW.org

A center that provides access to resources and information on community-based services and interventions for people with ASD and their families, through a national dissemination network, regional events, training and technical assistance, and the web. Supported by the Administration on Developmental Disabilities/Administration for Children and Families.

CADDRE (Centers for Autism and Developmental Disabilities Research and Epidemiology)

www.cdc.gov/ncbddd/autism/caddre.html

Regional centers of excellence for ASD and other developmental disabilities, which are currently conducting the largest U.S. study of ASD risk factors. Supported by CDC.

National Children's Study

www.nationalchildrensstudy.gov

A population-based study of environmental influences on child health and development that could be used to investigate the relationship between genetic and environmental risk markers and ASD diagnosis. Supported by NIH.

NDAR (National Database for Autism Research)

http://ndar.nih.gov

A secure bioinformatics platform for scientific collaboration and data sharing between ASD investigators. Supported by NIH.

NDAR Data Definition

http://ndar.nih.gov/ndarpublicweb/standards.go

Provides data definitions of ASD research terminology. Supported by NIH.

NICHD Brain and Tissue Bank

http://medschool.umaryland.edu/BTBank

A brain tissue repository to support and enhance the acquisition and distribution of tissue samples from deceased individuals diagnosed with intellectual and developmental disabilities for use in research studies. Supported by NIH.

NIF (Neuroscience Information Framework)

http://nif.nih.gov

A dynamic inventory of web-based neuroscience resources that enables discovery and worldwide access to these resources through an open source, networked environment. The NeuroLex project, within NIF, is a dynamic lexicon to improve communication among neuroscientists about their data by standardizing neuroscience terminology. Supported by NIH .

NIH Blueprint Non-Human Primate Atlas

www.blueprintnhpatlas.org/nhp

An atlas mapping the expression of particular genes to specific neuroanatomical locations across several time points in development in the rhesus monkey. Supported by NIH.

NIH Pediatric MRI Data Repository

http://nih-pediatricmri.org

A multi-site longitudinal study using technologies (anatomical magnetic resonance imaging [MRI], diffusion tensor imaging [DTI], and magnetic resonance spectroscopy [MRS]) to map pediatric brain development. Supported by NIH.

NIMH Center for Collaborative Genetic Studies of Mental Disorders

http://nimhgenetics.org

A repository of biospecimens from individuals with mental illnesses such as schizophrenia, bipolar disorder, autism spectrum disorders, depression, and obsessive-compulsive disorders. Supported by NIH.

NIMH Transcriptional Atlas of Human Brain Development

www.developinghumanbrain.org

A foundational resource created using funds from the American Recovery and Reinvestment Act (ARRA) for studying transcriptional mechanisms involved in human brain development. Supported by NIH.

NITRC (Neuroimaging Informatics Tools and Resources Clearinghouse)

www.nitrc.org

A neuroimaging tools repository, NITRC facilitates finding and comparing neuroimaging resources for functional and structural neuroimaging analyses. Supported by NIH.

Non-Government Resources

AGRE (Autism Genetic Resource Exchange)

www.agre.org

A repository for biomaterials and associated phenotype and genotype information from more than 1,000 individuals with an ASD diagnosis and their families. Supported by Autism Speaks.

ALLEN Human Brain Atlas

www.brain-map.org

A unique multi-modal atlas of the human brain that integrates anatomic data (MRI, DTI, histology) and gene expression data (microarray, in situ hybridization), coupled with a suite of visualization and mining tools, to create an open public resource for brain researchers and other scientists across a wide range of specialties, including autism. Maintained by the Allen Institute for Brain Science.

Autism Genome Project

www.autismspeaks.org/science/research/initiatives/autism_genome_project.php

A study to find the genes associated with inherited risk for autism. Supported by Autism Speaks and other partners, including the Health Research Board of Ireland, Genome Canada, the United Kingdom's Medical Research Council (MRC), and the Hilibrand Foundation.

Autism Induced Pluripotent Stem Cell (iPSC) Biorepository (ASCB)

http://www.nhnscr.org/autism.html

A biorepository of fibroblast and iPSC lines cultured from patients with idiopathic autism as well as patients with FMR1 gene mutations. Maintained by the National Human Neural Stem Cell Resource at the Children's Hospital of Orange County and fully supported by the NIH.

Autism Tissue Program

www.brainbank.org

An ASD brain tissue repository. Supported by Autism Speaks.

Autism Treatment Network

www.autismspeaks.org/science/programs/atn

A network of hospitals and physicians dedicated to developing a model of comprehensive medical care for children and adolescents with autism. A program of Autism Speaks funded in part through grants from HRSA and NIH.

Co iriell Institute's Autism Research Resource

http://ccr.coriell.org/sections/Collections/AUTISM/?SsId=13

A biobank of cell lines and DNA samples from autistic individuals and family members with corresponding detailed clinical diagnoses. The biobank is maintained and fully supported by Coriell Institute for Medical Research, in collaboration with the University of Medicine and Dentistry, Robert Wood Johnson Medical School, New Jersey.

High Risk Baby Siblings Research Consortium

www.autismspeaks.org/science/research/initiatives/babysibs.php

A consortium studying the infant siblings of children with ASD in order to identify early behavioral and biomedical markers of the disorder. Supported by Autism Speaks and NIH.

IAN (Interactive Autism Network)

www.ianproject.org

An online registry of more than 35,000 people who have or are related to those with ASD. Collaboratively supported at the Kennedy Krieger Institute by Autism Speaks, the Simons Foundation, and NIH.

ISAAC (Internet System for Assessing Autistic Children)

www.autismtools.org/index.cfm

A web-based application for administering and managing health research projects/studies and the associated data. Supported by Autism Speaks.

REDCap (Research Electronic Data Capture)

http://project-redcap.org

Two secure, web-based applications (REDCap and REDCap Survey) designed to support data capture for research studies. Maintained by the REDCap Consortium, comprised of 194 active institutional partners.

SFARI Gene/AutDB (Autism Database)

http://gene.sfari.org/

www.mindspcc.org/autdb_rcad.html

A publicly available webportal for ongoing collection, manual annotation, and visualization of genes associated with autism from the published literature. SFARI Gene is licensed by the Simons Foundation from MindSpec.

Simons Simplex Collection

https://sfari.org/simons-simplex-collection

A repository of genetic samples and phenotypic data from families where parents without ASD give birth to a child with the disorder. Supported by the Simons Foundation Autism Research Initiative (SFARI).

References

[1] Abrahams, BS; Geschwind, DH. Advances in autism genetics: on the threshold of a new neurobiology. *Nat Rev Genet*. 2008 May; 9, 341-355.

[2] Agenda from Autism and the Environment Meeting: New Ideas for Advancing the Science. Autism Speaks and the National Institute on Environmental Health Science (NIEHS). 2010 Sept 10; Durham, NC. Available at: http://www.niehs.nih.gov/news/ events/highlight/autism/ index.cfm.

[3] Akechi, H; Senju, A; Kikuchi, Y; Tojo, Y; Osanai, H; Hasegawa, T. The effect of gaze direction on the processing of facial expressions in children with autism spectrum disorder: an ERP study. *Neuropsychologia*. 2010 Aug; 48(10), 2841-51.

[4] Akshoomoff, N; Pierce, K; Courchesne, E. The neurobiological basis of autism from a developmental perspective. *Dev Psychopath*. 2002; 14, 613-634.

[5] Alarcón, M; Abrahams, BS; Stone, JL; Duvall, JA; Perederiy, JV; Bomar, JM; Sebat, J; Wigler, M; Martin, CL; Ledbetter, DH; Nelson, SF; Cantor, RM; Geschwind, DH. Linkage, association, and gene-expression analyses identify CNTNAP2 as an autism-susceptibility gene. *Am J Hum Genet*. 2008 Jan; 82(1), 150-9.

[6] Altun, C; Guven, G; Akgun, OM; Akkurt, MD; Basak, F; Akbulut, E. Oral health status of disabled individuals attending special schools. *Eur J Dent*. 2010 Oct; 4(4), 361-6.

[7] Altun, C; Guven, G; Yorbik, O; Acikel, C. Dental injuries in autistic patients. *Pediatr Dent*. 2010 Jul-Aug; 32(4), 343-6.

[8] Amminger, GP; Berger, GE; Schäfer, MR; Klier, C; Friedrich, MH; Feucht, M. Omega-3 fatty acids supplementation in children with autism: a double-blind randomized, placebo-controlled pilot study. *Biol Psychiatry*. 2007 Feb 15; 61(4), 551-3.

[9] Anderson, JS; Lange, N; Froehlich, A; DuBray, MB; Druzgal, TJ; Froimowitz, MP; Alexander, AL; Bigler, ED; Lainhart, JE. Decreased left posterior insular activity during auditory language in autism. *Am J Neuroradiol*. 2010 Jan; 31(1), 131-9.

[10] Association of University Centers on Disabilities website. Available at: http://www.aucd.org/template/index.cfm.

[11] Atladóttir, HO; Pedersen, MG; Thorsen, P; Mortensen, PB; Deleuran, B; Eaton, WW; Parner, ET. Association of family history of autoimmune diseases and autism spectrum disorders. *Pediatrics*. 2009 Aug; 124(2), 687-94.

[12] Autism Speaks. Autism Treatment Network Annual Report for 2009. Available at: http://www.autismspeaks.org/docs/sciencedocs/atn/ATN_Annual_Report_2009_ FINAL_ DRAFT_030810.pdf.
[13] Baccarelli, A; Bollati, V. Epigenetics and environmental chemicals. *Curr Opin Pediatr*. 2009, 21(2), 243-51.
[14] Bailey, A; Le Couteur, A; Gottesman, I; Bolton, P; Simonoff, E; Yuzda, E; Rutter, M. Autism as a strongly genetic disorder: evidence from a British twin study. *Psychol Med*. 1995 Jan; 25(1), 63-77.
[15] Bakkaloglu, B; O'Roak, BJ; Louvi, A; Gupta, AR; Abelson, JF; Morgan, TM; Chawarska, K; Klin, A; Ercan-Sencicek, AG; Stillman, AA; Tanriover, G; Abrahams, BS; Duvall, JA; Robbins, EM; Geschwind, DH; Biederer, T; Gunel, M; Lifton, RP; State, MW. Molecular cytogenetic analysis and resequencing of contactin associated protein-like 2 in autism spectrum disorders. *Am J Hum Genet*. 2008 Jan; 82(1), 165-73.
[16] Barnea-Goraly, N; Lotspeich, LJ; Reiss, AL. Similar white matter aberrations in children with autism and their unaffected siblings: a diffusion tensor imaging study using tract-based spatial statistics. *Arch Gen Psychiatry*. 2010 Oct; 67(10), 1052-60.
[17] Barry, C; Huskamp, H; Goldman, H. A political history of federal mental health and addiction insurance parity. *Milbank Q*. 2010 Sept; 88(3), 404-433.
[18] Boris, M; Kaiser, CC; Goldblatt, A; Elice, MW; Edelson, SM; Adams, JB; Feinstein, DL. Effect of pioglitazone treatment on behavioral symptoms in autistic children. *J Neuroinflammation*. 2007 Jan 5; 4(3).
[19] Braunschweig, D; Ashwood, P; Krakowiak, P; Hertz-Picciotto, I; Hansen, R; Croen, LA; Pessah, IN; Van de Water, J. Autism: maternally derived antibodies specific for fetal brain proteins. *Neurotoxicology*. 2008 March; 29(2), 226-231.
[20] Brieber, S; Herpertz-Dahlmann, B; Fink, GR; Kamp-Becker, I; Remschmidt, H; Konrad, K. Coherent motion processing in autism spectrum disorder (ASD): an fMRI study. *Neuropsychologia*. 2010 May; 48(6), 1644-51.
[21] Buie, T; Fuchs, GJ 3rd; Furuta, GT; Kooros, K; Levy, J; Lewis, JD; Wershil, BK; Winter, H. Recommendations for evaluation and treatment of common gastrointestinal problems in children with ASDs. *Pediatrics*. 2010 Jan; 125 Suppl 1, S19-29.
[22] Buie, T; Campbell, DB; Fuchs, GJ 3rd; Furuta, GT; Levy, J; Vandewater, J; Whitaker, AH; Atkins, D; Bauman, ML; Beaudet, AL; Carr, EG; Gershon, MD; Hyman, SL; Jirapinyo, P; Jyonouchi, H; Kooros, K; Kushak, R; Levitt, P; Levy, SE; Lewis, JD; Murray, KF; Natowicz, MR; Sabra, A; Wershil, BK; Weston, SC; Zeltzer, L; Winter, H. Evaluation, diagnosis, and treatment of gastrointestinal disorders in individuals with ASDs: a consensus report. *Pediatrics*. 2010 Jan; 125 Suppl 1, S1-18.
Centers for Disease Control and Prevention (CDC); Autism and Developmental Disabilities Monitoring Network - Surveillance Year 2002 Principal Investigators. Prevalence of autism spectrum disorders - Autism and Developmental Disabilities Monitoring Network, 14 sites, United States, 2002. *MMWR Surveill Summ*. 2007 Feb 9; 56(1), 12-28.
[23] Centers for Disease Control and Prevention (CDC); Autism and Developmental Disabilities Monitoring Network Surveillance Year 2006 Principal Investigators. Prevalence of autism spectrum disorders - Autism and Developmental Disabilities Monitoring Network, United States, 2006. *MMWR Surveill Summ*. 2009 Dec 18; 58(10), 1-20.

[24] Chappel, SL; Somers, BC. Employing persons with autism spectrum disorders: A collaborative effort. *J Vocational Rehab*. 2010; 32(2), 117-124.

[25] Chez, MG; Burton, Q; Dowling, T; Chang, M; Khanna, P; Kramer, C. Memantine as adjunctive therapy in children diagnosed with autistic spectrum disorders: an observation of initial clinical response and maintenance tolerability. *J Child Neurol*. 2007 May; 22(5), 574-9.

[26] Children's Health Insurance Program Reauthorization Act of 2009. Government Printing Office. 2009 Feb 4. Available at: http://frwebgate. access.gpo.gov/cgi-bin/getdoc.cgi?dbname=111_cong_public_laws& docid=f:publ003.111.pdf%20.

[27] Chowdhury, M; Benson, B; Hillier, A. Changes in restricted repetitive behaviors with age: a study of high-functioning adults with autism spectrum disorders. *Res Autism Spectr Disord*. April-June 2010; 4(2), 210-216.

[28] Cohen, IL; Tsiouris, JA; Flory, MJ; Kim, SY; Freedland, R; Heaney, G; Pettinger, J; Ted-Brown, W. A large-scale study of the psychometric characteristics of IBR modified overt aggression scale: findings and evidence for increased self-destructive behaviors in adult females with autism spectrum disorder. *J Autism Dev Disord*. 2010 May; 40(5), 599-609.

[29] Cook, EH Jr; Scherer, SW. Copy-number variations association with neuropsychiatric conditions. *Nature*. 2008 Oct 16; 455(7215), 919-23.

[30] Council on Children with Disabilities, Section on Developmental Behavioral Pediatrics, Bright Futures Steering Committee, Medical Home Initiatives for Children with Special Needs Project Advisory Committee. Identifying infants and young children with developmental disorders in the medical home: an algorithm for developmental surveillance and screening. *Pediatrics*. 2006 Jul; 118(1), 405-20.

[31] Coury, D. Medical treatment of autism spectrum disorders. *Curr Opin Neurol*. 2010 Apr; 23(2), 131-6.

[32] Craig, MC; Zaman, SH; Daly, EM; Cutter, WJ; Robertson, DM; Hallahan, B; Toal, F; Reed, S; Ambikapathy, A; Brammer, M; Murphy, CM; Murphy, DG. Women with autistic-spectrum disorder: magnetic resonance imaging study of brain anatomy. *Br J Psychiatry*. 2007 Sep; 191, 224-8.

[33] Danielsson, S; Gillberg, IC; Billstedt, E; Gillberg, C; Olsson, I. Epilepsy in young adults with autism: a prospective population-based follow-up study of 120 individuals diagnosed in childhood. *Epilepsia*. 2005 Jun; 46(6), 918-23.

[34] Dawson, G; Munson, J; Webb, SJ; Nalty, T; Abbott, R; Toth, K. Rate of head growth decelerates and symptoms worsen in the second year of life in autism. *Biol Psychiatry*. 2007 Feb 15; 61(4), 458-64.

[35] Dawson, G; Rogers, S; Munson, J; Smith, M; Winter, J; Greenson, J; Donaldson, A; Varley, J. Randomized, controlled trial of an intervention for toddlers with autism: the Early Start Denver Model. *Pediatrics*. 2010 Jan; 125(1):e17-23.

[36] Derosier, ME; Swick, DC; Davis, NO; McMillen, JS; Matthews, R. The efficacy of a social skills group intervention for improving social behaviors in children with high functioning autism spectrum disorders. *J Autism Dev Disord*. 2010 Nov 2. [Epub ahead of print]

[37] Dinstein, I; Thomas, C; Humphreys, K; Minshew, N; Behrmann, M; Heeger, DJ. Normal movement selectivity in autism. *Neuron*. 2010 May 13; 66(3), 461-9.

[38] Dölen, G; Osterweil, E; Rao, BS; Smith, GB; Auerbach, BD; Chattarji, S; Bear, MF. Correction of fragile X syndrome in mice. *Neuron*. 2007 Dec 20; 56(6), 955-62.

[39] Durand, CM; Betancur, C; Boeckers, TM; Bockmann, J; Chaste, P; Fauchereau, F; Nygren, G; Rastam, M; Gillberg, IC; Anckarsäter, H; Sponheim, E; Goubran-Botros, H; Delorme, R; Chabane, N; Mouren-Simeoni, MC; de Mas, P; Bieth, E; Rogé, B; Héron, D; Burglen, L; Gillberg, C; Leboyer, M; Bourgeron, T. Mutations in the gene encoding the synaptic scaffolding protein SHANK3 are associated with autism spectrum disorders. *Nat Genet*. 2007 Jan; 39(1), 25-7.

[40] Dziobek, I; Bahnemann, M; Convit, A; Heekeren, HR. The role of the fusiform-amygdala system in the pathophysiology of autism. *Arch Gen Psychiatry*. 2010 Apr; 67(4), 397-405.

[41] Ecker, C; Marquand, A; Mourão-Miranda, J; Johnston, P; Daly, EM; Brammer, MJ; Maltezos, S; Murphy, CM; Robertson, D; Williams, SC; Murphy, DG. Describing the brain in autism in five dimensions--magnetic resonance imaging-assisted diagnosis of autism spectrum disorder using a multiparameter classification approach. *J Neurosci*. 2010 Aug 11; 30(32), 10612-23.

[42] Ehninger, D; Han, S; Shilyansky, C; Zhou, Y; Li, W; Kwiatkowski, DJ; Ramesh, V; Silva, AJ. Reversal of learning deficits in a Tsc2+/- mouse model of tuberous sclerosis. *Nat Med*. 2008 Aug; 14(8), 843-8.

[43] Esbensen, AJ; Bishop, S; Seltzer, MM; Greenberg, JS; Taylor, JL. Comparisons between individuals with autism spectrum disorders and individuals with Down Syndrome in adulthood. *Am J Intellect Dev Disabil*. 2010 July; 115(4), 277-90.

[44] Esbensen, AJ; Greenberg, J; Seltzer, MM; Aman, MG. A longitudinal investigation of psychotropic and non-psychotropic medication use among adolescents and adults with autism spectrum disorders. *J Autism Dev Disord*. 2009 September; 39(9), 1339-1349.

[45] Esch, BE; Carr, JE. Secretin as a treatment for autism: a review of the evidence. *J Autism Dev Disord*. 2004 Oct; 34(5), 543-56.

[46] Eskenazi, B; Marks, AR; Bradman, A; Harley, K; Barr, DB; Johnson, C; Morga, N; Jewell, NP. Organophosphate pesticide exposure and neurodevelopment in young Mexican-American children. *Environ Health Perspect*. 2007 May; 115(5), 792-8.

[47] Federal Register. Interim Final Rules Under the Paul Wellstone and Pete Domenici Mental Health Parity and Addiction Equity Act of 2008; Final Rule. 2010 Feb 2. Available at: http://edocket.access.gpo.gov/2010/pdf/ 2010-2167.pdf.

[48] Fischbach, GD; Lord, C. The Simons Simplex Collection: a resource for identification of autism genetic risk factors. *Neuron*. 2010 Oct 21; 68(2), 192-5.

[49] Forum on Neuroscience and Nervous System Disorders, Institute of Medicine. Autism and the Environment: Challenges and Opportunities for Research, Workshop Proceedings. Washington, DC: The National Academies Press; 2008.

[50] Frankel, F; Myatt, R; Sugar, C; Whitham, C; Gorospe, CM; Laugeson, E. A randomized controlled study of parent-assisted Children's Friendship Training with children having autism spectrum disorders. *J Autism Dev Disord*. 2010 July; 40(7), 827-42.

[51] Frazier, TW; Youngstrom, EA; Haycook, T; Sinoff, A; Dimitriou, F; Knapp, J; Sinclair, L. Effectiveness of medication combined with intensive behavioral intervention for reducing aggression in youth with autism spectrum disorder. *J Child Adolesc Psychopharmacol*. 2010 Jun; 20(3), 167-77.

[52] Fujiura, GT; Roccoforte, JA; Braddock, D. Costs of family care for adults with mental retardation and related developmental disabilities. *Am J Ment Retard.* 1994 Nov; 99(3), 250.

[53] Ganz, ML. The lifetime distribution of the incremental societal costs of autism. *Arch Pediatr Adolesc Med.* 2007 Apr; 161(4), 343-9.

[54] Giarelli, E; Wiggins, LD; Rice, CE; Levy, SE; Kirby, RS; Pinto-Martin, J; Mandell, D. Sex differences in the evaluation and diagnosis of autism spectrum disorders among children. *Disabil Health J.* 2010 Apr; 3(2), 107-116.

[55] Gillberg, C; Billstedt, E; Sundah, V; Gillberg, IC. Mortality in autism: a prospective longitudinal community-based study. *J Autism Dev Disord.* 2010 Mar; 40(3), 352-7.

[56] Government Accountability Office. Oral health: efforts under way to improve children's access to dental services, but sustained attention needed to address ongoing concerns. 2010 Nov. Available at: http:// www.gao.gov/new.items/d1196.pdf.

[57] Grether, JK; Anderson, MC; Croen, LA; Smith, D; Windham, GC. Risk of autism and increasing maternal and paternal age in a large North American population. *Am J Epidemiol.* 2009 Nov 1; 170(9), 1118-1126.

[58] Groen, W; Teluij, M; Buitelaar, J; Tendolkar, I. Amygdala and hippocampus enlargement during adolescence in autism. *J Am Acad Child Adolesc Psychiatry.* 2010 Jun; 49(6), 552-60.

[59] Guy, J; Gan, J; Selfridge, J; Cobb, S; Bird, A. Reversal of neurological defects in a mouse model of Rett syndrome. *Science.* 2007 Feb 23; 315(5815), 1143-7.

[60] Hamilton, SM; Spencer, CM; Harrison, WR; Yuva-Paylor, LA; Graham, DF; Daza, RA; Hevner, R; Overbeek, PA; Paylor, R. Multiple autism-like behaviors in a novel transgenic mouse model. *Behav Brain Res.* 2011; 218, 29-41.

[61] Hazlett, HC; Poe, M; Gerig, G; Smith, RG; Provenzale, J; Ross, A; Gilmore, J; Piven, J. Magnetic resonance imaging and head circumference study of brain size in autism: birth through age 2 years. *Arch Gen Psychiatry.* 2005 Dec; 62(12), 1366-1376.

[62] Health and Human Services (HHS) Press Release. HHS announces new grants and programs from the Affordable Care Act to help people navigate health and long-term care options. 2010, Sep 27. Available at: http://www.hhs.gov/news/press/2010pres/09/20100927a.html.

[63] Hertz-Picciotto, I; Delwiche, L. The rise in autism and the role of age at diagnosis. *Epidemiology.* 2009 Jan; 20(1), 84-90.

[64] Hertz-Picciotto, I; Green, PG; Delwiche, L; Hansen, R; Walker, C; Pessah, IN. Blood mercury concentrations in CHARGE Study children with and without autism. *Environ Health Perspect.* 2010 Jan; 118(1), 161-6.

[65] Hollander, E; Bartz, J; Chaplin, W; Phillips, A; Sumner, J; Soorya, L; Anagnostou, E; Wasserman, S. Oxytocin increases retention of social cognition in autism. *Biol Psychiatry.* 2007 Feb 15; 61(4), 498-503.

[66] Hove, O; Havik, OE. Developmental level and other factors associated with symptoms of mental disorders and problem behaviour in adults with intellectual disabilities living in the community. *Soc Psychiatry Psychiatr Epidemiol.* 2010 Jan; 45(1), 105-13.

[67] Ibrahim, SH; Voigt, RG; Katusic, SK; Weaver, AL; Barbaresi, WJ. Incidence of gastrointestinal symptoms in children with autism: a population-based study. *Pediatrics.* 2009 Aug; 124(2), 680-6.

[68] Immunization Safety Review Committee. *Immunization Safety Review: Vaccines and Autism*. Washington, DC: The National Academies Press; 2004.

[69] Innovation Center website. *Centers for Medicare & Medicaid Services*. Available at: http://www.innovations.cms.gov.

[70] Interagency Autism Coordinating Committee (IACC). *2008 IACC Autism Spectrum Disorder Research Portfolio Analysis Report*. 2010 April 30. Available at: http://iacc.hhs.gov/portfolio-analysis/2008/index. shtml.

[71] Interagency Autism Coordinating Committee (IACC). *2009 IACC Autism Spectrum Disorder Research Portfolio Analysis Report* (Draft). 2010 Oct 22. Available at: http://iacc.hhs.gov/events/2010/102210/ 2009_portfolioanalysis_draft.pdf.

[72] Institute of Educational Sciences, U.S. Department of Education. *Early Childhood Education Intervention for Children with Disabilities: Lovaas Model of Applied Behavior Analysis*, August 2010.

[73] Jamain, S; Quach, H; Betancur, C; Råstam, M; Colineaux, C; Gillberg, IC; Soderstrom, H; Giros, B; Leboyer, M; Gillberg, C; Bourgeron, T. Mutations of the X-linked genes encoding neuroligins NLGN3 and NLGN4 are associated with autism. *Nat Genet.* 2003 May; 34(1), 27-9.

[74] Järbrink, K; Fombonne, E; Knapp, M. Measuring the parental, service and cost impacts of children with autistic spectrum disorder: a pilot study. *J Autism Dev Disord.* 2003; 33(4), 395-402.

[75] Johnson, N; Oliff, P; Williams, E. *An update on state budget cuts.* Center on Budget and Policy Priorities. 2010 Nov 5. Available at: http:// www.cbpp.org/files/3-13-08sfp.pdf.

[76] Johnson, S; Hollis, C; Kochhar, P; Hennessey, E; Wolke, D; Marlow, N. Autism spectrum disorders in extremely preterm children. *J Pediatr.* 2010 Apr; 156(4), 525-31.e2.

[77] Kaiser, MD; Delmolino, L; Tanaka, JW; Shiffrar, M. Comparison of visual sensitivity to human and object motion in autism spectrum disorder. *Autism Res.* 2010 Aug; 3(4), 191-5.

[78] Kaiser, MD; Hudac, CM; Shultz, S; Lee, SM; Cheung, C; Berken, AM; Deen, B; Pitskel, NB; Sugrue, DR; Voos, AC; Saulnier, CA; Ventola, P; Wolf, JM; Klin, A; Vander Wyk, BC; Pelphrey, KA. Neural signatures of autism. *Proc Natl Acad Sci U S A.* 2010 Dec 7; 107(49), 21223-8.

[79] Kasari, C; Gulsrud, AC; Wong, C; Kwon, S; Locke, J. Randomized controlled caregiver mediated joint engagement intervention for toddlers with autism. *J Autism Dev Disord.* 2010 Sep; 40(9), 1045-56.

[80] Kikuchi, Y; Senju, A; Akechi, H; Tojo, Y; Osanai, H; Hasegawa, T. Atypical disengagement from faces and its modulation by the control of eye fixation in children with autism spectrum disorder. *J Autism Dev Disord.* 2010 Aug 17. [Epub ahead of print]

[81] King, BH; Hollander, E; Sikich, L; McCracken, JT; Scahill, L; Bregman, JD; Donnelly, CL; Anagnostou, E; Dukes, K; Sullivan, L; Hirtz, D; Wagner, A; Ritz, L. Lack of efficacy of citalopram in children with autism spectrum disorders and high levels of repetitive behavior: citalopram ineffective in children with autism. *Arch Gen Psychiatry.* 2009 Jun; 66(6), 583-90.

[82] King, M; Bearman, P. Diagnostic change and the increased prevalence of autism. *Int J Epidemiol*. 2009 Oct; 38(5), 1224-34.

[83] King, TM; Tandon, SD; Macias, MM; Healy, JA; Duncan, PM; Swigonski, NL; Skipper, SM; Lipkin, PH. Implementing developmental screening and referrals: lessons learned from a national project. *Pediatrics*. 2010 Feb; 125(2), 350-60.

[84] Kliemann, D; Dziobek, I; Hatri, A; Steimke, R; Heekeren, HR. Atypical reflexive gaze patterns on emotional faces in autism spectrum disorders. *J Neurosci*. 2010 Sep 15; 30(37), 12281-7.

[85] Klin, A; Lin, DJ; Gorrindo, P; Ramsay, G; Jones, W. Two-year olds with autism orient to non-social contingencies rather than biological motion. *Nature*. 2009 May 14; 459(7244), 257-261.

[86] Knapp, M; Romeo, R; Beechum, J. Economic cost of autism in the UK. *Autism*. 2009 May; 13(3), 317-336.

[87] Kogan, MD; Blumberg, SJ; Schieve, LA; Boyle, CA; Perrin, JM; Ghandour, RM; Singh, GK; Strickland, BB; Trevathan, E; van Dyck, PC. Prevalence of parent-reported diagnosis of autism spectrum disorder among children in the US, 2007. *Pediatrics*. 2009 Nov; 124(5), 1395-403.

[88] Koh, HC; Milne, E; Dobkins, K. Contrast sensitivity for motion detection and direction discrimination in adolescents with autism spectrum disorders and their siblings. *Neuropsychologia*. 2010 Dec; 48(14), 4046-56.

[89] Kolevzon, A; Mathewson, KA; Hollander, E. Selective serotonin reuptake inhibitors in autism: a review of efficacy and tolerability. *J Clin Psychiatry*. 2006 Mar; 67(3), 407-14.

[90] Krauss, M; Gulley, S; Sciegaj, M; Wells, N. Access to specialty medical care for children with mental retardation, autism and other special health care needs. *Ment Retard*. 2003; 41(5), 329-339.

[91] Kumar, A; Sundaram, SK; Sivaswamy, L; Behen, ME; Makki, MI; Ager, J; Janisse, J; Chugani, HT; Chugani, DC. Alterations in frontal lobe tracts and corpus callosum in young children with autism spectrum disorder. *Cereb Cortex*. 2010 Sep; 20(9), 2103-13.

[92] Kumar, RA; KaraMohamed, S; Sudi, J; Conrad, DF; Brune, C; Badner, JA; Gilliam, TC; Nowak, NJ; Cook, EH Jr; Dobyns, WB; Christian, SL. Recurrent 16p11.2 microdeletions in autism. *Hum Mol Genet*. 2008 Feb 15; 17(4), 628-38.

[93] Lai, MC; Lombardo, MV; Chakrabarti, B; Sadek, SA; Pasco, G; Wheelwright, SJ; Bullmore, ET; Baron-Cohen, S; MRC AIMS Consortium, Suckling, J. A shift to randomness of brain oscillations in people with autism. *Biol Psychiatry*. 2010 Dec 15; 68(12), 1092-9.

[94] Landa, RJ; Holman, KC; Garrett-Mayer, E. Social and communication development in toddlers with early and later diagnosis of autism spectrum disorders. *Arch Gen Psychiatry*. 2007 Jul; 64(7), 853-64.

[95] Lang, R; Regester, A; Lauderdale, S; Ashbaugh, K; Haring, A. Treatment of anxiety in autism spectrum disorders using cognitive behaviour therapy: A systematic review. *Dev Neurorehabil*. 2010 Feb; 13(1), 53-63.

[96] Laumonnier, F; Bonnet-Brilhault, F; Gomot, M; Blanc, R; David, A; Moizard, MP; Raynaud, M; Ronce, N; Lemonnier, E; Calvas, P; Laudier, B; Chelly, J; Fryns, JP; Ropers, HH; Hamel, BC; Andres, C; Barthélémy, C; Moraine, C; Briault, S. X-linked

mental retardation and autism are associated with a mutation in the NLGN4 gene, a member of the neuroligin family. *Am J Hum Genet.* 2004 Mar; 74(3), 552-7.

[97] Levy, SE; Hyman, SL. Use of complementary and alternative treatments for children with autistic spectrum disorders is increasing. *Pediatr Ann.* 2003 Oct; 32(10), 685-91.

[98] Lintas, C; Altieri, L; Lombardi, F; Sacco, R; Persico, AM. Association of autism with polyomavirus infection in postmortem brains. *J Neurovirol.* 2010 Apr; 16(2), 141-9.

[99] Lister, R; Pelizzola, M; Dowen, RH; Hawkins, RD; Hon, G; Tonti-Filippini, J; Nery, JR; Lee, L; Ye, Z; Ngo, QM; Edsall, L; Antosiewicz-Bourget, J; Stewart, R; Ruotti, V; Millar, AH; Thomson, JA; Ren, B; Ecker, JR. Human DNA methylomes at base resolution show widespread epigenomic differences. *Nature.* 2009 Nov 19; 462(7271), 315-22.

[100] Loo, CY; Graham, RM; Hughes, CV. Behaviour guidance in dental treatment of patients with autism spectrum disorder. *Int J Paediat Dent.* 2009 Nov; 19(6), 390-8.

[101] Lord, C; McGee, J (Eds.). Educating Children with Autism. Washington, DC: The National Academies Press; 2001.

[102] Loth, E; Gómez, JC; Happé, F. When seeing depends on knowing: adults with Autism Spectrum Conditions show diminished top-down processes in the visual perception of degraded faces but not degraded objects. *Neuropsychologia.* 2010 Apr; 48(5), 1227-36.

[103] Mandell, D; Palmer, R. Differences among states in the identification of autistic spectrum disorders. *Arch Pediatr Adolesc Med.* 2005 Mar; 159(3), 266-269.

[104] Mandell, D; Morales, K; Marcus, S; Stahmer, A; Doshi, J; Polsky, D. Psychotropic medication use among Medicaid-enrolled children with autism spectrum disorders. *Pediatrics.* 2008 Mar; 121(3), e441-448.

[105] Mandell, DS; Ittenbach, RF; Levy, SE; Pinto-Martin, JA. Disparities in diagnosis received prior to a diagnosis of autism spectrum disorder. *J Autism Dev Disord.* 2007 Oct; 37(9), 1795-1802.

[106] Marshall, CR; Noor, A; Vincent, JB; Lionel, AC; Feuk, L; Skaug, J; Shago, M; Moessner, R; Pinto, D; Ren, Y; Thiruvahindrapduram, B; Fiebig, A; Schreiber, S; Friedman, J; Ketelaars, CEJ; Vos, YJ; Ficicioglu, C; Kirkpatrick, S; Nicolson, R; Sloman, L; Summers, A; Gibbons, CA; Teebi, A; Chitayat, D; Weksberg, R; Thompson, A; Vardy, C; Crosbie, V; Luscombe, S; Baatjes, R; Zwaigenbaum, L; Roberts, W; Fernandez, B; Szatmari, P; Scherer, SW. Structural variation of chromosomes in autism spectrum disorder. *Am J Hum Genet.* 2008 Feb; 82(2), 477-488.

[107] Mazumdar, S; King, M; Liu, KY; Zerubavel, N; Bearman, P. The spatial structure of autism in California, 1993-2001. *Health Place.* 2010 May; 16(3), 539-46.

[108] McClannahan, LE; MacDuff, GS; Krantz, PJ. Behavior analysis and intervention for adults with autism. *Behav Modif.* 2002 Jan; 26(1), 9-26.

[109] McDonough, JT; Revell, G. Accessing employment supports in the adult system for transitioning youth with autism spectrum disorders. *J Vocational Rehab.* 2010 Apr; 32, 89-100.

[110] McDougle, CJ; Scahill, L; Aman, MG; McCracken, JT; Tierney, E; Davies, M; Arnold, LE; Posey, DJ; Martin, A; Ghuman, JK; Shah, B; Chuang, SZ; Swiezy, NB; Gonzalez, NM; Hollway, J; Koenig, K; McGough, JJ; Ritz, L; Vitiello, B. Risperidone for the core symptom domains of autism: results from the study by the autism network of the

research units on pediatric psychopharmacology. *Am J Psychiatry*. 2005 Jun; 162(6), 1142-8.

[111] McVicar, KA; Ballaban-Gil, K; Rapin, I; Moshé, SL; Shinnar, S. Epileptiform EEG abnormalities in children with language regression. *Neurology*. 2005 Jul; 65(1), 129-31.

[112] Mehler, MF; Purpura, DP. Autism, fever, epigenetics and the locus coeruleus. *Brain Res Rev*. 2009 Mar; 59(2), 388-92.

[113] Miller, DT; Adam, MP; Aradhya, S; Biesecker, LG; Brothman, AR; Carter, NP; Church, DM; Crolla, JA; Eichler, EE; Epstein, CJ; Faucett, WA; Feuk, L; Friedman, JM; Hamosh, A; Jackson, L; Kaminsky, EB; Kok, K; Krantz, ID; Kuhn, RM; Lee, C; Ostell, JM; Rosenberg, C; Scherer, SW; Spinner, NB; Stavropoulos, DJ; Tepperberg, JH; Thorland, EC; Vermeesch, JR; Waggoner, DJ; Watson, MS; Martin, CL; Ledbetter, DH. Consensus statement: chromosomal microarray is a first-tier clinical diagnostic test for individuals with developmental disabilities or congenital anomalies. *Am J Hum Genet*. 2010 May 14; 86(5), 749-64.

[114] Montes, G; Halterman, JS. Association of childhood autism spectrum disorders and loss of family income. *Pediatrics*. 2008 Apr; 121(4), e821-6.

[115] Morgan, JT; Chana, G; Pardo, CA; Achim, C; Semendeferi, K; Buckwalter, J; Courchesne, E; Everall, IP. Microglial activation and increased microglial density observed in the dorsolateral prefrontal cortex in autism. *Biol Psychiatry*. 2010 Aug 15; 68(4), 368-76.

[116] Mostafa, GA; El-Hadidi, ES; Hewedi, DH; Abdou, MM. Oxidative stress in Egyptian children with autism: relation to autoimmunity. *J Neuroimmunol*. 2010 Feb 26; 219(1-2), 114-8.

[117] Mouridsen, SE; Rich, B; Isager, T. Epilepsy and other central nervous system diseases in atypical autism: a case control study. *J Neural Transm*. 2011 Jan 5. [Epub ahead of print]

[118] Munir, K. Psychiatry of intellectual and developmental disability in the US: time for a new beginning. *Psychiatry*. 2009 Nov; 8(11), 448-452.

[119] Nagarajan, RP; Patzel, KA; Martin, M; Yasui, DH; Swanberg, SE; Hertz-Picciotto, I; Hansen, RL; Van de Water, J; Pessah, IN; Jiang, R; Robinson, WP; LaSalle, JM. MECP2 promoter methylation and X chromosome inactivation in autism. *Autism Res*. 2008 Jun; 1(3), 169-78.

[120] National Association of State Directors of Developmental Disabilities Services (NASDDDS), Human Services Research Institute. *National Core Indicators Annual Summary Report 2008-2009*. 2010 Dec. Available at: http://www.nasddds.org/pdf/2008-2009NCI-Report.pdf.

[121] National Core Indicators Project website. *National Association of State Directors of Developmental Disabilities Services (NASDDDS) and the Human Services Research Institute (HSRI)*. Available at: http://www2. hsri.org/nci.

[122] National Governors Association & National Association of State Budget Officers. *The Fiscal Survey of States – Fall 2010*. 2010: Washington, DC. Available at: http://www. nasbo.org/LinkClick.aspx?fileticket=C6q1M3 kxaEY%3d&tabid=38.

[123] National Vaccine Advisory Committee (NVAC). *Recommendations on the Centers for Disease Control and Prevention Immunization Safety Office Draft 5-Year Scientific Agenda*. 2009 June 2. Available at: http://www.hhs.gov/nvpo/nvac/NVAC RecommendationsISOScientificAgendaFinal.pdf.

[124] New, JJ; Schultz, RT; Wolf, J; Niehaus, JL; Klin, A; German, TC; Scholl, BJ. The scope of social attention deficits in autism: prioritized orienting to people and animals in static natural scenes. *Neuropsychologia.* 2010 Jan; 48(1), 51-9.

[125] Norris, M; Lecavalier, L. Screening accuracy of Level 2 autism spectrum disorder rating scales: a review of selected instruments. *Autism.* 2010 Jul; 14(4), 263-84.

[126] Oregon Health & Science University – Participatory Action Research (PAR) Toolkit. *Oregon Health & Science University.* Available at: http://www.ohsu.edu/oidd/partoolkit/index.html.

[127] Ozonoff, S; Iosif, AM; Baguio, F; Cook, IC; Hill, MM; Hutman, T; Rogers, SJ; Rozga, A; Sangha, S; Sigman, M; Steinfeld, MB; Young, GS. A prospective study of the emergence of early behavioral signs of autism. *J Am Acad Child Adolesc Psychiatry.* 2010 Mar; 49(3), 256-66.e1-2.

[128] Palmer, RF; Blanchard, S; Jean, C; Mandell, D. School district resources and identification of children with autistic disorder. *Am J Public Health.* 2005; 95(1), 125-130.

[129] Palmer, RF; Blanchard, S; Wood, R. Proximity to point sources of environmental mercury release as a predictor of autism prevalence. *Health Place.* 2009 Mar; 15(1), 18-24.

[130] Palmer, RF; Blanchard, S; Stein, Z; Mandell, D; Miller, C. Environmental mercury release, special education rates, and autism disorder: an ecological study of Texas. *Health Place.* 2006 Jun; 12(2), 203-9.

[131] Palmieri, L; Papaleo, V; Porcelli, V; Scarcia, P; Gaita, L; Sacco, R; Hager, J; Rousseau, F; Curatolo, P; Manzi, B; Militerni, R; Bravaccio, C; Trillo, S; Schneider, C; Melmed, R; Elia, M; Lenti, C; Saccani, M; Pascucci, T; Puglisi-Allegra, S; Reichelt, KL; Persico, AM. Altered calcium homeostasis in autism-spectrum disorders: evidence from biochemical and genetic studies of the mitochondrial aspartate/glutamate carrier AGC1. *Mol Psychiatry.* 2010 Jan; 15(1), 38-52.

[132] Palmieri, L; Persico, AM. Mitochondrial dysfunction in autism spectrum disorders: cause or effect? *Biochem Biophys Acta.* 2010 Jun-Jul; 1797(6-7), 1130-7.

[133] Pardo, CA; Vargas, DL; Zimmerman, AW. Immunity, neuroglia and neuroinflammation in autism. *Int Rev Psychiatry.* 2005 Dec; 17(6), 485-95.

[134] Patient Protection and Affordable Care Act. *Government Printing Office.* 2010 March 23. Available at: http://www.gpo.gov/fdsys/pkg/PLAW-111 publ148/pdf/PLAW-111publ148.pdf.

[135] Pinto, D; Pagnamenta, AT; Klei, L; Anney, R; Merico, D; Regan, R; Conroy, J; Magalhaes, TR; Correia, C; Abrahams, BS; Almeida, J; Bacchelli, E; Bader, GD; Bailey, AJ; Baird, G; Battaglia, A; Berney, T; Bolshakova, N; Bölte, S; Bolton, PF; Bourgeron, T; Brennan, S; Brian, J; Bryson, SE; Carson, AR; Casallo, G; Casey, J; Chung, BH; Cochrane, L; Corsello, C; Crawford, EL; Crossett, A; Cytrynbaum, C; Dawson, G; de Jonge, M; Delorme, R; Drmic, I; Duketis, E; Duque, F; Estes, A; Farrar, P; Fernandez, BA; Folstein, SE; Fombonne, E; Freitag, CM; Gilbert, J; Gillberg, C; Glessner, JT; Goldberg, J; Green, A; Green, J; Guter, SJ; Hakonarson, H; Heron, EA; Hill, M; Holt, R; Howe, JL; Hughes, G; Hus, V; Igliozzi, R; Kim, C; Klauck, SM; Kolevzon, A; Korvatska, O; Kustanovich, V; Lajonchere, CM; Lamb, JA; Laskawiec, M; Leboyer, M; Le Couteur, A; Leventhal, BL; Lionel, AC; Liu, XQ; Lord, C; Lotspeich, L; Lund, SC; Maestrini, E; Mahoney, W; Mantoulan, C; Marshall, CR;

McConachie, H; McDougle, CJ; McGrath, J; McMahon, WM; Merikangas, A; Migita, O; Minshew, NJ; Mirza, GK; Munson, J; Nelson, SF; Noakes, C; Noor, A; Nygren, G; Oliveira, G; Papanikolaou, K; Parr, JR; Parrini, B; Paton, T; Pickles, A; Pilorge, M; Piven, J; Ponting, CP; Posey, DJ; Poustka, A; Poustka, F; Prasad, A; Ragoussis, J; Renshaw, K; Rickaby, J; Roberts, W; Roeder, K; Roge, B; Rutter, ML; Bierut, LJ; Rice, JP; Salt, J; Sansom, K; Sato, D; Segurado, R; Sequeira, AF; Senman, L; Shah, N; Sheffield, VC; Soorya, L; Sousa, I; Stein, O; Sykes, N; Stoppioni, V; Strawbridge, C; Tancredi, R; Tansey, K; Thiruvahindrapduram, B; Thompson, AP; Thomson, S; Tryfon, A; Tsiantis, J; Van Engeland, H; Vincent, JB; Volkmar, F; Wallace, S; Wang, K; Wang, Z; Wassink, TH; Webber, C; Weksberg, R; Wing, K; Wittemeyer, K; Wood, S; Wu, J; Yaspan, BL; Zurawiecki, D; Zwaigenbaum, L; Buxbaum, JD; Cantor, RM; Cook, EH; Coon, H; Cuccaro, ML; Devlin, B; Ennis, S; Gallagher, L; Geschwind, DH; Gill, M; Haines, JL; Hallmayer, J; Miller, J; Monaco, AP; Nurnberger, JI Jr; Paterson, AD; Pericak-Vance, MA; Schellenberg, GD; Szatmari, P; Vicente, AM; Vieland, VJ; Wijsman, EM; Scherer, SW; Sutcliffe, JS; Betancur, C. Functional impact of global rare copy number variation in autism spectrum disorders. *Nature.* 2010 Jul 15; 466(7304), 368-72.

[136] Piven, J; Rabins, P; Berry-Kravis, E; Bodfish, J; Buckwalter, K; Callahan, C; Coyle, J; Dawson, G; Dilworth-Anderson, P; Folstein, S; Fombonne, E; Heller, T; Hyman, SL; Lord, C; Lyketsos, C; Mandell, D; Murphy, D; Samsted, E; Silverman, W; Tyler, C; Autism-in-the-Elderly Working Group. Autism spectrum disorders in older adults: toward defining a research agenda. *N Engl J Med.* 2010. Manuscript submitted for publication.

[137] Presentation to the IACC on the Autism Treatment Network (ATN). Dawson, G. *Autism Treatment Network: Improving the Quality of Medical Care for Children with ASD.* 2010 April 30; Washington, DC. Available at: http://iacc.hhs.gov/events/2010/full-committee-mtg-minutes-april30.shtml#geraldine-dawson.

[138] Presentation to the IACC on the meeting convened by the *Eunice Kennedy Shriver* National Institute of Child Health and Human Development. Kau A, James R. Disparities in the Identification of Children with Autism Spectrum Disorders: A Meeting Report. 2010 Oct 22; Bethesda, MD. Available at: http://www.iacc.hhs.gov/events/2010/ slides_alice_kau_102210.pdf.

[139] Presentation to the IACC on Wandering and ASD. McIlwain L, Fournier W, National Autism Association. Wandering & Autism: the need for data and resources. 2010 Oct 22. Available at: http://iacc.hhs.gov/events/2010/slides_fournier_mcilwain_102210.pdf.

[140] Price, CS; Thompson, WW; Goodson, B; Weintraub, ES; Croen, LA; Hinrichsen, VL; Marcy, M; Robertson, A; Eriksen, E; Lewis, E; Bernal, P; Shay, D; Davis, RL; DeStefano, F. Prenatal and infant exposure to thimerosal from vaccines and immunoglobulins and risk of autism. *Pediatrics.* 2010 Oct; 126(4), 656-64.

[141] Prouty, R; Alba, K; Scott, N; Lakin, C. Where people lived while receiving services and supports from state developmental disabilities programs in 2006. *Intellect Dev Disabil.* 2008 Nov; 46(1), 82-85.

[142] Qiu, A; Adler, M; Crocetti, D; Miller, MI; Mostofsky, SH. Basal ganglia shapes predict social, communication, and motor dysfunctions in boys with autism spectrum disorder. *J Am Acad Child Adolesc Psychiatry.* 2010 Jun; 49(6), 539-51, 551.e1-4.

[143] Rauh, VA; Garfinkel, R; Perera, FP; Andrews, HF; Hoepner, L; Barr, DB; Whitehead, R; Tang, D; Whyatt, RW. Impact of prenatal chlorpyrifos exposure on neurodevelopment in the first 3 years of life among inner-city children. *Pediatrics.* 2006 Dec; 118(6), e1845-59.

[144] Rice, C; Nicholas, J; Baio, J; Pettygrove, S; Lee, LC; Van Naarden Braun, K; Doernberg, N; Cunniff, C; Newschaffer, C; Meaney, FJ; Charles, J; Washington, A; King, L; Kolotos, M; Mancilla, K; Mervis, CA; Carpenter, L; Yeargin-Allsopp, M. Changes in autism spectrum disorder prevalence in 4 areas of the United States. *Disabil Health J.* 2010 Jul; 3(3), 186-201.

[145] Roberts, EM; English, PB; Grether, JK; Windham, GC; Somberg, L; Wolff, C. Maternal residence near agricultural pesticide applications and autism spectrum disorders among children in the California Central Valley. *Environ Health Perspect.* 2007 Oct; 115(10), 1482-9.

[146] Ruble, L; Heflinger, C; Renfrew, J; Saunders, R. Access and service use by children with autism spectrum disorders in Medicaid Managed Care. *J Autism Dev Disord.* 2005 Feb; 35(1), 3-13.

[147] Saemundsen, E; Juliusson, H; Hjaltested, S; Gunnarsdottir, T; Halldorsdottir, T; Hreidarsson, S; Magnusson, P. Prevalence of autism in an urban population of adults with severe intellectual disabilities – a preliminary study. *J Intellect Disabil Res.* 2010 Aug; 54(8), 727-35.

[148] Schall, CM; McDonough, JT. Autism spectrum disorders in adolescence and early adulthood: characteristics and issues. *J Vocational Rehab.* 2010; 32, 81-88.

[149] Schumann, CM; Bloss, CS; Barnes, CC; Wideman, GM; Carper, RA; Akshoomoff, N; Pierce, K; Hagler, D; Schork, N; Lord, C; Courchesne, E. Longitudinal magnetic resonance imaging study of cortical development through early childhood in autism. *J Neurosci.* 2010 Mar 24; 30(12), 4419-27.

[150] Scott-van Zeeland, AA; Abrahams, BS; Alvarez-Retuerto, AI; Sonnenblick, LI; Rudie, JD; Ghahremani, D; Mumford, JA; Poldrack, RA; Dapretto, M; Geschwind, DH; Bookheimer, SY. Altered functional connectivity in frontal lobe circuits is associated with variation in the autism risk gene CNTNAP2. *Sci Transl Med.* 2010 Nov 3; 2(56), 56ra80.

[151] Sebat, J; Lakshmi, B; Malhotra, D; Troge, J; Lese-Martin, C; Walsh, T; Yamrom, B; Yoon, S; Krasnitz, A; Kendall, J; Leotta, A; Pai, D; Zhang, R; Lee, YH; Hicks, J; Spence, SJ; Lee, AT; Puura, K; Lehtimäki, T; Ledbetter, D; Gregersen, PK; Bregman, J; Sutcliffe, JS; Jobanputra, V; Chung, W; Warburton, D; King, MC; Skuse, D; Geschwind, DH; Gilliam, TC; Ye, K; Wigler, M. Strong association of de novo copy number mutations with autism. *Science.* 2007 Apr 20; 316(5823), 445-9.

[152] Shattuck, PT; Durkin, M; Maenner, M; Newschaffer, C; Mandell, DS; Wiggins, L; Lee, LC; Rice, C; Giarelli, E; Kirby, R; Baio, J; Pinto-Martin, J; Cuniff, C. Timing of identification among children with an autism spectrum disorder: findings from a population-based surveillance study. *J Am Acad Child Adolesc Psychiatry.* 2009 May; 48(5), 474-483.

[153] Shattuck, PT; Grosse, S. Issues related to the diagnosis and treatment of autism spectrum disorders. *Ment Retard Dev Disabil Res Rev.* 2007; 13(2), 129-135.

[154] Silverman, JL; Yang, M; Lord, C; Crawley, JN. Behavioural phenotyping assays for mouse models of autism. *Nat Rev Neurosci.* 2010 Jul; 11(7), 490-502.

[155] Simons Foundation. *Panel discussion of anecdotal evidence that fever alleviates symptoms of autism*. 2010 February 5. Available at: https:// sfari.org/workshop-reports/-/journal_content/56/12736/100401-WORKSHOP-FEVER-AUTISM.

[156] Smith, KR; Matson, JL. Psychopathology: differences among adults with intellectually disabled, comorbid autism spectrum disorders and epilepsy. *Res Dev Disabil.* 2010 May-June; 31(3), 743-9.

[157] Smith, KR; Matson, JL. Behavior problems: differences among intellectually disabled adults with co-morbid autism spectrum disorders and epilepsy. *Res Dev Disabil.* 2010 Sept-Oct; 31(5), 1062-9.

[158] Smith, V; Gifford, K; Ellis, E. Hoping for economic recovery, preparing for health reform: a look at Medicaid spending, coverage and policy trends. Results from a 50-state Medicaid budget survey for state fiscal years 2010 and 2011. *Kaiser Commission on Medicaid and the Uninsured and Health Management Associates.* 2010 Sept. Available at: http://www.kff.org/medicaid/upload/8105.pdf.

[159] Spezio, ML; Adolphs, R; Hurley, RS; Piven, J. Analysis of face gaze in autism using "Bubbles". *Neuropsychologia.* 2007 Jan; 45(1), 144-51.

[160] Stahmer, A; Mandell, D. State infant/toddler program policies for eligibility and services provision for young children with autism. *Adm Policy Ment Health.* 2007; 34(1), 29-37.

[161] Steffenburg, S; Gillberg, C; Hellgren, L; Andersson, L; Gillberg, IC; Jakobsson, G; Bohman, M. A twin study of autism in Denmark, Finland, Iceland, Norway and Sweden. *J Child Psychol Psychiatry.* 1989 May; 30(3), 405-16.

[162] Strauss, KA; Puffenberger, EG; Huentelman, MJ; Gottlieb, S; Dobrin, SE; Parod, JM; Stephan, DA; Morton, DH. Recessive symptomatic focal epilepsy and mutant contactin-associated protein-like 2. *N Engl J Med.* 2006 Mar 30; 354(13), 1370-1377.

[163] Summary of NIH Workshop on Nonverbal School-Aged Children with Autism; 2010 April 13-14; *Rockville*, MD. Available at: http://www.nidcd.nih.gov/funding/programs/10autism.

[164] Summary of the Massachusetts Act Early State Team Autism Summit. Association of University Centers on Disabilities. 2010 Nov 10. Available at: http://www.aucd.org/template/event.cfm?event_id=2456& id=547&parent=547.

[165] Taylor, JL; Seltzer, MM. Changes in the autism behavioral phenotype during the transition to adulthood. *J Autism Dev Disord.* 2010 Dec; 40(12), 1431-46.

[166] Taylor, JL; Seltzer, MM. Employment and post-secondary educational activities for young adults with autism spectrum disorders during the transition to adulthood. *J Autism Dev Disord.* 2010 Jul 17. [Epub ahead of print]

[167] Tolosa, E; Gaig, C; Santamaria, J; Compta, Y. Diagnosis and the premotor phase of Parkinson disease. *Neurology.* 2009 Feb 17; 72(7 Suppl), S12-20.

[168] van Meter, KC; Christiansen, LE; Delwiche, LD; Azari, R; Carpenter, TE; Hertz-Picciotto, I. Geographic distribution of autism in California: a retrospective birth cohort analysis. *Autism Res.* 2010 Feb; 3(1), 19-29.

[169] Virués-Ortega, J. Applied behavior analytic intervention for autism in early childhood: meta-analysis, meta-regression and dose-response meta-analysis of multiple outcomes. *Clin Psychol Rev.* 2010 Jun; 30(4), 387-99.

[170] Vismara, LA; Rogers, SJ. Behavioral treatments in autism spectrum disorder: what do we know? *Annu Rev Clin Psychol.* 2010 Apr 27; 6, 447-68.

[171] Viswanathan, M; Ammerman, A; Eng, E; Gartlehner, G; Lohr, K; Griffith, D; Rhodes, S; Samuel-Hodge, Maty, S; Lux, L; Webb, L; Sutton, S; Swinson, T; Jackman, A; Whitener, L. *Community-Based Participatory Research: Assessing the Evidence.* Prepared for the Agency for Healthcare Research and Quality (AHRQ). 2004 July. Available at http://www.ahrq.gov/downloads/pub/evidence/pdf/cbpr/ cbpr.pdf.

[172] von dem Hagen, EA; Nummenmaa, L; Yu, R; Engell, AD; Ewbank, MP; Calder, AJ. Autism spectrum traits in the typical population predict structure and function in the posterior superior temporal sulcus. *Cereb Cortex.* 2010 May 3. [Epub ahead of print]

[173] Videocast of the NICHD Workshop on Disparities of Children with Autism Spectrum Disorders (ASDs). 2010 Aug 19. Available at: http:// videocast.nih.gov/summary.asp? live=9453.

[174] Wang, K; Zhang, H; Ma, D; Bucan, M; Glessner, JT; Abrahams, BS; Salyakina, D; Imielinski, M; Bradfield, JP; Sleiman, PM; Kim, CE; Hou, C; Frackelton, E; Chiavacci, R; Takahashi, N; Sakurai, T; Rappaport, E; Lajonchere, CM; Munson, J; Estes, A; Korvatska, O; Piven, J; Sonnenblick, LI; Alvarez Retuerto, AI; Herman, EI; Dong, H; Hutman, T; Sigman, M; Ozonoff, S; Klin, A; Owley, T; Sweeney, JA; Brune, CW; Cantor, RM; Bernier, R; Gilbert, JR; Cuccaro, ML; McMahon, WM; Miller, J; State, MW; Wassink, TH; Coon, H; Levy, SE; Schultz, RT; Nurnberger, JI; Haines, JL; Sutcliffe, JS; Cook, EH; Minshew, NJ; Buxbaum, JD; Dawson, G; Grant, SF; Geschwind, DH; Pericak-Vance, MA; Schellenberg, GD, Hakonarson, H. Common genetic variants on 5p14.1 associate with autism spectrum disorders. *Nature.* 2009 May 28;459(7246), 528-33.

[175] Wehmeyer, MI; Shogren, KA; Smith, TEC; Zager, D; Simpson, R. Research-based principles and practices for educating students with autism: self-determination and social interactions. *Education Train Autism Dev Disabil.* 2010; 45(4), 476-86.

[176] Weiss, LA; Arking, DE. Gene Discovery Project of Johns Hopkins & the Autism Consortium, Daly MJ, Chakravarti A. A genome-wide linkage and association scan reveals novel loci for autism. *Nature.* 2009 Oct 8; 461(7265), 802-8.

[177] Weiss, LA; Shen, Y; Korn, JM; Arking, DE; Miller, DT; Fossdal, R; Saemundsen, E; Stefansson, H; Ferreira, MA; Green, T; Platt, OS; Ruderfer, DM; Walsh, CA; Altshuler, D; Chakravarti, A; Tanzi, RE; Stefansson, K; Santangelo, SL; Gusella, JF; Sklar, P; Wu, BL; Daly, MJ. Association between microdeletion and microduplication at 16p11.2 and autism. *N Engl J Med.* 2008 Feb 14; 358(7), 667-75.

[178] Weiss, MJ; Harris, SL. Teaching social skills to people with autism. *Behav Modif.* 2001 Oct; 25(5), 785-802.

[179] Wetherby, AM; Watt, N; Morgan, L; Shumway, S. Social communication profiles of children with autism spectrum disorders late in the second year of life. *J Autism Dev Disord.* 2007 May; 37(5), 960-75.

[180] Wiggins, LD; Baio, J; Rice, C. Examination of the time between first evaluation and first autism spectrum diagnosis in a population-based sample. *J Dev Behav Pediatr.* 2006 Apr; 27(2 Suppl), S79-87.

[181] Windham, GC; Zhang, L; Gunier, R; Croen, LA; Grether, JK. Autism spectrum disorders in relation to distribution of hazardous air pollutants in the San Francisco Bay area. *Environ Health Perspect.* 2006 Sep; 114(9), 1438-44.

[182] Woods, JS; Armel, SE; Fulton, DI; Allen, J; Wessels, K; Simmonds, PL; Granpeesheh, D; Mumper, E; Bradstreet, JJ; Echeverria, D; Heyer, NJ; Rooney, JP. Urinary porphyrin

excretion in neurotypical and autistic children. *Environ Health Perspect.* 2010 Oct; 118(10), 1450-7.

[183] Yokotani, K. Educational level signals unobserved abilities of people with high functioning autism spectrum disorders. *Psychological Reports.* 2010 Aug; 107(1), 227-35.

[184] Young, J; Corea, C; Kimani, J; Mandell, D. Autism Spectrum Disorders (ASDs) Services: Final Report on Environmental Scan. Prepared for the Centers for Medicare & Medicaid Services. 2010 March 9. Available at: http://www.impaqint.com/files/4-content/1-6-publications/1-6-2-project-reports/finalasdreport.pdf.

[185] Zikopoulos, B; Barbas, H. Changes in prefrontal axons may disrupt the network in autism. *J Neurosci.* 2010 Nov 3; 30(44), 14595-609.

In: Autism Spectrum Disorders ISBN 978-1-62257-076-8
Editors: Gregory L. Campbell and Anthony O. Phillips

Chapter 6

THE COMBATING AUTISM ACT: OVERVIEW AND FUNDING*

Amalia K. Corby-Edwards

SUMMARY

Autism spectrum disorder (ASD) and autism are general terms for a group of developmental disabilities that cause impairments in social skills and communication, and are often characterized by certain atypical behaviors. The federal government has a role in the financing (through Medicaid and State Children's Health Insurance Programs) and delivery (through funding of developmental disabilities programming in schools, Title V Maternal and Child Health funding, and other sources) of treatment for ASD. The number of autism cases and their appropriate diagnosis and treatment affect federal and state expenditures. As such, Congress has shown interest in financing research on ASD prevalence, causes, and optimal treatment for individuals with ASD.

On September 26, 2011, the 112th Congress passed the Combating Autism Reauthorization Act (CARA, P.L. 112-32), which reauthorized funding for autism research authorized under the Combating Autism Act of 2006 (CAA, P.L. 109-416). The CAA was enacted to address public and congressional concern with growing rates of autism; to increase existing autism research funding authorizations; and to stimulate state-level coordination of health, education, and disability programs. The CAA authorizes funding for ASD surveillance, research, and education at the Department of Health and Human Services (HHS), at the Centers for Disease Control and Prevention (CDC), the Health Resources and Services Administration (HRSA), and the National Institutes of Health (NIH).

The CAA authorizes funding for the CDC to administer a grant program for states and other entities to conduct surveillance on ASD and developmental disabilities, and to establish regional centers of excellence in ASD epidemiology. These funds have been used to develop

* This is an edited, reformatted and augmented version of the Congressional Research Service Publication, CRS Report for Congress R42369, dated February 22, 2012.

a multi-state network for the collection, analysis, and reporting multiple years of state and local data on ASD prevalence to the CDC.

The CAA authorizes funding for the HRSA to support autism education, intervention, and early detection. These activities are designed to increase ASD awareness, to reduce barriers to screening and diagnosis, and to promote evidence-based interventions.

NIH is authorized under the CAA to conduct and fund basic scientific research on autism and other developmental disabilities. In addition, NIH is tasked with the coordination of all research, screening, intervention, and education efforts through the Interagency Autism Coordinating Committee.

The Combating Autism Act authorized appropriations for these activities from FY2007 through FY2011. The Combating Autism Reauthorization Act of 2011 extends authorizations of appropriations at FY2011 levels for FY2012 through FY2014. This report presents an overview of the CAA and CARA, HHS funding and activities under the CAA and CARA for FY2007 through FY2012 and the FY2013 President's budget request, other federal activities related to autism, and selected issues for Congress.

INTRODUCTION

Autism spectrum disorder (ASD) and autism are general terms for a group of developmental disabilities that cause impairments in social skills and communication, and are often characterized by certain atypical behaviors.[1] Autism spectrum disorders include autistic disorder, Asperger disorder, and pervasive developmental disorder-not otherwise specified.[2] These conditions have overlapping symptoms that differ in terms of onset, severity, and nature. ASDs are referred to as "spectrum disorders" because they encompass a range of behaviorally defined conditions. The complex nature of these conditions creates diagnostic challenges; there are no consistent genetic[3] or biologic markers[4] to facilitate diagnosis.

Autism has been linked to abnormal biology and chemistry in the brain; however, the cause or causes of these abnormalities remain unknown. According to the Centers for Disease Control and Prevention (CDC), as many as 1 in 110 eight-year-olds currently have an autism spectrum disorder, with boys affected more than four times as often as girls.[5] This represents an increase from past autism rates, and has generated public interest in the causes of autism. The increased prevalence has also focused attention on the demand for effective treatment and support services for individuals with these conditions. In addition, some have questioned whether the current rates of ASD reflect increased awareness and diagnosis, a true increase in the incidence of ASD, or a combination of these factors.[6]

For many, autism is a lifelong illness whose symptoms often manifest before age three. Autistic children and adults generally display a unique set of symptoms, but common traits associated with autism include difficulty talking, repeated behaviors, and aversion to loud noises. ASD impedes an individual's communication skills, making it difficult to learn or to integrate socially. There are no medical treatments for autism itself; however, medications and behavioral therapy can help mitigate certain symptoms. While there is currently no known cause or cure for autism, research to determine the cause or causes may identify risk factors, some of which may be modifiable. Other studies may determine optimal methods of screening and diagnosis, identify the most effective mental and behavioral health therapies, and find the best medical treatments for individuals with ASD.

The federal government has a role in the financing (through Medicaid and State Children's Health Insurance Programs) and delivery (through funding of developmental disabilities programming in schools, Title V Maternal and Child Health funding, and other sources) of treatment for ASD.[7]

The number of cases and their appropriate diagnosis and treatment affect federal and state expenditures.[8] As such, Congress has shown interest in financing research on ASD prevalence, causes, and optimal treatment for individuals with ASD. This interest in ASD surveillance and research has been demonstrated through inclusion of autism research provisions in the Children's Health Act (CHA, P.L. 106-310) in 2000, enactment of the Combating Autism Act in 2006 (CAA, P.L. 109-416), and the recent enactment of the Combating Autism Reauthorization Act (CARA, P.L. 112-32) by the 112th Congress.

This report presents an overview of the CAA and CARA, Department of Health and Human Services (HHS) funding and activities under the CAA and CARA, other federal activities related to autism, and selected issues for Congress.

THE COMBATING AUTISM ACT (CAA)

The precursor to the CAA was the Children's Health Act of 2000 (CHA), which addressed a number of child health issues. Title I of the CHA authorized the Secretary of HHS (the Secretary) to conduct certain activities relevant to autism and developmental disabilities. It established funding for autism surveillance at the CDC and established the National Center on Birth Defects and Developmental Disabilities. Under the CHA, the National Institutes of Health (NIH) was authorized to expand and intensify its autism research efforts and to establish Centers of Excellence for autism research. The CHA also established an Autism Coordinating Committee to coordinate research within NIH, and authorized funds for HHS to establish and implement an information and education campaign for health care providers and the general public.

Enacted in 2006 and subsequently reauthorized by the Combating Autism Reauthorization Act of 2011, the CAA is intended to address growing concern about the increasing prevalence of autism spectrum disorders, and to stimulate research into possible autism causes and treatments. It authorized funding from FY2007 through FY2011 for autism research, screening, early intervention, and education. CARA reauthorized this funding through FY2014.

The CAA authorizes the Secretary to expand, intensify, and coordinate existing ASD research activities; to expand surveillance and epidemiological research; to increase awareness of ASD; and to provide access to screening and early intervention services. It authorizes expanded research activities at NIH, and created the Interagency Autism Coordinating Committee (IACC) to coordinate all federal autism research efforts (this expanded the mission of the Autism Coordinating Committee described above). At the CDC, the CAA authorizes surveillance and establishes ASD awareness programs. At the Health Resources and Services Administration (HRSA), the CAA authorizes expanded federal efforts in autism education, early detection, and intervention. The CAA also required a report to Congress on implementation and progress four years after enactment, which was provided to Congress on January 7, 2011.[9] CARA requires a report to Congress two years after enactment.

The following sections summarize the programs and funding authorized under the CAA and subsequently reauthorized by CARA.

Surveillance and Epidemiological Research

The CAA authorizes the CDC to award competitive grants for the collection, analysis, and reporting of state-level epidemiological data on ASD and other developmental disabilities. The CDC must establish guidelines for reporting these data, in collaboration with other public and private entities. The CDC is also required to coordinate the federal response to potential or alleged clusters of ASD or developmental disabilities (DD).

The CAA also requires the CDC to award grants or cooperative agreements for the establishment of regional centers of excellence in the epidemiology of ASD and other developmental disabilities. The purpose of the centers of excellence is to collect and analyze information on the number, incidence, correlates, and causes of ASD and other DD. The centers are required to collect and report data according to the guidelines established by CDC. In addition, centers are required to develop an area of special research expertise (such as genetics, epigenetics, or environmental epidemiology), and to identify suitable cases and controls for research into potential causes or risk factors for ASD.

Autism Education, Early Detection, and Intervention

The CAA authorizes the Secretary to provide grants for projects designed to (1) increase awareness of ASD; (2) reduce barriers to screening and diagnosis; (3) promote evidence-based interventions for individuals with ASD or other developmental disabilities; (4) train health care professionals to use valid, reliable screening tools; and (5) provide early intervention if needed. The Secretary must use an interdisciplinary approach that also focuses on specific issues for children who are not receiving early diagnosis and interventions. These activities are carried out through HRSA.

The Secretary must, subject to funding, provide information and education on ASD to increase public awareness of developmental milestones; promote research into the development and validation of reliable screening tools; promote early screening of high-risk individuals; increase the number of individuals who are able to diagnose or rule out ASD; increase the number of individuals who are able to provide evidence-based interventions; and promote the use of evidence-based interventions for high-risk individuals.

The Secretary must, subject to funding, collaborate with a number of federal programs for low-income individuals to provide culturally competent information regarding ASD and developmental disabilities, in collaboration with the Department of Education and the Department of Agriculture. These programs include Head Start; Early Start; Healthy Start;

programs under the Child Care and Development Block Grant Act of 1990; Medicaid, including the Early and Periodic Screening, Diagnosis, and Treatment Program (EPSDT); the State Children's Health Insurance Plan (CHIP); the Maternal and Child Health Block Grant; Individuals with Disabilities Education Act Parts B and C; and the Special Supplemental Nutrition Program for Women, Infants, and Children (WIC).

The CAA authorizes the Secretary to require states to designate a lead agency responsible for disseminating the information described above available to individuals in the state. This information may be provided through toll-free numbers, Internet websites, mailings, or other means, as determined by the governor of each state. In addition, the Secretary, through the states, must promote and assist the development and use of screening tools. The Secretaries of HHS and the Department of Education must provide for the collection, storage, coordination, and public availability of screening tools and educational materials. The CAA also authorizes the Secretary to fund grants to expand existing interdisciplinary training and leadership programs (authorized in Title V of the Social Security Act). The Secretary must also promote best practices in autism screening and diagnosis.

Centers of Excellence in Autism Research, and Research Coordination

The CAA authorizes the Secretary of HHS to expand, intensify, and coordinate ASD research activities at NIH, and to consolidate existing program activities if necessary. It directs NIH to investigate the cause, diagnosis, early detection, prevention, services, supports, intervention, and treatment of ASD.

The CAA also authorizes the Interagency Autism Coordinating Committee (IACC) at NIH to coordinate all ASD research, screening, intervention, and education efforts within HHS. Members of the IACC are appointed for a term of four years and may be reappointed once. Members must include representatives of the following: Administration for Children and Families (ACF), CDC, Centers for Medicare and Medicaid Services (CMS), HRSA, NIH, HHS Office on Disability, Substance Abuse and Mental Health Services Administration (SAMHSA), and the Department of Education. No fewer than six members, or one-third of the committee (whichever is greater) must be non-federal public members, including people with autism, parents of people with autism, and leaders of national autism organizations.

The IACC is required to meet at least twice per year in public session. It is responsible for formulating and annually updating the strategic plan for ASD research, and presenting those recommendations to the Secretary and to Congress. The IACC must also monitor all federal ASD activities, make recommendations to the Secretary and to NIH regarding changes to these activities, and make recommendations on public participation in decision making to the Secretary.

Combating Autism Reauthorization Act (CARA)

Funding for CAA programs was authorized through FY2011; the Combating Autism Reauthorization Act (CARA), which extends funding at current levels through FY2014, was signed into law on September 30, 2011. CARA authorizes appropriations through FY2014 for CAA activities, but does not include funding or authorizations for an expansion of research and/or other services as some autism advocates had requested.[10]

FUNDING

Table 1 presents authorizations of appropriations for the provisions of the CAA and CARA. The table includes authorizations of appropriations from FY2007 through FY2014. **Table 2** provides details of funding for CAA activities, as reported by HHS.[11] The table also includes proposed funding levels in the President's FY2013 budget for HRSA and CDC.[12] NIH does not have an autism-specific budget line. For CAA activities, FY2011 funding totaled $229 million. Funding for FY2012 activities is estimated at $232 million, a $3 million increase.

CAA authorizations and funding are presented in two separate tables because funding for autism-related activities is not specifically limited to the authorizations shown in **Table 1**, and may be more or less in a given year. In addition, agencies typically do not have disease-specific budget lines. Autism-related activities may also be funded at CDC and NIH through general authorizations. The information on agency level spending in **Table 2** is compiled from the Moyer Report, a report published by the HHS Office of the Assistant Secretary for Financial Resources. The Moyer Report presents information as reported by the agencies on spending for selected diseases and conditions, including autism.

Table 1.AuthorizationsofAppropriations in the Combating Autism Act of 2006 and the Combating Autism Reauthorization Act of 2011
Dollars in millions

	FY2007	FY2008	FY2009	FY2010	FY2011	FY2012	FY2013	FY2014
Developmental Disabilities and Surveillance Program (PHSA 399AA)	15.0	16.5	18.0	19.5	21.0	22.0	22.0	22.0
Autism Education, Early Detection, and Intervention (PHSA 399BB)	32.0	37.0	42.0	47.0	52.0	48.0	48.0	48.0
Interagency Autism Coordinating Committee, Autism Centers of Excellence (PHSA 399CC, 409C, and 404H)	100.0	114.5	129.0	143.5	158.0	161.0	161.0	161.0
Total	147.0	168.0	189.0	210.0	231.0	231.0	231.0	231.0

Source: For FY2007 through FY2011, CAA, P.L. 109-416; FY2012 through FYFY2014, CARA, P.L. 112-32.

Notes: Appropriations are authorized in Section 399EE of the PHSA.

Table 2. Funding for Activities Related to the Combating Autism Act Dollars in millions

	FY2007	FY2008	FY2009	FY2010	FY2011	FY2012	FY2013 Request
Centers for Disease Control and Prevention[a]	14.8	16.2	20.4	22.1	21.4	21.3	21.3
Health Resources and Services Administration[b]	0	36.4	42.0	47.9	47.9	47.1	47.1
National Institutes of Health[c]	126.8	118.1	254.2	159.6	159.6	163.0	N/A
Total	141.6	170.7	316.6	229.6	228.9	231.4	N/A`

Sources: Compiled by the Congressional Research Service from the FY2011 Moyer Material, Office of the Assistant Secretary for Financial Resources, HHS, February 2010; the FY2012 Moyer Material, Office of the Assistant Secretary for Financial Resources, HHS, March 2011, and the accompanying Conference Report, H.Rept. 112-331, to the FY2012 Consolidated Appropriations Act, P.L. 112-74.

a. For the FY2013 CDC budget request for autism activities, see http://www.cdc.gov/fmo/topic/Budget%20Information/appropriations_budget_form_pdf/FY2013_CDC_CJ_Final.pdf.

b. Prior to FY2008, HRSA autism activities were funded within the Special Projects of Regional and National Significance (SPRANS) set-aside of funds from the Maternal and Child Health Block Grant, and were not provided a separate line of funding. For the FY2013 HRSA budget request for autism activities, see http://www.hrsa.gov/about/ budget/budget justification2013.pdf.

c. NIH funding for autism activities is authorized in PHSA Sections 399CC, 409C, and 404H. Autism does not have a specific budget line in the NIH budget; therefore, an autism specific request for FY2013 is unavailable. NIH autism funding for FY2008-2012 is based on NIH's Research, Condition, and Disease Categories (RCDC) tracking system. See http://report.nih.gov/rcdc/. Funding for FY2007 was reported in the Moyer report, cited above.

Federally funded autism research not authorized under the CAA, including activities carried out by the Departments of Defense and Education, is discussed below in the section "Other Federal Activities Related to Autism Research."

Autism Activities under the Combating Autism Act

The activities carried out by CDC, HRSA, and NIH under the CAA are summarized below. As discussed previously, CDC focuses on surveillance and epidemiological research, NIH on basic science and research coordination, and HRSA on autism education, detection, and early intervention. For further detail on agencies' autism-related activities and publications, refer to the IACC's Report to Congress on Activities Related to Autism Spectrum Disorder and Other Developmental Disabilities Under the Combating Autism Act of 2006.[13]

Centers for Disease Control and Prevention (CDC)

Under the Combating Autism Act, the CDC is responsible for ASD and developmental disabilities surveillance and epidemiological research. Under the CHA and CAA, CDC formed the National Center on Birth Defects and Developmental Disabilities, the Autism and Developmental Disabilities Monitoring Network (ADDM), and the Centers for Autism and Developmental Disabilities Research and Epidemiology (CADDRE), an ASD education campaign for caregivers and health professionals, and has collaborated on the International Autism Epidemiology Network (IAEN).[14] CDC also coordinates with other agencies, including HRSA and the Department of the Army, on other epidemiologic ASD research.

The National Center on Birth Defects and Developmental Disabilities established the ADDM network for the collection, analysis, and reporting of state-level epidemiological data on ASD and other developmental disabilities. ADDM monitors the prevalence of ASD among eight-year-olds at selected sites. The sites, which are regional or state-based public or private nonprofit entities, collect data on ASD prevalence using uniform surveillance methods, which include screening health and education records at multiple sources. Pilot surveillance sites were established with funding from the Children's Health Act; the program was expanded to additional sites under the CAA. ADDM has published two widely cited reports on ASD prevalence, one in 2007 and another in 2009.[15]

Under the CAA, CDC established a grant program for states or other entities (e.g., private nonprofits institutions, including institutions of higher education and hospitals) to establish regional centers of excellence in ASD. These centers, called the Centers for Autism Developmental Disabilities Research and Epidemiology (CADDRE), are part of a multi-site collaborative study examining the risk factors for ASD and other developmental disabilities.[16] The CADDRE network is currently working on the Study to Explore Early Development (SEED), which seeks to characterize ASD-related traits.[17]

CDC has partnered with the autism advocacy organization Autism Speaks to compile statistics on the global prevalence of autism. This partnership is called the International Autism Epidemiology Network.[18] The IAEN has produced a fact sheet that summarizes global autism prevalence from 2000 to 2008.[19]

In addition to research and surveillance activities, CDC has established a health communication campaign, entitled "Learn the Signs. Act Early," to improve early identification of children with ASD. The campaign is intended to educate parents, health care professionals, and early educators on the developmental milestones of early childhood.

Health Resources and Services Administration (HRSA)

Under the CAA, the Maternal and Child Health Bureau of HRSA must ensure that children with ASD are screened, diagnosed, and receive appropriate treatment. It is also tasked with addressing the shortage of trained professionals who provide autism treatment. HRSA received funding to address the five following objectives: (1) to increase awareness of ASD; (2) to reduce barriers to screening and diagnosis; (3) to promote evidence-based interventions for individuals with ASD or other developmental disabilities; (4) to train health care professionals to use valid, reliable screening tools; and (5) to provide early intervention if needed. To address these objectives, HRSA established or increased support for four programs: Leadership Education in Neurodevelopmental Disabilities (LEND), Developmental Behavioral Pediatric training programs, state implementation programs, and research programs.

HRSA has used CAA funding to support 43 LEND programs and 10 Developmental Behavioral Pediatric training programs by public and private nonprofit agencies in FY2011. The programs focus on the use of screening and diagnostic tools, and continuing education for health care providers that serve women, children, and families. These programs are designed to address the shortage of qualified professionals available to assess and assist autistic individuals.

The governor of each state must designate a lead agency to coordinate the HRSA-funded activities in that state. HRSA state-level grantees have used their funds to implement state autism plans, promote autism awareness, and develop model systems of services for children with ASD and developmental disabilities.[20] The primary focus of state implementation grants is to improve access to ASD and developmental disabilities screening and diagnostic services.

HRSA has established Autism Intervention Research programs, focusing on interventions to improve the health and well-being of children and adolescents with ASD and other developmental disabilities. These grants are provided to develop research networks among public and non-profit private institutions that focus on evidence-based research and the development of best practices in physical health, behavioral health, and the general health and well-being of individuals with ASD. Autism Intervention Research programs develop evidence-based guidelines and test and validate tools for measuring treatment outcomes.

National Institutes of Health (NIH)

CAA funding at NIH supports intramural and extramural research[21] at multiple institutes and centers. Under the CAA, NIH-funded researchers are tasked with studying potential risk factors and causes of autism, and to coordinate and consolidate its research on ASD and other developmental disabilities with other agencies.

NIH supports and coordinates the Autism Centers of Excellence Program, consisting of 11 research centers and networks that focus on identifying the causes of ASD and developing treatments. This includes research on biomarkers, genetic susceptibility, pharmacotherapy, language development, early intervention, and risk and protective factors. Another study, the Early Autism Risk Longitudinal Investigation, is looking into the interaction of environmental and genetic factors in ASD.[22]

NIH has sponsored a number of scientific workshops and symposia on ASD-related research. NIH also supports ASD research infrastructure, including biobanking (storage and archiving of biological samples) support, and the establishment of a common database (the National Database for Autism Research) to warehouse data collected in NIH-funded ASD studies.

The Children's Health Act required NIH to form a committee to coordinate research among the Institutes. The CAA broadened the mission of the coordinating committee to include other entities, both within and outside of HHS. The Interagency Autism Coordinating Committee (IACC), chaired by the director of the National Institute for Mental Health, is intended to facilitate the exchange of information on autism activities among the member agencies, and coordinates HHS autism-related programs and initiatives. The CAA required the IACC to present a strategic plan for ASD research, focusing on gaps, opportunities, and new knowledge in the autism research field. The strategic plan must be updated annually. The

2011 IACC Strategic Plan, released on February 28, 2011, includes a new focus on interventions for non-verbal people with ASD, health promotion efforts, and safety.[23]

OTHER FEDERAL ACTIVITIES RELATED TO AUTISM RESEARCH

Federal funding for autism research is not limited to the Combating Autism Act, and is supported by the Department of Defense and the Department of Education in addition to HHS. Many of the stakeholders in the IACC do not receive funding under the CAA, but through their participation in autism research, these stakeholders have an interest and a guiding role. Following is a brief description of the autism-related research activities of the other federal participants in the IACC.

Other HHS Agencies

Certain HHS agencies employ general authorities to direct funds as needed to address public health concerns. For example, CDC may provide funding for autism programs under its general authorities to fund public health activities. Other relevant activities may focus broadly on developmental disabilities and receive funding under different authorities. Within HHS, ACF, CMS, the Office on Disability, and SAMHSA conduct activities that contribute to the growing body of research on ASD. The CAA does not authorize appropriations for these agencies.

ACF is the HHS agency responsible for federal programs that promote the economic and social well-being of families, including Head Start and Temporary Assistance for Needy Families. The agency participates in the IACC and provides services for children with ASD through funds authorized under the Developmental Disabilities Assistance and Bill of Rights Act of 2000 (P.L. 106-402). ACF funds state Developmental Disabilities Councils; Protection and Advocacy Agencies; Centers for Excellence in Developmental Disabilities Education, Research, and Services; and Projects of National Significance.[24]

CMS administers the Medicare, Medicaid, and State Children's Health Insurance Program. The agency participates in the IACC and supports autism education, early detection, and intervention services under the CAA through Medicaid's EPSDT program.[25] CMS has also conducted several studies on best practices in autism treatment, and is planning to issue a report of all state services available to individuals with ASD.

The HHS Office on Disability is primarily a policy office that supports coordination of resources across HHS and federal agencies to support individuals with disabilities, including those with autism.[26]

Finally, SAMHSA is the HHS agency responsible for supporting mental health and substance abuse programs.[27] The agency provides services to children with ASD through the Child Mental Health Initiative, a grant program mandated by Congress to serve children and youth with serious emotional disorders. This program provides grants for the development of coordinated support systems for children who are referred to the program.

Non-HHS Agencies

Federal autism activities are not limited to HHS agencies. Other federal entities use general authorities and previously established programs to address ASD. These entities include the Department of Defense (DOD) and the Department of Education.

The DOD does not receive funds under the CAA. However, it maintains a congressionally directed research program for ASD research, which was first funded in FY2007.[28] The program, which supports a range of scientific and clinical research on autism, received $41 million in total funding from FY2007 to FY2012.[29]

The Department of Education does not receive appropriations under the CAA.[30] However, it funds a number of research programs and collects data on individuals served by special education programs. Programs and services in the Department of Education are geared toward individuals with disabilities in general, and not autism or developmental disabilities specifically.

Coordination of Public and Private Autism Research Funding

In 2010, the IACC conducted an analysis of autism research spending by private and federal entities that are represented on the IACC.[31] Analysts found that private entities funded 24% of autism research in the United States in 2009, while the federal government funded 76%. The report also gauged relevance of the funded projects to the topic areas that were identified in the IACC strategic plan.[32] These objectives for 2009 were (1) When should I be concerned? (2) How can I understand what is happening? (3) What caused this to happen and can it be prevented? (4) Which treatments and interventions will help? (5) Where can I turn for services? (6) What does the future hold, particularly for adults? (7) What other infrastructure and surveillance needs must be met? The vast majority (95%) of ASD research aligned with research questions in the IACC strategic plan, with the largest proportion of research focused on the causes and prevention of ASD. Research on access to ASD-related services and lifespan issues received the least amount of funding.

Issues for Congress

During CAA enactment and reauthorization, several issues were highlighted, some of which are of general interest to Congress when deciding whether to support disease-specific legislation. Specifically, concerns were raised about barriers to data sharing and confidentiality across state and federal government entities; the coordination of surveillance and research, across both agencies and diseases; and the pros and cons of Congress directing funding to specific diseases (or groups of diseases). These concerns apply not only to autism research policy, but can be applied broadly to any disease-specific legislation, and the consequent policy decisions may affect access to care and treatment for individuals with autism.

Coordination of research and sharing of the resulting data is an ongoing interest of Congress. Researchers call for accurate case estimates in order to study common characteristics of autistic individuals and potential risk factors for autism. Federal and state-funded programs provided through health care providers and schools must provide certain services for individuals with ASD, and need accurate estimates to anticipate the need for those services. However, enumerating autism cases for researchers, health care providers, and schools has presented an ongoing challenge at the state, local, and federal levels.[33]

During the reauthorization process, some Members of Congress raised the concern that continuing to pass disease-specific legislation allows Congress to prioritize one disease (or group of diseases, in this case developmental disabilities) over another, and that priority-setting should be left to the agencies that perform the research. The issue of prioritizing one developmental disability over another has also been raised among researchers and families of children with developmental disabilities and other conditions. Advocates for CARA argued that allowing authorization of these programs to lapse would interrupt the progress made under the CAA.

Autism services research, such as the development and adoption of new screening tools and implementation of best practices in autism therapy, has effects on both health care cost and coverage decisions made at the government and individual level. The Patient Protection and Affordable Care Act (ACA, P.L. 111-148) includes provisions that may affect coverage for individuals with autism, including prohibitions on the cancellation of coverage by an insurer due to a preexisting condition, elimination of lifetime caps on insurance benefits and annual limits on coverage, and eligibility for tax subsidies to assist low- and middle-income individuals in the purchase of coverage from state health insurance exchanges. In addition, Medicaid eligibility will be broadened to include single adults. The long-range impact of health reform on individuals with ASD (specifically, the coverage of recommended treatments for ASD) is unknown.

APPENDIX. LIST OF ACRONYMS

ACA	Patient Protection and Affordable Care Act, P.L. 111-148
ACF	Administration for Children and Families
ADDM	Autism and Developmental Disabilities Monitoring Network
ASD	Autism Spectrum Disorder
CAA	Combating Autism Act
CADDRE	Centers for Autism and Developmental Disabilities Research and Epidemiology
CARA	Combating Autism Reauthorization Act
CDC	Centers for Disease Control and Prevention
CHA	Children's Health Act
CHIP	State Children's Health Insurance Program
CMS	Centers for Medicare and Medicaid Services
DD	Developmental Disabilities
DOD	Department of Defense

EPSDT	Early Periodic Screening, Diagnosis, and Treatment Program
HHS	Department of Health and Human Services
HRSA	Health Resources and Services Administration
IACC	Interagency Autism Coordinating Committee
IAEN	International Autism Epidemiology Network
LEND	Leadership Education in Neurodevelopmental Disabilities
NIH	National Institutes of Health
SAMHSA	Substance Abuse and Mental Health Services Administration
WIC	State Supplemental Nutrition Program for Women, Infants, and Children

End Notes

[1] National Institute of Mental Health, *What Are Autism Spectrum Disorders?* http://www.nimh.nih.gov/health/publications/autism/what-are-the-autism-spectrum-disorders.shtml.

[2] As defined by the *Diagnostic and Statistical Manual of Mental Disorders—Fourth Edition.*

[3] A genetic marker is a DNA sequence with a known physical location on a chromosome. Genetic markers can help link an inherited disease with the responsible gene.

[4] A biologic marker is a measurable and quantifiable parameter that serves as an indicator for health and physiology assessments, such as disease risk, environmental exposures, metabolic processes, etc. For example, the presence of antibodies in a blood sample may indicate an infection.

[5] Autism and Developmental Disabilities Monitoring Network, *Prevalence of Autism Spectrum Disorders*, United States, 2006, Atlanta, GA, December 18, 2009, http://www.cdc.gov/mmwr/preview/mmwrhtml/ss5810a1.htm.

[6] National Institute of Mental Health, "Autism: The Whys of Increased Prevalence," press release, November 23, 2009, http://www.nimh.nih.gov/media/video/bearman.shtml.

[7] See CRS Report RL33202, *Medicaid: A Primer*, by Elicia J. Herz; CRS Report R40444, *State Children's Health Insurance Program (CHIP): A Brief Overview*, by Elicia J. Herz and Evelyne P. Baumrucker; and CRS Report R41833, *The Individuals with Disabilities Education Act (IDEA), Part B: Key Statutory and Regulatory Provisions*, by Ann Lordeman.

[8] Ganz M, "The Lifetime Distribution of the Incremental Societal Costs of Autism," *Arch Pediatr Adolesc Med*, vol. 161, no. 4 (April 2007), pp. 343-349.

[9] Office of Autism Research Coordination, National Institutes of Health, Report to Congress on Activities Related to Autism Spectrum Disorder and Other Developmental Disabilities Under the Combating Autism Act of 2006, U.S. Department of Health and Human Services, December 2010, http://iacc.hhs.gov/reports/reports-to-congress/FY2006-2009/index.shtml.

[10] A number of bills addressing expansion of research, global surveillance, and services for individuals with autism have been introduced in the 112th Congress.

[11] FY2012 Moyer Material, Office of the Assistant Secretary for Financial Resources, HHS, March 2011.

[12] Health Resources and Services Administration, *Justification of Estimates for Appropriations Committees*, Fiscal Year 2013, February 13, 2012, http://www.hrsa.gov/about/budget/ budgetjustification2013.pdf; and Centers for Disease Control and Prevention, *Justification of Estimates for Appropriations Committees*, Fiscal Year 2013, February 13, 2012, http:// www.cdc.gov/fmo/topic/Budget%20Information/appropriations_budget_formpdf/FY2013_CDC_CJ_Final.pdf.

[13] Office of Autism Research Coordination, National Institutes of Health, *Report to Congress on Activities Related to Autism Spectrum Disorder and Other Developmental Disabilities Under the Combating Autism Act of 2006*, U.S. Department of Health and Human Services, December 2010, http://iacc.hhs.gov/reports/reports-to-congress/FY2006-2009/index.shtml.

[14] See http://www.autismepidemiology.net/.

[15] Prevalence of Autism Spectrum Disorders, Autism and Developmental Disabilities Monitoring Network, Six Sites, United States, 2000, Autism and Developmental Disabilities Monitoring Network, Atlanta, GA, February 9, 2007, http://www.cdc.gov/mmwr/preview/mmwrhtml/ ss5601a1.htm; Prevalence of Autism Spectrum Disorders, Autism and Developmental Disabilities Monitoring Network, United States, 2006, Autism and Developmental Disabilities Monitoring Network, Atlanta, GA, December 18, 2009, http://www.cdc.gov/ mmwr/preview/mmwrhtml/ss5810a1.htm.

[16] See http://www.cdc.gov/ncbddd/autism/caddre.html.

[17] See http://www.cdc.gov/ncbddd/autism/seed.html.

[18] Centers for Disease Control and Prevention and Autism Speaks, "International Autism Epidemiology Network," press release, 2009, http://www.autismepidemiology.net/.

[19] International Autism Epidemiology Network, "Autism Prevalence Around the World (2000-2008)," press release, 2009, http://www.worldautismawarenessday.org/atf/.

[20] See http://mchb.hrsa.gov/programs/autism/statedempolicy.html.

[21] *Extramural research* is performed by non-federal scientists using NIH grant or contract money; *intramural research* is performed by NIH scientists in the NIH laboratories and Clinical Center.

[22] See http://www.earlistudy.org/.

[23] Interagency Autism Coordinating Committee, *2011 Strategic Plan for Autism Spectrum Disorder Research*, January 2011, http://www.iacc.hhs.gov/strategic-plan/2011/IACC_ 2011_Strategic_Plan.pdf.

[24] See the Administration on Developmental Disabilities, ACF: http://www.acf.hhs.gov/ programs/add/.

[25] See CRS Report RL33202, *Medicaid: A Primer*, by Elicia J. Herz.

[26] See the Office on Disability: http://www.hhs.gov/od/index.html.

[27] See SAMHSA: http://www.samhsa.gov/.

[28] U.S. Congress, Senate Committee on Appropriations, *Department of Defense Appropriations Bill, 2007*, report to accompany H.R. 5631, 109th Cong., 2nd sess., July 25, 2006, 109-292 (Washington: GPO, 2006), p. 223.

[29] Congressionally Directed Medical Research Programs: http://cdmrp.army.mil/arp/default. shtml.

[30] However, individuals with autism are entitled to a free and appropriate public education under the Individuals with Disabilities Education Act (IDEA, P.L. 101-476, as amended), and public school systems provide services for children with autism from ages 6 to 21. Currently, 300,000 children with autism receive services under IDEA, and more than 6,000 individuals with autism participate in their vocational rehabilitation programs.

[31] Office of Autism Research Coordination, Interagency Autism Coordinating Committee, *2009 Autism Spectrum Disorder Research Portfolio Analysis Report*, June 2011, http://iacc.hhs. gov/portfolio-analysis/2009/ 2009_portfolio_analysis.pdf.

[32] Interagency Autism Coordinating Committee, *2011 Strategic Plan for Autism Spectrum Disorder Research*, January 2011, http://www.iacc.hhs.gov/strategic-plan/2011/IACC_ 2011_Strategic_Plan.pdf.

[33] U.S. Government Accountability Office, *Federal Autism Activities: Funding for Research has Increased, but Agencies Need to Resolve surveillance Challenges*, 06-700, July 2006, p. 12, http://www.gao.gov/new.items/ d06700.pdf.

INDEX

B

C

G

H

I

Q

R

S

T

U

V

W

X

Y

Z